Practical Research Methods in Education

Practical Research Methods in Education is a hands-on guide which critically explores and scrutinizes research methods used in educational enquiry. Drawing on the research, practical experience and reflections of active researchers, each chapter offers explanations, examples, tasks for students to undertake and suggestions for further reading, all of which are designed to strengthen understanding of practical methods of data collection in educational and social-science research.

This insightful book offers:

- Detailed illustration of a range of data-collection methods and approaches used in educational research
- Chapters written by active researchers, experienced in addressing challenges of carrying out practical research in education
- Examples, study tasks and suggestions for further reading in each chapter
- An exploration of critical reflection and decision-making in relation to research methodology in education
- Close attention to research ethics

Exploring practical methods of data-collection for educational and social-science research, *Practical Research Methods in Education* is a unique and valuable resource for any students interested and engaged in the planning and completion of their own investigations.

Mike Lambert was Principal Lecturer in Education at the University of Wolverhampton, UK, where he developed a two-year undergraduate course on doing educational research. He has supervised the research work of many undergraduate and postgraduate students.

Practical Research Methods in Education

An Early Researcher's Critical Guide

Edited by Mike Lambert

Foreword by Jyothsna Latha Belliappa

Routledge
Taylor & Francis Group

LONDON AND NEW YORK

First published 2019
by Routledge
2 Park Square, Milton Park, Abingdon, Oxon, OX14 4RN

and by Routledge
52 Vanderbilt Avenue, New York, NY 10017

Routledge is an imprint of the Taylor & Francis Group, an informa business

British Library Cataloguing-in-Publication Data
A catalogue record for this book is available from the British Library

Library of Congress Cataloging-in-Publication Data
A catalogue record has been requested for this book

ISBN: 978-0-8153-9355-9 (hbk)
ISBN: 978-0-8153-9356-6 (pbk)
ISBN: 978-1-351-18839-5 (ebk)

Typeset in Galliard
by Newgen Publishing UK

Contents

List of illustrations

Figures

Tables

Contributors

Brendan Bartram is Reader in Education at the University of Wolverhampton, England. He was awarded a National Teaching Fellowship by the Higher Education Academy in 2012. His research and publications cover a wide range of issues, related primarily to higher-education practice, pedagogy and policy. Much of this work has involved a comparative dimension, examining such themes as (international) student mobility, behaviour, support and motivation. His book *Attitudes to Modern Foreign Language Learning: Insights from Comparative Education*, published by Continuum, examined second-language learning in the UK, USA, Australia, Germany and the Netherlands. Brendan has been Honorary Secretary of British Association of International and Comparative Education (BAICE) and is a member of the British Education Studies Association (BESA).

Jyothsna Latha Belliappa is an international educator and researcher with over twenty years' experience in primary, higher secondary and tertiary education. Her research interests include gender, work, personal life and education. She has published on these and other subjects, including qualitative research methods, pedagogy and sexual harassment. Her book *Gender, Class and Reflexive Modernity*, which examines how middle-class women create a sense of self by drawing on multiple discourses prevalent within contemporary India, is published by Palgrave Macmillan. Her PhD in Women's Studies was awarded by the University of York, England. Jyothsna has acted as research consultant to industry, educational institutions and the not-for-profit sector. She currently teaches at Srishti Institute of Art, Design and Technology, Bangalore, India, and supports schools in embedding gender in their curriculum.

Marte Blikstad-Balas is Professor at the Faculty of Education, University of Oslo, Norway. Her main research interest concerns how traditional and digital texts are used in different school contexts. She also has a particular interest in research methodologies, in particular qualitative methods and video research, and she has been a part of several video studies of students in school settings across grades and subjects. Marte is involved in teaching research methods at both Master's and PhD levels. She has written a range of academic articles about students' literacy practices and methodological issues.

Zeta Brown is Reader in Education for Social Justice at the University of Wolverhampton, England, and is leader of the 'Children, Young People and Families' research cluster for the University's Education Observatory. She is an executive member and currently

Chair of the British Education Studies Association (BESA). Zeta's research predominately focuses on agendas and policies in early-years and primary education.

Joke Dewilde is Associate Professor of Multilingualism in Education at the Faculty of Education, University of Oslo, Norway. She defended her PhD there with a dissertation on bilingual migrant teachers in Norwegian schools. In subsequent work, she has investigated young people's multilingual literacy practices and identity construction in and outside of school. Currently, she is leading a research project on multicultural school and community events. In general, she is concerned with developing context- and participant-sensitive methodologies to explore voices from the margins.

Michael Jopling is Professor of Education and Director of the Education Observatory in the Institute of Education at the University of Wolverhampton, England. He has been involved in research in all areas of education, using a range of methods and approaches, but his research interests and publications centre on school collaboration, multi-agency support for vulnerable groups, education policy and leadership, and how to engage teachers and practitioners in research and enquiry.

Mike Lambert is a writer and researcher in education and author of *A Beginner's Guide to Doing Your Education Research Project*, published by Sage. After working as a teacher and project leader in the UK and elsewhere, he was Principal Lecturer in Education at the University of Wolverhampton, UK, where he developed modules and materials in research methods. He has particular interest in the education of students with special educational needs and disabilities and has worked internationally for voluntary organizations in this field. His PhD thesis for the University of Warwick, England, focused on pedagogy for gifted students.

Helen Lyndon is currently Postgraduate Programme Lead for the Centre for Research in Early Childhood (CREC) in Birmingham, England. She taught initially in primary-school education, specializing in mathematics, then undertook a Master's degree in early-years education whilst teaching in children's centres. She went on to work in higher education on undergraduate and postgraduate courses relating to early-childhood education. Her doctoral research, almost complete, focuses on pedagogic mediation, including development of listening methods for daily practice with young children. Helen is the UK Country Coordinator for the European Early Childhood Research Association (EECERA).

Julian McDougall is Professor in Media and Education, Head of the Centre for Excellence in Media Practice and Programme Leader for the Educational Doctorate in Creative and Media Education at Bournemouth University, England. He convenes the annual International Media Education Summit and is Principal Fellow of the Higher Education Academy. He edits the journal *Media Practice and Education*, and is author/editor of a range of books, chapters, journal articles and reports. Julian has completed a variety of research projects for funding councils, charities, commercial clients and non-profit organizations in the fields of media, education and pedagogy, literacy, cultural theory and technology.

Jane O'Connor is Reader in Childhood Studies at Birmingham City University, England, where she leads the 'Cultures in Education' research group. She is the author of *The Cultural Significance of the Child Star* and co-editor of *Childhood and Celebrity*, both published by Routledge. Jane has written extensively in the areas of representations of childhood and children in the media and is currently leading an international project exploring young children's use of touchscreen technology. She teaches on MA and EdD programmes and supervises a wide range of PhD projects in the area of Childhood Studies.

Gavin Rhoades is Principal Lecturer (Head of Student Transitions) in the Faculty of Education, Health and Wellbeing at the University of Wolverhampton, England. Prior to joining the University, he was Assistant Headteacher at secondary schools in Staffordshire and Cumbria. His research interests, including current doctoral study, are focused on issues around student satisfaction and retention in higher education.

Tunde Rozsahegyi is Senior Lecturer in Special Educational Needs, Disability and Inclusion Studies at the University of Wolverhampton, England. Previously, she trained and worked as a 'conductor', specialist educator of children and adults with disabilities through Conductive Education, at the Pető Institute in Budapest, Hungary, then played a key role in establishing the National Institute for Conductive Education in Birmingham, England. Tunde has a strong interest in early education and support for children with special educational needs and disabilities and has written a range of material on this topic. Tunde's PhD thesis for the University of Warwick, England, examined developmental needs of young children with cerebral palsy.

Jo Winwood is Senior Lecturer in Special Educational Needs, Disability and Inclusion Studies at the University of Wolverhampton, England, teaching at undergraduate and postgraduate levels. She worked previously in mainstream and special schools. Her particular area of interest is the role of the Special Educational Needs Co-ordinator (SENCO) and her doctoral thesis examined this issue. She has worked internationally, supporting the development of inclusion for all children and young people.

Foreword

Jyothsna Latha Belliappa

It is a pleasure and a privilege to welcome *Practical Research Methods in Education* to the field of educational enquiry. I first came across Mike Lambert's work a few years ago, when I was teaching research methods to postgraduate students of education in India. This resulted in a stimulating transcontinental correspondence on the subject and first-hand experience of the real-world approach encapsulated in this edited collection. I am therefore delighted to be writing the foreword for this new book.

In recent times, such enquiry in India (and in many other countries) has become increasingly saturated with both qualitative and quantitative research which shapes policy and practice. On the qualitative side, there is an increase in studies of the experiences of educators and learners, of parents' expectations and involvement, and of the impact of educational policies on institutions and communities. In terms of quantitative research, we have international standardized tests, such as the somewhat controversial Programme for International Student Assessment (PISA), which assesses scholastic performance in mathematics, science and reading, and more localized tests such as the Annual Status of Education Report (ASER), which measures literacy and numeracy skills of children in India. Studies such as these influence a wide range of policies and programmes and have a direct impact on all phases of educational provision.

As part of their training as scholars and educators, therefore, students need to develop critical knowledge and understanding of research and of the methods with which it is carried out. The same could be said to apply to teachers and other practitioners, all of whom have a role to play in making the practice of education, as indicated in this book's introduction, less subject to short-lived fashion and more cumulatively 'research-based'.

One of the most effective ways to do this is by engaging thoughtfully and critically in an enquiry of one's own. Indeed, a research project, including research-methods training and a final-year dissertation, now invariably forms a core component of undergraduate degrees. In turn, students engaging in postgraduate study need to revisit concepts and remind themselves of the critical stance which one needs to adopt when considering research methodology. Practising educators also gain from closer understanding of ways of formally evaluating their own work and that of others. This book will therefore be of value to all educators undertaking research, be it as part of a course of study or to support reflective practice in classrooms and elsewhere.

In addition, *Practical Research Methods in Education* is a particularly refreshing addition to more theoretical and conceptual guides on research methods, as it addresses in a very pragmatic way – using real-life and real-research examples – some of the challenges that novice and more experienced researchers invariably face. These include choosing methods appropriate to the research question, evaluating their strengths and drawbacks, and making informed choices about how they should be used. The chapters in this book critically discuss the many considerations which need to be taken into account in this process, including research objectives, sampling, combining methods, analysis, validity and generalizability, as well as the level of participation desired from those contributing data to the study.

Each chapter is written by an experienced research practitioner, who not only explains the research method in question but also draws on personal experiences of employing it in their enquiry and grappling with the problems with which it is associated. In this manner, the book goes beyond a simple 'cook-book' approach which merely tells students how to use a given method. As a course instructor, I will find its critical approach, as well as its specific questions for reflection, particularly useful in stimulating classroom discussion and helping students to make decisions in relation to their own research projects.

One key characteristic of education research is that it is often conducted amongst potentially vulnerable subjects, including, of course, children and young people. Even research projects that do not directly involve them may impact on decision-making in education policy and practice, the consequences of which young people will then either enjoy or endure. Researchers in education therefore need to engage with a variety of ethical questions, not only when actually conducting research but also with regard to how its findings might be employed. I am pleased to see that this collection not only alerts readers to many of these ethical issues but also considers critically how they can be addressed. Overall, the contributors recognize that enthusiasm for answers should never override a commitment to the well-being of one's research subjects and the contexts in which they learn and live their lives.

I am heartened, too, to note that this volume includes not only traditional methods which continue to have relevance, such as questionnaires, interviews and observations, but also newer or less well understood approaches, such as video and 'Mosaic', the latter having become increasingly popular internationally in early-childhood education. Readers are thus introduced to a wide range of methods and approaches applicable to research.

Written throughout in a lucid, engaging but rigorous style, the collection will appeal to both first-time and more experienced researchers. It will also be invaluable to busy lecturers who seek inspiration for conversation, debate and instruction in their modules and courses. I look forward to using *Practical Research Methods in Education* in my own teaching and recommending it to students for many years to come. I warmly recommend it to you too.

Editor's introduction

Mike Lambert

Welcome, readers, to *Practical Research Methods in Education: An Early Researcher's Critical Guide*. Whatever your motivation for picking up this book – planning a research project, choosing methods or actually carrying out your data collection – this book will help you to understand and use research methodology in your educational investigation.

Importance of research methodology

There's a lot of it about (educational research, that is). Now, if you are doing almost any kind of higher-education course in education, you will be required to learn about research methods, plan an investigative project, collect data, and write up and submit a report on how you did it and its findings. Non-studying educators, too, will invariably find themselves involved in formal, school-based or more extended evaluations of classroom intervention and its outcomes. The practice of education is hardly 'research-based', as hoped for by Professor David Hargreaves in a seminal lecture in 1996 in England (published as Hargreaves, 2007), but it seems a shade more research-oriented than it was before.

Concerns remain, however, most notably that educational enquiry still has a limited impact on educational practice (see, for example, Norwich, 2015). The contrast with research in the health sciences, raised by Hargreaves, remains pertinent in this and other ways. Medical researchers and practitioners (they are often though not always the same people) set up trials, engage with patients and track their progress, with strong consideration of ethics throughout. As a patient, you may be invited to be part of research through the course of your treatment and follow-up. Reports may be published explaining what is found out and how this relates to previous research results. Outcomes prominently inform what is done in hospitals and doctors' surgeries, and also influence us, the public, when considering personal health in our daily lives. Nevertheless, despite peer-review safeguards, methodologically flawed medical research can still find its way into the public domain (see Forster, 2017, for discussion on one fraught issue of this kind) and there is much questioning of research findings overall – Ioannidis (2005) is a seminal paper on this issue.

There is no doubt that educational research has considerable methodological challenges of its own, and that these affect the extent to which notice is taken of its findings. Setting up experiments, with one learner group getting a new pedagogical approach and others not, can appear both difficult to achieve and ethically unsound, and outcomes are rarely noteworthy enough to be taken up by a wider educational world. Repeating such research, so that knowledge gained becomes cumulative, is even more problematic – education, in

England at least, is still easily criticized for its fads and novelties (Ward, 2018). It may also still be the case that many educators are more comfortable doing things than systematically, collaboratively and critically researching their actions, and still conscious of 'the low value of research as a guide to the solution of practical problems' (Hargreaves, 2007:4). As for students and children, how straightforward is it for them to be engaged in evaluation of the specifics of their experiences, and how many, indeed, are invited to do this for extended periods of their education?

Such issues can make identifying and using suitable methodologies in any research project a particularly perplexing task. Indeed, education can appear almost too complicated for systematic investigation, so much about relationships between individuals, in particular between those who mostly lead and those who mostly are guided. Practice endures too a problematic gulf between official (or even research) agendas and the professional or personal instincts of practitioners, parents and learners themselves. For many, still, 'common sense and a feel for educational practice may ultimately be more important than knowing anything about research' (Lambert, 2012:1).

This book

Which is where *Practical Research Methods in Education* comes in. Whether you are undertaking a first research project, perhaps at undergraduate level, or tackling a Master's degree or doctorate, or undertaking a specific funded investigation, or even doing unaccredited practitioner research of your own, you will undoubtedly face the challenges (and a few sleepless nights, perhaps) associated with choosing suitable research methods, designing their implementation, using them and – not least – writing up what you have discovered so it is meaningful to others and even influential in relation to understanding, thinking and wider practice in education.

This book's aim is to help you through these processes. Each chapter focuses on one research method, starting with those most frequently adopted, then moving on to approaches which combine and cultivate these further. The final chapters look at overall designs for research – perhaps in ideal worlds these would be decided first, but in practice most researchers need understanding of specific data-collection methods early on, so they can establish an overall framework which structures and deepens their investigation later.

All the chapters take a dual approach. First (it is usually first) each discusses the characteristics of a chosen methodology, then analyses the author's own use of it in her or his own research. This not only gives the opportunity to examine a procedure from both theoretical and practical points of view but also makes the scrutiny personal, almost heartfelt. The authors have 'been through it', they know what they have been enthused by and worried about, including the thorny questions of ethics. They know how they have dealt with challenges and can see where these processes have succeeded in tackling limitations of their approach, and crucially where perhaps these have not (hence it is a 'critical guide'). The authors share their anxieties and solutions with you, the readers, so you can feel and resolve them too.

The chapters

Brendan Bartram starts this process in Chapter 1 by looking carefully at the frequent use of *questionnaires*. He draws on his own use of this approach in three research projects, one using paper-based questionnaires, another online, and the third based on a word-association technique.

Jo Winwood continues in Chapter 2 with a close look at another common approach, that of *interviews*. She draws for her critical gaze on those she carried out to examine the role of special educational needs coordinators (SENCOs) in English schools. Chapter 3 is an examination by Tunde Rozsahegyi of *observation* as a research technique, whereby participants, even very young children, show their beliefs, perspectives, abilities and understanding in how they act and react in practical situations.

I take this lead further in Chapter 4 by scrutinizing the challenges of *involving children* in research, drawing on my own experiences including their perspectives and experiences in curricular investigation but struggling sometimes with the ethical and other considerations when doing so.

Marte Blikstad-Balas then takes us into deeper territory in Chapter 5, drawing on her own research to examine the challenges and the benefits of *using video data* to capture the detail of practical educational activity and give opportunities for its constant review.

These first chapters focus mainly on the gathering of qualitative data, but in Chapter 6, Michael Jopling usefully reminds us of the strong and varied contribution which *quantitative data* can make to understanding educational practice and opinion and encourages readers to incorporate collection of such data into their methodologies.

Jane O'Connor then looks in Chapter 7 at how *document analysis* can reveal much about dominant but often hidden textual discourses and, in doing so, address issues of social inequality and stereotyping.

In Chapter 8, Julian McDougall extends this critical gaze even further by examining how aspects of the lived experience of students, educators and researchers can be drawn out by use of creative methods – in his words, by '*doing text*'.

The next two chapters look at wider approaches which can incorporate one or more of the data-gathering techniques already covered. Firstly, Gavin Rhoades and Zeta Brown present and critically scrutinize the *Q-methodology* approach, a systematic but flexible methodology for exploring people's opinions, perspectives and attitudes. Then Helen Lyndon explains how an influential participatory methodology, the *Mosaic approach*, can serve both early-childhood research and evaluation and development of professional practice.

Joke Dewilde extends the scope again in Chapter 11 by examining *ethnography* as an approach which gets closer to participants' real experiences by the researcher's involvement in those experiences.

Tunde Rozsahegyi presents *case study*, a frequently adopted if often misunderstood research design which involves boundaried, in-depth investigation. In the last chapter, I share my own practical interest in another popular if diverse and sometimes disputed approach, that of *grounded theory*.

In *Closing words*, characteristics which have emerged from all the chapters are drawn together, most notably the importance of decision-making, of critical perspectives and of ethical considerations relating to whatever methods or approach are chosen for educational enquiry.

I and all the authors trust that you will find much to appreciate and be rewarded by in this critical guide to practical research methods in education.

References

Forster, K. (2017) Are vaccines safe to give to children? *The Independent*, 11 May 2017. [Online] www.independent.co.uk/news/health/vaccines-are-they-safe-to-give-children-dangers-advice-facts-mmr-autism-donald-trump-anti-vaxxers-a7719491.html (accessed 10 October 2018).

Hargreaves, D.H. (2007) Teaching as a research-based profession: Possibilities and prospects. In: M. Hammersley (Ed.) *Educational Research and Evidence-Based Practice*. Milton Keynes: Open University/London: Sage.

Ioannidis, J.P.A. (2005) Why most published research findings are false. *PLoS Medicine*, 2(8), e124. https://doi.org/10.1371/journal.pmed.0020124 (accessed 1 October 2018).

Lambert, M. (2012) *A Beginner's Guide to Doing Your Education Research Project*. London: Sage.

Norwich, B. (2015) Educational psychology, neuroscience and lesson study: Translating research knowledge into practice requires teacher research. *Knowledge Cultures*, 3(2), 172–190.

Ward, H. (2018) Teachers are still falling for 'fads', warns senior Ofsted official. *TES*, 1 March 2018. [Online] www.tes.com/news/teachers-are-still-falling-fads-warns-senior-ofsted-official (accessed 1 October 2018).

Chapter 1

Using questionnaires

Brendan Bartram

Introduction

This chapter explores the online and offline use of questionnaires as a research tool in education and offers a critical discussion of their benefits and limitations in relation to design and data analysis. The discussion draws on examples from my own experiences of using questionnaire surveys in quantitative and qualitative research projects. Special consideration is additionally afforded to a relatively under-utilized but very helpful form of questionnaire, based on a word-association technique. This innovative method arguably has advantages for novice and experienced researchers alike and its use and potential are again illustrated by examples derived from my own practical experiences of investigating educational issues.

Merits and limitations

When we think about investigating educational phenomena, questionnaires are perhaps one of the first research tools that spring to mind. Their use in the social sciences as a whole is very well established and students of education soon become particularly familiar with studies, reports and papers whose findings are based on data collected in this way. There are very good reasons for their ubiquity (Munn and Drever, 2004), as will be discussed below, though like any other research technique, they come with their own challenges and are not necessarily suitable for all types of enquiry. Nonetheless, their merits are many, with issues of time and scale chief among them: questionnaires often allow researchers to collect large amounts of data from sizeable groups of respondents in a relatively short amount of time. The large datasets which can be generated from standardized questions give researchers the option of using statistical means of analysis and representation, and where the sample size is both large and diverse, they offer the additional possibility of analysing and comparing particular sub-groups which may be of interest, defined, for example, by gender, age, professional roles, location or nationality. Whether or not statistical means of analysis are applied, it is nearly always possible to analyse and present findings succinctly and clearly using figures and percentages, for instance: 'Eighty per cent of respondents agreed that university students should sit exams'. Questionnaires can also be particularly useful when the aim of the research is to capture a surface impression of the extent to which groups of people agree or disagree on an issue, or to establish the range of thoughts and views in relation to certain topics, for example: 'Fifteen out of 20 respondents felt that exams were stressful, while only five suggested they were an enjoyable challenge'.

As such, questionnaires are an ideal tool when we are confident of a high return rate, and they often work particularly well in combination with interviews, which allow questionnaire data to be fleshed out with greater depth and detail. One factor often considered to facilitate a higher number of returns is related to an important ethical consideration: the anonymity and confidentiality that questionnaires offer. Well-designed versions usually highlight this feature in an attempt to encourage completion based on honest and frank responses, with respondents confident that their personal views will not be identifiable.

These factors are some of the central advantages of questionnaires, but, as with all data-collection instruments, there are certain limitations which researchers need to bear in mind. Some of these are simply the reverse side of their strengths. For example, just as questionnaires are well suited to collecting large amounts of data, they are often designed only at a descriptive, surface level (Yes/No selection, tick-box items, etc.). Although more open questions can be included, they are not always an effective means of gathering in-depth and detailed responses and this can sometimes limit the usefulness of the data collected and what can be claimed these data reveal. Given that questionnaires are predominantly a written means of data gathering, this is also an important consideration where the target population may face challenges or concerns in relation to literacy skills and confidence. And while questionnaires can sometimes produce very high numbers of returns, they are also notorious for low rates of completion. This can be for a range of reasons, in addition to the aforementioned literacy concerns. For instance, the very anonymity of the method, combined with the communication distance often involved, especially with online versions, allows disinclined respondents to opt out and hide very easily (ethically important but unfortunate for the eager researcher) and, in an age where all of us are increasingly asked to share our views on what we buy, use and experience, the notion of 'questionnaire fatigue' is something to which most of us can relate.

Further limitations relate to the fundamental issues of design and construction. Although assembling a set of questions on a topic may seem a relatively straightforward task, this is often far from the case. First of all, decisions need to be made about the type of questions to include. These can be open, closed, scaled, multi-choice, based on sentence completion, or indeed a mixture of some or all of these. Where researchers decide on a combination of question types, they run the risk of deterring respondents by producing a confusing mixture of formats. They may also end up setting themselves something of a challenge later on, when they have to decide how to analyse, interpret and represent a wide variety of response types.

There is also the very basic issue of question phrasing. This is something notoriously difficult to get right, and many questionnaire designers fall into the trap of failing to avoid leading questions ('Do you agree that exams should be scrapped?'), double questions ('Do you think exams are difficult and invalid ways to assess students?'), and overly complex, ambiguous and sometimes even offensive questions. Such potential pitfalls highlight the need for careful piloting to ensure that the planned questionnaire is as clear, valid and effective as possible. Cohen *et al.* (2018) also offer useful guidance in terms of question sequencing, suggesting that it is generally better to begin with unthreatening, factual questions (collecting demographic or 'categorical' details, for example), followed by a set of closed questions, before finishing with the most demanding open ones. Clarity of presentation and instruction are, of course, additional, vital considerations in this respect.

The importance of piloting is just one particular aspect of the logistical challenge posed by questionnaires. Trialing the planned instrument sometimes raises difficult questions with regard to time, place and arrangements for collection and return, let alone issues of negotiating access to a relevant sample, all of which need careful, advance consideration. These apply equally to administration of the 'live' questionnaire, and especially when the researcher is unable to be personally present (questionnaires may quite often be distributed by headteachers or school staff, for example). In this respect, electronic questionnaires mitigate some of these challenges, though they present the additional challenge of selectivity – the fact that some potential respondents, receiving the questionnaire link via email, opt not to take part may mean that those that do are not necessarily representative of the broader target population. For example, an electronic questionnaire about the cross-curricular use of information technology in secondary schools may see far more responses from active enthusiasts than from the disgruntled or indifferent (or perhaps *vice versa*). The potential for such selectivity effects must be carefully borne in mind when considering the validity of the findings generated and what can be claimed on this basis.

Trustworthiness and validity

One of the advantages of using questionnaires is that it allows you to get data from a large number of respondents. To what extent might having many respondents automatically increase the trustworthiness or validity of the data you collect?

Ethics

Clearly too, there are a number of ethical considerations that researchers will need to consider when using questionnaires, in addition to those of anonymity and confidentiality mentioned above. One relates to the issue of informed consent and voluntary participation, which is particularly pertinent when school children or college and university students, for example, are asked to complete a questionnaire. In this kind of 'captive' situation, it would be very easy for respondents to feel coerced into completion. This may be because they feel under pressure to comply with what they are asked to do, or even to fit in with what others in the group appear happy to go along with. This is a difficult issue to address completely, but it highlights the researcher's responsibility to emphasize the voluntary nature of completion, to provide assurances of confidentiality, and to highlight the lack of any consequences for non-participation. As alluded to earlier, questions will also need to be sensitively and appropriately constructed so as to avoid causing offence, embarrassment or a perception of invasion of privacy. To do this would be to breach all ethical codes in research, and it stands to reason that such reactions will do little to encourage respondent participation.

Addressing ethical concerns

As well as the issues identified here, what other ethical concerns need to be considered when using questionnaires? In what ways might you address these in your own research?

The following sections now focus on a number of projects which I have been involved in that have used different types of questionnaires to collect data. Many of the issues discussed above are examined in the context of the specifics at the heart of the various research studies, and there are some discussion questions at the end to focus your reflections and ideas.

Using written questionnaires to investigate university students' reasons for non-participation in international placements

This research study (Bartram, 2013) examined the views of undergraduates studying on education-related courses at a university in the West Midlands, England. Second-year students undertook a year-long module which offered an optional, two-week, international placement in the Netherlands or Finland. However, very few students chose to take advantage of this opportunity, despite well-publicized, preparatory sessions and online information. One of the study's key aims was to uncover the reasons behind the students' reluctance.

The research used a paper-based questionnaire as well as interviews to collect data. The questionnaire consisted of three types of questions. As suggested above, it began with a set designed to establish key categorical features (gender, age, ethnicity, previous experience abroad), followed by closed, tick-box questions, and finally some open-ended questions which invited the students to elaborate on their reasons for not choosing to do an international placement. The questionnaire (after piloting with colleagues for feedback) was administered mid-module, post-dating the point at which students needed to declare their intention to participate, or not, in the placement. It was handed out to willing respondents, all of whom had decided not to take up a placement abroad, at the end of a taught session on the module. Students were fully briefed on the nature and intentions of the research, informed that completing the questionnaire was entirely voluntary and given assurances of anonymity. As had been anticipated, a high response rate was received, with a total of 106 students agreeing to participate – 11 chose not to. I suggested that non-respondents should work on a preparatory task for the following week's lecture so that their non-participation was hidden and any feelings of embarrassment could be averted.

At this stage, students were additionally asked to indicate their willingness to take part in follow-up interviews by adding their email address to a post-it note that they could hand in separately to preserve their anonymity. The questionnaire responses were analysed using a spreadsheet package so that they could be isolated and interrogated against the background features indicated above. This was useful in identifying overall patterns that were later followed up in the individual interviews.

To address the study's aim, students were asked to tick any number of items from a list of possible reasons for their non-participation. These related to factors identified in the literature and were arranged in the questionnaire in random order so as to avoid simple repetition of previously established rankings. Table 1.1 shows the number of responses per item and presents them in the rank order which resulted. As such, the questionnaire provided a useful, straightforward and effective means of establishing and presenting a clear overview and hierarchy of factors deterring these students from undertaking an international placement.

Table 1.1 Students' reasons for non-participation in international placements (Bartram, 2013)

Reasons for not applying for international placement	Ranking	No. of responses
Financial concerns	1	71
Lack of interest	2	23
Lack of confidence	3	20
Anxiety about leaving friends/family	4	19
Childcare difficulties	5=	18
Fear of the unknown	5=	18
Anxiety about language skills	5=	18
Anxiety about travel	6=	12
Not perceived to enhance employability	6=	12
Anxiety about being abroad	7	11
Perceived lack of relevance	8	9
Not perceived to enhance CV	9	8

Using online questionnaires to investigate students' reasons for entering higher education in England, Germany and Portugal

This research project (Bartram, 2016a; 2016b) explored and compared students' reasons for attending university in three different countries. A set of seven intrinsic and extrinsic motivational components had been identified from models in the literature: motivation, prompted by a perceived lack of alternatives; a desire for self-development; economic benefits; qualification and career motives; attendance, driven by social pressures associated with family and peers; the appeal of the social dimension of university life; and altruism – a desire to help other people in future.

The project focused on undergraduates at one institution in each of the countries, and as such, the findings were not necessarily representative of national pictures (inasmuch as those exist). To provide a degree of relatability (Hammersley, 1997), however, the universities involved – in the West Midlands, North-Rhine Westphalia and the Algarve – were purposively selected on the basis of their relative typicality: large, multi-faculty, state-run institutions, offering a wide range of courses at BA, MA and doctorate levels, and recruiting students from a wide range of backgrounds. The students surveyed were all studying broadly similar subjects – this was an attempt to provide as valid a basis for comparison as possible, given the potential dissimilarity in motivations between students from different disciplines. A two-stage survey approach was adopted, consisting of an online questionnaire, followed by individual email interviews.

The questionnaire aimed to capture a picture of students' motives by using a version of Neill's (2004) motivation survey. It consisted of 35 questions, seven of which collected categorical details. The remaining 'Likert-scale' items required respondents to express levels of agreement (1–5), with statements based around the components mentioned above. The intention was to provide an initial, numerical indication of key areas in order to highlight broader commonalities and differences regarding the relative importance of these motivational elements.

Table 1.2 Personal development and altruistic motives for university enrolment: Combined percentage scores for top two boxes: 'Strongly Agree' and 'Agree' (Bartram, 2016a; 2016b)

Personal development: I went to university because…	Germany	Portugal	England
I want to explore new ideas	78.1	93	91.4
I want to challenge myself	65.6	86.1	87.4
For my personal growth and development	96.8	100.0	97.8
I love learning	45.0	64.2	66.6
Average percentage	*71.3*	*86*	*85.8*
Altruism: I went to university because …	Germany	Portugal	England
I genuinely want to help others	59.3	71.3	89.5
I want to contribute to society	48.3	81.4	79.1
I want to help solve society's problems	25.7	75.7	39.5
I want to be more useful to society	32.1	89.2	79.1
Average percentage	*41.3*	*79.4*	*71.8*

After piloting and adjustments, respondents completed a 'plain-English' version of the questionnaire. Though an initial consideration was to opt for German and Portuguese translations (a costly undertaking), discussions with colleagues persuaded me that this kind of English-language version should pose few problems, given that students in both countries had studied English as a compulsory, pre-university subject and that completing the survey involved only receptive language skills.

In total, 351 students completed the questionnaire: 150 English students (43 per cent of the overall sample, and thus the largest grouping); 99 Germans (28 per cent) and 102 Portuguese (29 per cent). The online software package used enabled filtering by country of origin and converted responses into percentage totals. Responses to items belonging to the same motivational categories were then brought together to allow comparison of patterns, consistencies and emphases across the data. It was decided that the percentage figures produced by the data could only be included for the purposes of tentative indication, rather than statistical statement of fact – limitations imposed by the self-selective nature of the sample, the variation in national group sizes and the single institutional and subject-area composition could support only fallibilistic interpretation (Schwandt, 2015), rather than scientific measurement.

An example of the data relating to two of the motivational categories, Table 1.2, is presented by way of illustration. This shows combined percentages for the top two boxes, 'Strongly agree' and 'Agree', for students from each country, rounded to one decimal place, and indicates that the questionnaire was useful in highlighting some interesting, overall differences and similarities between the national sub-samples.

Using a word-association questionnaire to compare school students' attitudes to modern foreign language learning

This piece of research compared and examined secondary-school students' attitudes to learning different languages in England, Germany and the Netherlands. It began by using what is known as a 'word-association' questionnaire to establish key attitudinal features among the chosen school communities. Word-association questionnaires involve participants providing responses to given stimulus words or expressions – Ryan and Bernhard (2000:770) describe these kinds of free lists as 'particularly useful for identifying the items in a cultural domain'. Word-association techniques like this were employed by Mondario (1997) in her investigation of language attitudes among Hungarian students and by Cain and de Pietro (1997) in similar research carried out with French, Swiss and Bulgarian teenagers. In order to aid interpretation, Cain and de Pietro asked participants to mark responses with either a plus (+), minus (−) or equals (=) symbol to indicate whether they felt their chosen answer was positive, negative or neutral, potentially a useful way to avoid erroneous assumptions during data analysis.

For each language being investigated, teachers in each of the secondary schools in my study were asked to recruit around 30 volunteer students, male and female, from across the ability range. Once these students were assembled in the classroom, I discussed the task and dealt with any questions. The students subsequently wrote down their responses to 21 key educational and social notions, identified by the literature as being important in terms of attitudes towards modern foreign language learning, with 30 minutes to complete the task. They were reminded that the number and nature of their responses was entirely their choice, and once completed, the questionnaires were collected and sealed in envelopes.

The responses were examined, analysed and coded to produce categories of meaning that emerged directly from the secondary-school students themselves. These provisional categories were then compared across the schools to find similarities and differences in attitudes which had been expressed. This enabled the research process to begin in a fairly exploratory fashion, with students themselves volunteering vocabulary for analysis, rather than producing fixed responses to standardized questions based around pre-determined categories, something often considered a shortcoming in traditional questionnaires.

There are, however, several criticisms that could have been levelled at the use of this type of questionnaire in my research. One was its reductive quality, in that responses were often given as single-word items. To compensate for this, more students participated in this questionnaire phase than in later, focus-group interview stages. This meant that even though questionnaire responses were generally brief, they still contributed a rich and detailed descriptive vocabulary that served as a useful research basis which could be verified and subsequently explored. Another criticism related to the challenging, quantitative element involved in the analysis, with quite large numbers of students (408 across six schools) learning three different languages and responding to 21 individual items. From Silverman's (2013) point of view, however, simple numerical techniques such as this are potentially useful features in qualitative research, and once the students' responses had been categorized, it seemed sensible to acknowledge the number of contributions within each category, though I refrained from attaching any statistical significance to these. Had more time for questionnaire completion been available, it is possible that supplementary responses would have swelled other categories, thus altering the elements highlighted within the data. In this sense again, the findings offer only a fallible representation of student attitudes. Nonetheless, the numbers do provide some indication of attitudinal emphases within the sample, by making explicit the frequency of particular categories of comment and, as such, add to understanding of the issues on which the research was focused.

Piloting

As outlined above, the word-association task was devised to include various items based on educational, social and cultural factors, identified as being important in influencing attitudes. From the start, related items were not listed close together, in order to deter students from simply repeating similar responses to associated elements. After subsequent consultation with colleagues, it was decided to amend the order of some of the items, so that less contentious issues (for example, about use of information technology in the language classroom) were presented earlier in the task than potentially sensitive ones (such as those relating to attitudes towards German people). This was an attempt to make students more at ease completing the exercise. The task was then piloted with a group of 20 learners of German, aged 15–16, at an English school similar in size, intake and attainment levels to those participating in the study (but not included in the study itself), thus allowing a realistic indication of how the task would be received and approached. All those present agreed to participate in the pilot and as well as completing the task, they also gave feedback on the questionnaire itself, providing some interesting insights that were subsequently used as the basis for separate, specific research on student attitudes towards learning German (Bartram, 2004).

This feedback showed that there was some confusion about the annotation of responses, that is using the symbols (+), (−) and (=) to indicate whether students felt their responses were positive, negative or neutral, as in Cain and de Pietro's (1997) research. Although the cover sheet included instructions on this, and responses demonstrated that many students had clearly understood the process, it was decided that spending time discussing it more thoroughly during the introduction to the main study would be important. Nevertheless, even in this pilot, the annotation system proved to be a useful feature in interpretation. An example was identical-word responses to the item concerning the amount of German taught at the school, where the annotations helped to distinguish between students who were pleased with what they felt to be a welcome number of lessons: 'a lot (+)', and those who saw the situation as undesirable: 'a lot (−)'.

The questionnaire was then translated into German and Dutch, before being checked by native-speaker teachers in Germany and the Netherlands to ensure accuracy, clarity and currency of expression. Careful attention was also paid throughout the research to ensuring linguistic and conceptual equivalence in the translations (Osborn *et al.*, 2003), in order to preserve the validity of comparisons. Though logistical difficulties prevented whole-class trials in these two countries, colleagues there assisted in finding a small number of German and Dutch teenagers willing to complete the piloting task and provide feedback.

Analysis

Once the data had been collected, student responses were transcribed onto single sheets related to each item per school. This allowed a clear overview and facilitated categorization. Sample responses were discussed and reviewed with colleagues in an attempt to identify any omissions or bias in my analysis. The involvement of such critical friends at each stage, as recommended by Winter (1989), was not only helpful from a practical point of view but, by including a range of viewpoints, also contributed towards confirming analytical plausibility of the findings (Hammersley, 1997). Barring a few minor discrepancies, the process

Table 1.3 English and Dutch students' attitudes to their German lessons (Bartram, 2012)

Category	English responses		Dutch responses	
	No.	Examples	No.	Examples
Boring	22	Dull Very boring	13	Unbelievably boring Dull

Critical	21	It's mostly writing
		Rubbish
		Don't learn enough vocab
		I don't see a point in them
		Some students mess about
		   because they don't like
		   languages
		Too early in the morning
			16	No good explanations
				Don't do much
				We generally don't achieve our
				   objective
				We don't do anything in the lesson
				   (−), she's never there
				Our class is very noisy

Indifferent	10	OK (=) So-so	15	All right (=) OK (=)

Enjoyable	16	Fast paced (+)
		Can be rewarding
		Are really good but I'd never
		   say!
		Gives me a better understanding
		   of English
			25	Fun
				Lot of variety
				Useful
				Nice with videos
				Peaceful lessons
				Always follows the same pattern
				   (+)

produced both similar categories and numbers within those categories, thereby confirming that the method of analysis offered a fair degree of dependability (but not total reliability in a scientific sense). Item responses were then regrouped thematically to establish overall patterns. These were compared between schools in the same country to identify differences. As expected, these response patterns proved broadly similar, allowing the pooling of data before proceeding to compare the different national responses. Overall, this instrument yielded a wealth of useful data, although the time-consuming analysis proved a significant challenge and in hindsight, a smaller number of respondents at this stage (perhaps around 20, instead of 30 per language) would have reduced the time taken, without compromising the results.

Table 1.3 presents an overview of the English and Dutch students' attitudes to the questionnaire item, 'German lessons'. Bartram (2012) offers a full discussion of the entire study.

Ways of using questionnaires

1. What do you consider the strengths and limitations of the ways of using questionnaires described in these three research studies?
2. In what ways do you feel these research studies addressed (or failed to address) the design, usage and ethical issues discussed in the first part of the chapter?
3. Which of the three approaches (if any) might you favour for your own research, and for what reasons?

Conclusion

As illustrated, questionnaires offer the educational researcher many advantages. They are an adaptable, flexible and often efficient technique by which large amounts of data from multiple respondents can be collected fairly quickly. There is a variety of question types and formats which can be included to prompt responses. Nevertheless, there are pitfalls and limitations which can compromise their usefulness. Researchers need to consider very carefully, through piloting and other means, access to the intended sample, the choice, formulation and structure of questions, planned processes for data analysis and presentation, and the ethical implications of what they are undertaking. Finally, therefore, here are three main points of advice:

- Consider carefully whether the type of research you are planning is best served by using a questionnaire.
- Make sure that you pay close attention to issues of design clarity, user instruction, question construction and ethics.
- Give advance thought to how you plan to analyse the responses you will receive and how you will present this analysis in your final written study.

Recommended reading

Denscombe, M. (2017) *The Good Research Guide: For Small-Scale Social Research Projects*. Sixth edition. Milton Keynes: Open University Press.
Robson, C. and McCartan, K. (2016) *Real World Research*. Fourth edition. Chichester: John Wiley.

Both these texts provide useful discussions on designing and using questionnaires in educational research.

References

Bartram, B. (2004) Learning German: An investigation of pupil attitudes. *Deutsch: Lehren und Lernen*, 29, 21–24.
Bartram, B. (2012) *Attitudes to Modern Foreign Language Learning: Insights from Comparative Education*. London: Continuum.
Bartram, B. (2013) The 'graduate global citizen'? An examination of undergraduate Education students' reasons for non-participation in international placements. *Educationalfutures*, 5(2), 75–87. [Online] http://educationstudies.org.uk/wp-content/uploads/2013/11/brendan_bartram_2013.pdf (accessed 31 August 2017).
Bartram, B. (2016a) Economic motives to attend university: A cross-country study. *Research in Post-Compulsory Education*, 21(4), 394–408.
Bartram, B. (2016b) 'Career and money aside, what's the point of university?' A comparison of students' non-economic entry motives in three European countries. *Higher Education Quarterly*, 70(3), 281–300.
Cain, A. and de Pietro, J.F. (1997) Les représentations des pays dont on apprend la langue: Complément facultatif ou composante de l'apprentissage? In: M. Matthey (Ed.) *Les Langues et Leurs Images*. Neuchâtel: Institut de Recherche et de Documentation Pédagogique (IRDP).
Cohen, L., Manion, L. and Morrison, K. (2018) *Research Methods in Education*. Eighth edition. Abingdon: Routledge.

Hammersley, M. (1997) *Reading Ethnographic Research: A Critical Guide*. New York: Longman.

Mondario, A. (1997) L'image des langues dans le paysage socioéconomique hongrois. In: M. Matthey (Ed.) *Les Langues et Leurs Images*. Neuchâtel: Institut de Recherche et de Documentation Pédagogique (IRDP).

Munn, P. and Drever, E. (2004) *Using Questionnaires in Small-Scale Research: A Beginner's Guide*. Revised edition. Glasgow: Scottish Council for Research in Education.

Neill, J. (2004) *The University Student Motivation and Satisfaction Questionnaire Version 2* (TUSMSQ2). Centre for Applied Psychology, University of Canberra.

Osborn, M., Broadfoot, P., McNess, E., Planel, C., Ravn, B. and Triggs, P. (2003) *A World of Difference? Comparing Learners Across Europe*. Maidenhead: Open University Press.

Ryan, G.W. and Bernhard, H.R. (2000) Data management and analysis methods. In: N.K. Denzin and Y.S. Lincoln (Eds.) *Handbook of Qualitative Research*. Second edition. London: Sage.

Schwandt, T.A. (2015) *The SAGE Dictionary of Qualitative Enquiry*. Fourth edition. London: Sage.

Silverman, D. (2013) *Doing Qualitative Research*. London: Sage.

Winter, R. (1989) *Learning from Experience: Principles and Practice in Action-Research*. London: The Falmer Press.

Chapter 2

Using interviews

Jo Winwood

Introduction

Within school-based education, research is often about the experiences of children, most notably in relation to their learning. However, adults play a pivotal role in providing their educational experiences and developing effective provision. In my research in schools in England (Winwood, 2012), the role of the Special Educational Needs Co-ordinator (SENCO) in developing inclusive practice and school improvement was explored. Interviews in this research enabled the SENCOs to have a voice, reflecting their important professional involvement in the education system. The interviews also made it possible for the researcher and participants to develop a dialogue through which the SENCO role could be examined from a range of perspectives. Building on data collected earlier from questionnaires, they then allowed findings to be reached which were in-depth, which revealed personal experiences as well as professional understandings, and which were valuable to other SENCOs, settings and researchers.

This chapter examines different kinds of interviews and explores the benefits and limitations of using each of these to gather data from adults. It discusses which kind of interviews I used in my own research, how they were used, how a suitable interview schedule was developed, and how the data produced was analysed in order to reach worthwhile findings.

Interviews

Interviews enable participants to discuss their experiences and interpretations of particular situations. Cohen *et al.* (2018) point out that they are also an effective method to validate and explore in greater depth issues already raised by other techniques, adding additional insights and enriching the research through the generation of qualitative data. Grosvenor and Rose (2012) further support their use when investigation focuses on particular phenomena or a specific group of people and when detailed information is required from a small number of participants. An additional advantage is that most people already have some experience of being interviewed when seeking a job, or as part of work appraisal, and sometimes experience of actually carrying out interviews themselves. While a range of issues needs to be taken into account before interviews begin, they offer a very accessible method of data collection, and because of their familiarity, the process is likely to be less daunting for interviewees (Bryman, 2015).

There are three main types of interviews commonly identified in the literature. These are defined by the amount of pre-planning and structure they entail. It is worth looking at each of these in turn.

Structured interviews

In its simplest form, a 'structured' interview involves one person asking questions to another and then recording the responses, perhaps with written notes or electronically, all in a very pre-planned and controlled way. It is a formal exchange which follows a exact schedule – very specific questions are asked in a pre-determined order and in the same way to all participants. Answers are usually – but do not have to be – short (Yes or No, a specific fact, or a choice on a scale), with little or no guidance or feedback given by the interviewer. This means that data can be gathered relatively quickly from a large number of participants, and that results can be analysed easily too. In a structured interview, the interviewer is, as far as possible, a neutral participant, whose role it is to administer the questions but not to sway the interviewee's responses in any way. If done well, the researcher can then be confident that any variations in responses between different participants will only reveal differences in their insights, beliefs and experiences, with little or no influence on those responses from the interviewer or the interview process. Any reader who has taken part in a tele-marketing interview will recognize this structured method of collecting data.

Nevertheless, it is easy to presume in structured interviews, particularly when there is a small number of participants and the topic includes commonly used terms, that there is shared understanding amongst those participants of the language being used. However, research issues are invariably complex, and careful planning and piloting of questions in advance of the investigation is therefore needed to reveal different possible understandings of words, wording and terminology (Punch, 2009). Even within a formal schedule, questions can be open to different interpretations, depending on how they are asked or phrased. For instance, questions which aim to reveal facts, such as age or gender, can appear straightforward but can actually be unreliable or cause difficulty, for example, if a participant does not wish to reveal their true age or gender, or indeed, is transgender.

It is also possible, fairly common in fact, for there to be a few structured questions within other, more informal styles of interview (the types I describe below). I had an example of this in my own examination of staff perceptions of special educational needs, part of the SENCO research mentioned at the start. In response to initial, structured questions about 'working with disabled children', staff surprisingly reported that they had little experience in this area. However, as my later, more informal questioning revealed, they had answered in this way because they almost exclusively associated 'disability' with physical impairment, and defined other, non-physical conditions, such as autism, not as a disability but as 'special educational needs'. I had intended that the word, 'disabled', should cover all types, but this was not matched by the participants' interpretation of the term. The example reflects May's (2011) suggestion that researchers need to reach a situation where the interviewees' interpretation is similar to that of the researcher. In relation to structured questions or interviews, it also illustrates their limitations, in that some topics are too complex to be explored through a standard format and the researcher may therefore need to use an alternative approach.

Semi-structured interviews

Social-research topics exemplify this complexity. They often require more extensive qualitative data to be gathered to gain deeper insights into the experiences and perceptions of those involved. In these situations, less formalized, so-called 'semi-structured' interviews (or semi-structured questions within an interview) are often favoured. These provide the opportunity for more interaction and discussion between the interviewer and interviewee than is the case with structured interviews or questions. Interviewers can revisit points and ask supplementary questions to further increase insights obtained from interviewees' initial responses.

While structured interviews stick rigidly to a schedule, semi-structured interviews offer more of a 'middle ground' between that and having no pre-determined structure at all. As with structured interviews, an interview schedule is developed in advance, but this is more a general guide, leaving the interviewer free to ask secondary or supplementary questions for clarification of a point or for elaboration (Silverman, 2017). This schedule is usually shared with the participants before the interview is conducted, so that they are aware of the main questions which will be asked. This approach also offers a support mechanism for interviewers, as it can be easy to forget key questions when actively involved in the data-collection process. The schedule acts as an *aide-mémoire*, meaning that essential topics are not overlooked.

This degree of flexibility can raise questions about the validity of responses gained. However, a semi-structured approach can also help the development of a rapport between the interviewer and interviewee, which is particularly beneficial when exploring some topics, as participants are more likely to reveal their thoughts and opinions to a person who seems genuinely interested in them and their responses. Bell (2014) notes that although this makes the process subjective, it often leads to rich data which can be missing from more structured approaches.

Unstructured interviews

The third type of interview, 'unstructured' interviews, can be seen as an open but purposeful conversation, where the interviewer and interviewee freely discuss the topic being explored. Burton and Bartlett (2009) state that this approach puts the respondent at the centre of the process, with the interviewer having only a few prompts or questions to support the debate. They note that discussions between teachers and schoolchildren are an example of unstructured interviews, and although these might not be seen as a formal data-collection technique, they can easily be used to provide data during an action-research project or lesson study. The natural development of conversation and the insights revealed is one benefit of doing unstructured interviews, but researchers should remember that they are still gathering data for a purpose and therefore should try to ensure that relevant data which answers the study's research questions is collected.

In unstructured interviews, participants may even set the agenda themselves, so as to highlight the issues which matter most to them (Bell, 2014). A good example of this would be disabled people guiding an investigation into disability-related issues, reflecting a participatory approach. In this context, the researcher might start the process by identifying a broad area to explore and then invite disabled people directly involved in, or impacted by, this topic to guide, shape and participate in the research process, including carrying out interviews themselves. Within a broad framework for these interviews, the participants would have freedom to introduce, examine and discuss issues which they felt were relevant, and, at the same time, essential data relevant to the investigation would be gathered.

Focus-group interviews

This brings us to another type of interview which can utilize any of the approaches outlined above, although they are most usually associated with those which are semi-structured or unstructured. 'Focus-group' interviews are conducted with participants in a group, rather than individually. The interviewees are included in the group because of their interest or involvement in the topic being researched and may represent a range of opinions or perspectives on that topic. By bringing people together, researchers can encourage them to interact with each other and develop discussion, debate and exploration (Bryman, 2015). Agreement and disagreement amongst the participants will reveal interesting insights, and reaching a consensus might not be an aim of the method – the researcher's purpose might rather be for participants to review their opinions in light of what others say. Nevertheless, the dynamics of this kind of group can be hard to manage: the interviewer must allow all participants to have an opportunity to speak, as well as prevent anybody from dominating the discussions, especially in ways that might influence what others feel comfortable to say. There may well be issues of confidentiality and anonymity to deal with also, as each focus-group member will know who the other group members are and will hear their contributions to discussion.

My research

Although the SENCO role is common to every maintained mainstream and special school in England, my doctoral research aimed to discover what, if any, shared experiences SENCOs actually have when carrying out this role. Furthermore, I felt that an exploration of the experiences of being a SENCO would reveal how far the aspirations of government guidelines, most notably the *Special Educational Needs Code of Practice* (DfES, 2001), which first set out the SENCO role and which was still applicable at that time, were actually being realized.

The semi-structured nature of the interviews which I carried out enabled the SENCOs to discuss their experiences and perceptions of their role in this context. They also provided opportunities for both the interviewer and interviewee to engage in dialogue about the topic, to identify and analyse issues together and to jointly explore emergent points. Discussion of this kind could uncover events, feelings or responses that had not been observed or recognized in data I collected using other methods.

Indeed, semi-structured interviews offer an opportunity to gather substantial qualitative data, but for that reason they can be time-consuming, not only for the interviewer but also for interviewees. Researchers have to balance their desire to gather good-quality, useful data with other demands faced by their participants. This was very relevant to SENCOs in my research, as time pressure associated with their role was one of the challenges which both the literature review and my earlier questionnaire had identified. In part to take account of this challenge, the six interviewees were informed beforehand of the points for discussion which would be raised in their interviews. The participants also invited the researcher into their schools for preliminary visits before the interviews took place. These enabled me to consolidate the professional relationships that already existed between us, provided an insight into the day-to-day work which the SENCOs completed, and helped to develop a shared understanding of the pressures and expectations of the role in each setting before the interviews were conducted.

Types and topics

Four types of interviews are outlined in this chapter: structured, semi-structured and unstructured, as well as focus groups. Using this discussion, as well as other literature and your own ideas:

1. Identify advantages and limitations of using each kind of interview as a research method.
2. Identify advantages and limitations of using semi-structured interviews in the SENCO research described here.
3. Choose a research topic and a type of interview (or perhaps more than one type) which would enable you to collect relevant and useful data. Justify why you selected this for the research.

Interview schedule

Having decided on a type of interview which will enable relevant data to be gathered, the researcher has to develop a schedule which will form the basis of the interview process. This is likely to be made up of questions, but it could also include statements and themes for the participants to explore. This was the case in the schedule for my own research – it was not a rigid set of questions to be asked in order, but rather a set of headings, based on issues, themes and topics to be explored in the interview. I had identified these through a literature review and from my own experiences of being a SENCO. Examples of the themes which emerged included the following: the SENCO role as a career aspiration (previous experiences, roles, training, interests); a typical working week; leadership aspects of the role (working with colleagues, strategic elements of the role, management and paperwork); expectations of others and their implications for the status associated with the SENCO role. These themes acted as pointers around which interview questions were organized.

The sequence of questions is an important element of an interview schedule. Devising a clear structure is likely to put those involved at ease and enable useful data to be gathered. A popular way to do this is to start with an introduction which outlines the purpose of the study as well as how the interview will be conducted. Participants can also ask any questions they have at this point.

The interview itself can then start with straightforward questions, for example, about the type and size of school where the interviewee works. This approach creates confidence that questions can be answered and also helps the interviewer to understand some basic information about the interviewee and their experiences. This can then lead on to exploring the more complex issues surrounding the chosen topic. Active listening by the interviewer is important at this stage: revisiting points, asking for clarification and seeking further explanation for some responses. Any questions which might be considered sensitive or problematic should probably be left until the later stages of the interview, when a rapport has been established. Some participants might refuse to answer these more difficult questions, but the interviewer will already have gathered other data which can still be used. It is good practice to end the interview by asking if the participants have any queries or further information to give, by reiterating what will happen to their data, and, of course, by thanking them for their contribution to the research.

As indicated earlier, questions asked during the interview can be closed, open or answered using a scale. Closed questions may require only a 'Yes', 'No' or 'Don't know' response from the interviewee, or a specific fact, whereas open questions require longer responses, with the participant drawing on their knowledge and experiences to answer them, while still being able to control how much they reveal to the interviewer. Scale questions often make use of a 'Likert scale', where the participant selects an answer from several provided. Depending on the question, these might range from 'Strongly disagree' to 'Strongly agree', or could be numerical, for instance 1 to 5. Having an odd number of choices means that participants can select a neutral response in the middle, whereas an even number forces them to select either a negative or positive option. Likert-scale questions are still closed questions, but they provide more useful data for the researcher than the simple 'Yes', 'No' or 'Don't know' responses. Figure 2.1 shows two different examples, together with their questions.

Having thought about the type of questions and the order in which they will be asked, researchers also have to consider their focus. Questions should only be asked if they collect the data needed to answer the main research questions. Wording should encourage the participants to share relevant facts, thoughts and insights. In problematic areas, providing definitions for potentially ambiguous terms and technical language can help with this. The interviewer should also avoid overly long questions, as parts might be forgotten and overlooked, limiting the data that is gathered. It is also important to avoid asking two questions in one, for example: 'How satisfied are you with your pay and job conditions?' This can be done by separating each part – pay on the one hand, job conditions on the other – into two separate questions. In the SENCO research, two pilot interviews were carried out, with a teacher and an experienced teaching assistant, in order to find out the extent to which participants and the researcher would have shared understanding of the terms used in the interview questions and to try to ensure that these would be interpreted by participants in the main study in ways that would provide relevant data.

Interview questions can explore facts (such as work roles and tasks), how a professional role is behaviourally operationalized and what participants think about this experience (Robson and McCartan, 2016). This is what I did in my research. I started with questions to find out what type of school the participant was working at (mainstream or special, primary or secondary), the number of classes in that school, and the identity of the local authority, all as an introduction to the main part of the interview. These were

Overall, to what extent do you have enough time to complete the tasks which relate to special educational needs in your school?

Never	Rarely	Sometimes	Yes, mostly	Yes, always

How involved are you with leadership issues for special educational needs in your setting (1 = not at all, 6 = fully involved)?

1	2	3	4	5	6

Figure 2.1 Examples of questions and scales

followed by more complex, open questions about the type of tasks which the SENCO undertook and their day-to-day management of special educational needs within the school. These questions also explored their behaviour as SENCOs, an issue which had factual underpinnings, but which also started debates about what it meant to fulfil this role. At the end came questions which explored more deeply their perceptions of their role. These required reflection on their working lives as SENCOs, drawing on what they did in relation to areas such as leadership and collegiality, and on the ways in which others interpreted and responded to their work.

Finally, it is worth being aware of your own interest in your chosen research topic. Because of your commitment to it, your questions (or comments within the interview) might include unintended biases, which can lead respondents to give answers which do not reflect their actual opinions. Here is an example of the type of biased question which I had to avoid in my own research: 'Do you think that the excessive demands placed on SENCOs by the Code of Practice have deterred some from continuing in the role?' The question suggests that the Code of Practice does indeed place excessive demands on SENCOs, whereas it would be more useful to find out whether or not this was the case for the SENCO being interviewed (it might not be). Rewording the question, for instance by asking about the extent to which expectations of the role were demanding or not demanding, would avoid this inherent bias. Another example is this: 'Do you have difficulties completing all of the tasks outlined in the Government's Code of Practice?'. Again the question guides the participant towards identifying problems, when actually there might not be any. Overall, interview questions should aim to be neutral, offering respondents the opportunity to give their independent views on the issues being explored, uninfluenced by the researcher or by the wording of questions.

Writing an interview schedule

Using ideas presented in this section, write an interview schedule for a topic which is relevant to you. This could be a topic you intend to research or something more general, for instance (if you are a student) a campus issue, such as the cost of lunch. Once the schedule is written, try these further tasks:

1. Sort or colour-code your questions into facts, behaviours and feelings. Then organize them into a logical structure, starting with facts, then behaviours, then feelings.
2. Carefully examine the questions. Do they include words or phrases which might be ambiguous? Do any questions need to be broken into smaller parts, covering one area each? Is there bias in the way any are phrased? Overall, will they gather the kind of data which will help your research?
3. Pilot your schedule with friends, then evaluate what further changes you might need to make to it before using it for a proper investigation.

Conducting interviews

One other decision to make before actually conducting the interviews is how to capture what is said. Recording electronically through audio or even video can be very useful, as it means that you do not have to write anything during the interview and can focus fully on asking questions and furthering discussion. However, it will also be necessary to have permission from the participant to do this, and some, although willing to be interviewed, might not wish what they say to be documented in this way. All such data must be kept securely afterwards, so that it cannot be accessed by others, even inadvertently – storing files (including transcript files) on a password-protected computer is one way to achieve this. Recording also allows the researcher to listen closely and repeatedly to the interview afterwards and to become very familiar with its content, although transcribing even short interviews is a very laborious process.

Taking written notes while listening, on the other hand, may be more acceptable to some interviewees, but it will mean that some data is likely to be lost. It is worth adding to any written notes taken during the interview with further notes immediately afterwards, when you recall what was said. Another approach is for a friend or colleague to take notes while you yourself conduct the interview, although this third person must be acceptable to the interviewee and must agree to abide by any promises of anonymity and confidentiality which have been given. Again, written notes need to be stored, perhaps in a locked filing cabinet, so that others cannot read them. Any data, in whatever form, must only be used for the research outlined to participants at the start of the interview, unless additional permission is given.

Overall, collecting data through interviews is a very rewarding task, but it can also be rather nerve-wracking, both for yourself as the interviewer and for your interviewees. To deal with this, it is useful to consider your interviews as professional interactions and act accordingly. Here are some suggestions in relation to this:

- Be at the setting early to arrange furniture and chairs, check recording equipment (if it is to be used) and create a suitable environment.
- Welcome the interviewee or interviewees and outline how the interview will proceed. This is a good way to make everyone feel at ease and to show that participation is valued.
- Practise asking the questions in advance, so that at the interview itself you are familiar with the wording and order and can focus on the responses which your participants give.
- At the start of the interview, revisit ethical safeguards, such as confidentiality and anonymity, with your participants.
- Thank your interviewee or interviewees at the end and, if you wish, discuss the possibility of another meeting in the future, perhaps to clarify any points or eventually to share findings and outcomes of the research.

Practical issues

1. What is your view on the idea of treating interviews with adults as 'professional interactions'?
2. If you were advising another interviewer, what additional suggestions to those given here might you make?
3. What other practical issues might you wish to address before conducting any type of interview yourself?

Analysing interview data

Listening to recordings, reading transcripts or examining notes should enable the researcher to identify patterns in the responses provided by the interviewees. 'Codes', such as numbers, letters or colours, can be used to sort and group the data. Each code should relate to a specific idea which emerges and when sufficient data has been analysed, this should make it possible to identify the participants' common experiences and perspectives in the findings and instances where these diverge. Cohen *et al.* (2018) provide a detailed explanation of this kind of coding process.

Coding a transcript

Here is an example of recorded data from one of the SENCO interviews described in this chapter. The participant had been asked about her role in the school and, in particular, how she supported other staff in relation to special educational needs and inclusion. Use coding to identify themes emerging from this extract:

Participant: And then I've also still got children who I'm referring for statutory assessment and all the paperwork that that involves. I do training sessions quite regularly, I'm regularly involved in delivering CPD [continuing professional development], I'm regularly involved in working with newly qualified teachers. I very much have an open door, and often we'll have people coming in from the area, saying could we come and look at your school. We work with the cluster [of local schools], provide advice there – work, as I say, with specialist support teachers that come into school.

Interviewer: What kind of CPD do you do?

Participant: Well, in school, I do CPD around autism or dyslexia or differentiation for those sorts of subject areas.

Interviewer: And would that be staff meeting or …

Participant: Yes, we have twilight [after the school day] CPDs, we do our CPD now through twilight.

The 'Coding a transcript' example given here illustrates how coding and analysing data from semi-structured and unstructured interviews can take time and effort but also reveal very useful insights. Formal, structured interviews might reduce time spent on coding, but they are likely to reveal much less from their data, especially when the data is qualitative. Whatever kind of interview is chosen, analysis offers the researcher an opportunity to reflect on what they have learned, begin to make links to the literature review and develop a structure for the final written report.

Ethics

Ethical standards should be kept in mind and regularly revisited at every stage of the research process (Alderson, 2014), not only when interviews are actually being conducted. Projects evolve over time and different issues might arise which have not been considered at an earlier point. Furthermore, researchers have this responsibility not just in order to protect their participants but also so that they do not jeopardize research opportunities for other researchers in the future.

One ethical consideration which has already been mentioned is the need to create a professional tone and supportive environment for interviewees. The interviewer should appreciate that being interviewed can be a quite an intimidating process. Participants may feel pressure to 'say the right thing'. They may also inadvertently reveal more in the interview than they intended. In my research, I sought to address this by giving them the opportunity to review and amend the data they had provided. Being open and honest about both the purpose and the outcomes of the interviews is an essential part of the researcher's task in this respect.

Participants must also have the freedom not to answer any question if they do not wish to, and indeed to withdraw from an interview after it has started. Bell (2014) highlights how some people welcome the opportunity to discuss professional issues openly, whereas others find the process uncomfortable. Researchers should remember that interviews, even with seemingly 'safe' topics, have the potential to raise issues which participants consider sensitive and that visiting these may cause them anxiety or distress. For example, it is not uncommon for a teacher or teaching assistant who is carrying out research to explore an element of their own practice by interviewing colleagues in school. It could be difficult for some of these other members of staff to report their actual experiences and opinions, perhaps through fear of being too critical of the person interviewing them, or of other colleagues, or of the setting more broadly. They may also be conscious of a need to maintain professional, cooperative relationships after the completion of the research project. This raises questions about power and the impact of being an 'insider' on the data gathered. Both researcher and participants should therefore consider what impact, if any, involvement in the research might have on their working lives. Again, clear explanation about the purpose of the investigation and its broader aims should help to ensure that participants understand what it is about, for instance that it is about their experiences and perspectives, not a judgement or review of their own professional performance at the school, or that of others.

The SENCO research had some issues of this kind. Being asked about their work meant that participants had to consider both the challenges and the rewards of their role. Their responses provided useful insights into the lived experiences of being a SENCO, including negative or difficult aspects, but as the researcher and interviewer, I was unable to offer any support to the participants in terms of changing these more challenging elements. It may, however, have helped the SENCOs to 'voice' the difficulties and share their experiences with someone else. At the end of the research process, each SENCO received an executive summary of the findings in order to show that their opinions had been valued and so they could see how, through the research, these had contributed to a broader understanding of relevant issues in schools.

Conclusion

In conclusion, here are three recommendations which will further increase your understanding of interviews and strengthen their use in your own research work:

- Explore how others have designed interview schedules and questions – examples are widely available online. These will give you insight into common features and structure. Over time, however, you may start to feel that the quality of the schedules and questions you find is rather variable – some are good, some not so good. This is a positive sign, as it means that your critical perceptions and understanding are developing.

- Always pilot your interview questions with people not involved in your actual investigation in order to see how they interpret them and whether the data gathered will be what you require in order to address your research questions.
- During semi-structured interviews, engage in active listening – responding to participants' answers in order to gain further, deeper and clearer information.

Interviews offer a versatile and accessible method for data collection with potential for researchers to obtain enlightening insights into their chosen topic. They give participants opportunities to explore and debate their interpretations of the topic, as well as revealing how it impacts on them. While the data collected might include some worthwhile statistics or factual information, most researchers use interviews to gain rich, qualitative perspectives. Conducted well, they can provide real understandings of people's lived experiences, views and values.

Recommended reading

Newby, P. (2014) *Research Methods for Education*. Second edition. Abingdon: Routledge.

A clear introductory text, with useful supplementary material available online.

Thomas, G. (2017) *How to Do Your Research Project: A Guide for Students*. Third edition. London: Sage.

The book covers all of the main issues surrounding the completion of a research project, including use of interviews, and will be useful for beginner and more advanced researchers.

References

Alderson, P. (2014) Ethics. In: A. Clark, R. Flewitt, M. Hammersley and M. Robb (Eds.) *Understanding Research with Children and Young People*. London: Sage.

Bell, J. (2014) *Doing Your Research Project*. Sixth edition. Maidenhead: Open University Press.

Bryman, A. (2015) *Social Research Methods*. Fifth edition. Oxford: Oxford University Press.

Burton, D. and Bartlett, S. (2009) *Key Issues for Education Researchers*. London: Sage.

Cohen, L., Manion, L. and Morrison, K. (2018) *Research Methods in Education*. Eighth edition. Abingdon: Routledge.

DfES (2001) *Special Educational Needs Code of Practice*. Annesley: Department for Education and Science.

Grosvenor, I. and Rose, R. (2012) Interviews. In: R. Rose and I. Grosvenor (Eds.) *Doing Research in Special Education: Ideas into Practice*. Second edition. Abingdon: Routledge.

May, T. (2011) *Social Research: Issues, Methods and Process*. Fourth edition. Maidenhead: Open University Press.

Punch, K.F. (2009) *Introduction to Research Methods in Education*. London: Sage.

Robson, C. and McCartan, K. (2016) *Real World Research*. Fourth edition. Chichester: John Wiley.

Silverman, D. (2017) *Doing Qualitative Research*. Fifth edition. London: Sage.

Winwood, J. (2012) *Policy into Practice: The Changing Role of the Special Educational Needs Coordinator in England*. EdD thesis for University of Birmingham, UK.

Chapter 3

Observations

Tunde Rozsahegyi

Introduction

Following the discussion of questionnaires and interviews in the preceding chapters, here we explore the third of the most commonly used data-collection methods: observation. In contrast with the two others, both of which draw out the perceptions and opinions of research participants, observation offers a direct opportunity to gain closer understanding of what actually happens in real life.

Not only are observations an illuminating data source, they can also be particularly rewarding, for both novice and more experienced researchers. A chapter in Basit (2010) has the title: 'The charm of gathering data *in situ*', and Delamont (2016:102) reflects at length on the highly satisfying, multi-sensory nature of this method:

> I always want to stand or sit and watch something. The data gathered slowly by watching … are for me the sweetest jams and most aromatic oils and spices. Whenever I hear about a project, I want to go and sit there myself … As well as looking, use your ears, touch everything you can and pay attention to all bodily sensations such as heat and cold, smell the fieldsite, and when feasible, taste things.

Despite these attractions, however, utilizing the potential of observation and applying its processes in meaningful ways require considerable methodological and ethical deliberation. This chapter discusses these considerations. It does this firstly by outlining the purpose of observation as a data-gathering method in educational enquiry, explaining different types of observations which can be undertaken and illustrating ways of recording the resulting data. Specific issues of validity and ethics are also addressed. Issues are then revisited in a more practical way in the second part of the chapter, which shares the rationale and processes which I applied in my doctoral study. You are encouraged to apply ideas discussed in this chapter critically to your own research and to consider how observation, if appropriate, might be employed to address the research questions in your own investigation.

Observation in educational research

Prior to discussing observation as a research method, we should first distinguish it from the everyday actions of watching, absorbing, reacting and interacting. These are the all-encompassing, cumulative and largely impulsive means through which, from a very young age, we build our understanding and intelligence. We use these processes to construct outlooks and develop our judgements about people, physical entities and the social world, to 'interpret the world from our own personal perspective' (Simpson and Tuson, 2003:2).

For educators, more well-ordered kinds of observation are advocated as part of professional practice. One serves as a platform for comprehending and evaluating learners' growth and progression and for making pedagogical judgements and interventions to enhance their behaviour, curiosity and learning. Another is that of practitioners by other practitioners, as a part of training, mentoring and improvement of professional practice.

When an educational researcher employs 'observation' for a research study, the process becomes even more conscious and organized, and in some ways more intricate as well, qualitatively and quantitatively different to other kinds of watching and perceiving. Drawing on other writers, Cohen *et al.* (2018:542) point out that it is 'more than just looking. It is looking (often *systematically*) and noting *systematically* people, events, behaviours, settings, artefacts, routines, and so on' (my italics). They then helpfully go on to discuss specific aspects of educational practice where research observations can be particular enlightening. These include the physical features of the setting and how these change with different educational activities; human organization of the classroom, such as the adult-learner ratio or allocation of teaching assistants in lesson time; the frequency and nature of interactions between educators and learners or between learners themselves; and pedagogical features, such as employment of teaching strategies or use of resources.

Regardless of the natural appeal and informative nature of observation in educational research, there are several demands the researcher has to consider before engaging with data collection in this way. The first decision to be made is – as with any other data-gathering methods – whether it is an appropriate way of gathering evidence to answer the research questions. For instance, if a researcher is aiming to discover how secondary-school teachers plan for differentiated activities for diverse learner groups, other methods – document analysis or a focus-group discussion, for example – might reveal better information than observation. However, if a research question focused on how teachers' differentiated plans were actually implemented in real learning activities, the researcher might rightly decide to use observations alongside other sources to address this.

Using observation

If you have not yet started to plan a research project of your own, identify some educational topics that might usefully be investigated using observation as a data-collection method. Consider what might be gained from using this method. If you have started to plan a research project of your own, examine your research questions, then consider the following:

1. Could your research questions be usefully addressed by including observation as part of your methodological approach?
2. If yes, in what way might this strengthen or contribute to your investigation?
3. If observations would not be useful, explain why not.

Once observation is confirmed as an appropriate method of gathering data, research planning will need to address a further spectrum of practical issues. These include decisions on what role the observer should take, how the processes of observation might influence the behaviour of those being observed, how the observation data will be recorded, analysed and interpreted, and whether the observational strategies being planned are ethically and morally sound. A further question is deciding what *exactly* will be observed. Such contemplations will lay the foundation of a trustworthy study and are considered in the remaining sections of this chapter.

Participant or non-participant?

The first issue listed above concerns the role of the researcher when carrying out observations. Originating from different research traditions and situated at opposite ends of an intricate spectrum are two contrasting researcher roles in this respect: 'participant' and 'non-participant'.

Participant observation stresses the researcher's active involvement in, and interaction with, the context being observed. The notion is historically linked to ethnographic approaches whereby researchers 'share in the lives [of those being studied] rather than observe from a position of detachment … a *journey of discovery* in which the explanations for what is being witnessed emerge over a period of time' (Denscombe, 2017:83, italics in original). *Non-participant observation* is its opposite: the researcher seeks to remain separate from the context being observed as well as non-influential in its activity, an approach conventionally used in scientific investigations and testing (Papatheodorou *et al.*, 2013). In actual observational research, the boundaries between these two forms are increasingly blurred and overlapping, with many subtle, even complex combinations in between. Nevertheless, understanding the contrasts between the two, in particular the specific methodological and ethical issues which are linked to one or the other, will enable the educational researcher to plan, conduct and evaluate a resilient observational study which addresses the research questions which have been set.

Prior familiarity with the venue for the research and its personnel, together with an understanding of the processes of education, either in general or those relating to the specific setting, may make it easier for the researcher to incorporate participant observation, thereby taking an 'insider' position (Papatheodorou *et al.*, 2013). Actively engaging with the context during observation (although not necessarily during all observations) may then bring about a new, in-depth understanding of the research issue under scrutiny (Patton, 2015). However, in some circumstances it can be difficult for participant observers (who may actually work in the setting where they are doing their research) to discover aspects which they were not aware of before, or to change views which they might already hold. To reach new or revised discoveries with this approach, researchers 'need to be prepared to look beneath the surface and refine their judgements as a result of the observation' (Basit, 2010:124), by no means a straightforward task.

There are other potential drawbacks of this insider position. First, the participant observer may need to be involved in the research milieu for an extended period of time ('weeks, months, even years', according to Delamont, 2016:102), and cutting short the time needed may lead to superficial or patchy data. Second, with this approach not only is the researcher engaged in observing what is happening but is also part of, and contributing to, what happens. This dual role may not only make it difficult to identify noteworthy events but also mean that what would normally be natural circumstances are altered as the result of their involvement in activities. Finally, unless video or audio recording is used, the researcher in this situation usually has to note down data with a time delay, after the participant observation has ended, therefore relying a great deal on a good memory and raising questions of how reliable or comprehensive this might be.

In contrast, in *non-participant observation* the researcher remains uninvolved in the setting or its activities. This detached, passive role means adopting what Papatheodorou *et al.* (2013:75) explain as a 'fly-on-the-wall approach, by being unobtrusive and dissociated from the happenings, and attempting not to influence the situation at all'. The non-participant observer simply listens, watches and records what participants are saying and doing, thus gathering data from an outsider's point of view.

Not surprisingly, this kind of observation has its challenges too. As explained by Basit (2010:125), researchers 'need to do their homework before they observe a setting … they need to know the background of the particular context and group to be observed in order to make relevant and meaningful inferences from the observation'. In addition, as described by Baker (2006), non-participant observers usually remain stationary while observing so as to avoid interrupting or influencing activity. Aspects may, therefore, be missed, misheard or only partially seen. And although non-participant observation may be regarded as a useful way of gathering objective and neutral data about people and their interactions, there is the real possibility, an inevitability perhaps, that elements of subjectivity will creep into the ways in which the researcher comprehends, records and interprets the observed data.

In recognition of such challenges, and indeed to be as pragmatic with data-gathering as possible, there is increasing recognition that the notions of participant and non-participant observation actually frame many different kinds within a spectrum. Indeed, when favourable and necessary, researchers will often take a role in between these two extremes. In the description of Cohen *et al.* (2018:543), for example, the researcher may adopt the position of 'participant-as-observer' or of 'observer-as-participant'. While in both cases the researcher is involved in both observing and participating, in the former she or he is more engaged in activity than in observing it, and in the latter more concerned with watching than with participating. It is worth here taking note of Papatheodorou *et al.*'s (2013) reminder that with these and other adjusted roles the degree of objectivity of the researcher also changes and ethical considerations will alter too.

Structured or non-structured?

Observations can also be categorized according to what researchers focus on from the real-life events and scenarios taking place before or around them, also how the resulting data is recorded and remembered. Again, there are two ends to the spectrum: 'structured' and 'unstructured', with again – in practice – other, combined points in between. As Basit (2010) indicates, quantitative studies are more likely to adopt structured observations and collect numerical data which can be analysed statistically, and qualitative studies are more likely to use unstructured approaches, involving fieldnotes and narrative or thematic recording which might include data on non-verbal, even sensory aspects of what is observed (a reminder of Delamont's 'sweetest jams and most aromatic oils and spices', quoted at the start). When methodology is mixed, researchers may combine structured and unstructured observations, resulting in numerical as well as narrative data.

Structured observation is sometimes called 'systematic' observation and shares many similarities with structured interviews or surveys. It demands careful planning and preparation by the researcher to produce pre-determined categories indicating the kind of behaviour, event or activity which will be recorded. It is likely that data will be logged in numerical forms which 'facilitate the making of comparisons between settings and situations, and enable frequencies, patterns and trends to be noted or calculated' (Cohen *et al.*, 2018:545).

Most frequently, structured observation involves listing incidents on a pre-prepared observation form and having a system for recording when these occur, known as 'event sampling'. In an example offered by Basit (2010:132), the incidents include 'Teacher explains activity', 'Pupil asks questions' and 'Teacher and pupils laugh', then a mark is used to show each time such behaviour is observed. These accumulate and, when counted, provide numerical data for analysis.

Another example, based on 'time sampling', is provided by Mukherji and Albon (2017:112). It was designed to show when nursery staff members were interacting with children and when they were engaged in other activities away from children. The observed time period is split into 15-minute intervals and staff behaviour is listed as 'No interaction', 'Interacting with one child' and 'Interacting with more than one child'. Its use enables the researcher to chart both the frequency of relevant interaction and changes in that frequency over a period of time. When quantified, such data can be either analysed statistically or described in narrative form – in both cases, tables and charts would usually form part of data presentation in the written research report.

At the other end of this particular spectrum are *unstructured observations*, sometimes referred as 'naturalistic'. In contrast with structured forms, data is collected and recorded descriptively, as heard, seen and understood by the researcher. This may involve note-taking, writing descriptive accounts, maintaining research journals, or audio or video recording. These last electronic approaches, while in many ways providing the most extensive data, raise a range of practical as well as ethical issues which cannot be overlooked.

The main advantage of unstructured observation is the opportunity to represent events as they happen in a narrative format, using everyday language or self-designed, abbreviated codes, as described, for instance, by Mukherji and Albon (2017). Data emerges detailed but unstructured, and analysis is usually carried out in the way in which qualitative data is analysed in general (Simpson and Tuson, 2003). Cohen *et al.* (2018) give specific examples of such strategies, including identifying key notions, coding and categorizing, and establishing connections. However, such data is usually highly contextual, being focused on, and relevant to, an individual setting, particular people or specific processes. As a consequence, it can be hard to compare and contrast different sets of unstructured observational data collected on different occasions or in different places.

As noted earlier, a *semi-structured* approach is usually the most advantageous, and Mukherji and Albon (2017:143) provide a useful template which illustrates this. This is a design by a non-participant researcher who wanted to observe what happened before a child had a temper-tantrum, what kind of behaviour their temper-tantrums involved, and what happened afterwards. It is an event sample, so a record is made only when a temper-tantrum occurs – if there is none, no record is made. The chart has columns to note when and how frequently these tantrums take place but also to write narrative comments, making the overall form a pragmatic combination of the structured and unstructured recording procedures described above.

When working out how observation data is to be recorded, therefore, a first task is to consider closely the nature of your research enquiry. With this clarity, you may then choose to use an observation tool which has been developed and used in a different research study, or to adapt one of these, or to develop your own observation schedule with your own interests in mind (Basit, 2010).

Types of observation

You are planning to use observation in your research project, which will explore how the notion of 'sharing' is evident in young children's spontaneous play activities. Consider the following:

1. What would be the anticipated benefits and drawbacks for this project of:

    participant or non-participant observations?
    structured, semi-structured or non-structured observations?

2. Given your preferences, in what ways might you record your data? What kind of template might you use?

You may also wish to address the same questions in relation to a research project of your own.

Validity and ethics

As with all methods of data gathering, observation – in the different ways it can be carried out and the different means by which its data can be recorded – gives rise to special threats to credibility and trustworthiness of the research. For instance, observations can induce emotional reactions in researchers themselves, such as memories (positive or negative) or uncomfortable feelings, which 'may colour our perceptions and interpretations' (Papatheodorou et al., 2013:69) and result in compromised data and findings. Cohen et al. (2018:560) list a broad range of other, more practical threats, such as selective attention, selective data recording, misinterpretation of what is being observed, being judgemental, attention deficit, as well as the use of inappropriate data-recording strategies. Being on the look-out for these hazards when interrogating outcomes from piloting or when checking collected data with the participants who provided it can reduce them and their undesirable effects.

Furthermore, research participants may alter their behaviour as a response to being observed. One such reaction, whereby performance improves when those involved know they are being investigated, is known as the 'Hawthorne effect'. A review of evidence of this phenomenon, which is especially significant for health-science enquiry but applicable across wider fields, including education, is provided by McCambridge et al. (2014). In an attempt to avoid this kind of response, researchers may be tempted not to reveal information about their observations, for instance by keeping secret when they are taking place and what exactly is being watched. However, this raises both moral and ethical issues: in almost all circumstances there is an expectation and responsibility that the researcher should inform participants about the nature of the investigation so that the latter can give their 'informed' consent to take part. A different way to reduce the Hawthorne impact might be for the researcher, even in non-participant observations, to strengthen their natural role in the setting (Robson and McCartan, 2016), for instance by paying preliminary visits, explaining the whole context of the enquiry and being professional and reassuring in their approaches, thereby lessening both the 'novelty' and potentially rather intimidating nature of being researched.

In this and many other ways, it is the researcher's responsibility in carrying out observations to apply generic moral and ethical principles (BERA, 2018), as well as to operationalize these in relation to the specifics of the study. Ethical contemplations when doing observations include the effects of whatever role the researcher takes, how consent for such data gathering is obtained, and how the resulting data is stored and used. In addition, the researcher needs to work out how to pay heed to the participants' choices and how to make their contribution to the study a positive or even beneficial experience. Adhering to such guidance is not simply a matter of following procedures (Papatheodorou *et al.*, 2013) but part of the researcher's obligations to carry out 'good' research which shows respect to all involved. Some specific issues will be examined later in this chapter.

Observation in my own research

We now go on to consider how the ideas discussed above affected and informed an actual research project. This investigation (Rozsahegyi, 2014) focused on interrogating outlooks amongst parents, early-years practitioners and other educational stakeholders on the development and learning of young children with cerebral palsy. Its main aim was to enhance, or indeed to challenge, conventional medical and health-related views about disability in general and about cerebral palsy in particular. The study also sought to pin down ways in which early growth and development of these children could be supported in the family, childcare and early educational provision. Research questions focused on the children's multiple identities as conveyed by research participants, on views about processes and contexts providing support, and on ideas relating to future aspirations and priorities. As part of this, I wanted also to reveal how the range of perspectives was evident in children's everyday experiences, and it was this aspect which focused on collecting data from observations, used alongside other data-collection methods as part of a 'mixed-methods' approach (Plowright, 2011).

Six target children were selected for the research: four girls and two boys, with ages from 1 year 10 months to 4 years 11 months. Each was observed on three separate occasions, for anything between ten minutes to over an hour, and in different contexts – these could be home-based or setting-based, maintained, private or voluntary services, and mainstream, special or specialist provision. I termed my approach 'activity sampling', as my purpose was to observe a range of children's routines, such as play, mobility, snack-time and self-care.

Relationship to other methods

Parents, early-years practitioners and service managers had been interviewed earlier in the study. This data, together with data from a wider questionnaire which was completed by 50 parents of children with cerebral palsy and 85 practitioners working in relevant local services, revealed similarities and contrasts in outlooks. The observations themselves had more child-focused rationale, in that they provided a platform for exploring the nature of interplay between a target child and her or his immediate social and physical environment – data which could not be obtained directly by other means. They were also a tool for validating stakeholders' perspectives as revealed in the earlier data sources (Simons, 2009), in other words they provided an opportunity to confirm the applicability or non-applicability of outlooks evident in the questionnaire and interview data. Last but not least, involving children in this way gave them some kind of voice in a situation where it would have been difficult for them realistically (or ethically) to take part in other direct methods, such as interviewing, due to their very young age and developmental challenges (Basit, 2010).

Observing and recording

Participant observation as described above was considered for the research, as this role could have given me useful, close involvement in the experiences of these children. However, it was rejected because I felt that my own professional background and teaching experience with children with cerebral palsy may have resulted in me inputting into events more than was appropriate or helpful for the objectives of the research. It could also have influenced not simply the setting's routines and activities but the behaviour of its children and adults too, and I considered this to be both pedagogically and ethically undesirable. An outsider, non-participant position was therefore adopted, aiming for minimum interference with activities and with the children being observed, in the setting or in their home. Nevertheless, these being young children, Papatheodorou *et al.*'s (2013:75) disassociated, 'fly-on-the-wall' approach was not fully achievable – it would be a hard-hearted researcher (and perhaps even not a very good one) who would be able to ignore completely the children's friendly chat or non-verbal interaction. However, my overall non-participant position seemed to strengthen the opportunity to capture detailed data, perhaps increasing the chances of pinning down more in-depth and critical ideas.

Similar contemplations also underpinned the process of making decisions about how to record observation data. I recognized the potential benefits of unstructured methods and noted in particular how in research by Thomas *et al.* (1998), described in Thomas (2017:230–232), 'comments and interpretations' about ways in which physically disabled children were supported in mainstream settings could emerge from an unstructured recording technique. However, my piloting of this approach revealed that rather too much subjectivity and selectivity and too many personal judgements were edging into my notes. To reduce these negative aspects for the actual research, a semi-structured observation form was developed which enabled both 'looking *at*' and 'looking *for*', the former more structured in search of 'evidence', the latter more unstructured in search of 'meaning' (Clough and Nutbrown, 2012:59, italics in original). An early template from Sylva *et al.* (1980) was considered to be a helpful example to be adapted; Figure 3.1 shows the final version of the template that I used.

As can be seen, the template allowed me first of all to include some general notes about the setting. These were important as they clarified physical and social arrangements and the processes by which the child's individual needs were normally accommodated, and were part of my preparatory 'homework' for the observations, as recommended by Basit (2010:125) above. I had already collected details about the children themselves when interviewing their parents and practitioners, so only minimal information of that kind needed to be recorded on the observation form itself.

The main sections of the template guided consistent but extensive recording of how practitioner expectations were communicated to the child, how participation was facilitated socially, educationally and physically, what the child's responses were, and how practitioners acted upon these responses – all as witnessed from my non-participant position. In this way the template provided both structure and focus for the observations, as well as opportunity to make detailed and illustrative narrative notes.

Date of observation:			Setting:			
Initials of the child:		Gender:		Age:		
Pen-picture of the setting:						

Activity	Adult expectation	Responses			
		Child-to-adult	Adult-to-child	Child-to-adult	Themes and codes

Figure 3.1 Observation template used for doctoral research by Rozsahegyi (2014)

Analysing data

The form also allowed me (in the right-hand column) to start to analyse data almost as soon as I had collected it. This was a practical measure which eased my progress from data-collection in the field to its subsequent scrutiny and interpretation. It meant I could start data analysis immediately after observation of each individual child (an approach advocated by Cohen *et al.*, 2018), rather than waiting until a large amount of information relating to several children had accumulated. The analysis itself involved identifying and coding themes and peculiarities evident in the activities and interactions that I had observed. I subsequently found it possible to compare and contrast findings related to all six children and to establish emerging meanings, outlooks and understandings.

Trustworthiness and credibility

Several strategies were put in place in order to increase the trustworthiness of observation data, especially after the selectivity and personal-judgement problems identified in piloting. Consistency in observation notes (encouraged by the template's format), together with debriefing sessions with practitioners, did something to address potential subjectivity in my interpretation of what had been seen and heard in practice. Triangulation, derived from the mixed-methods approach, also had an important role to play, so that what was found out through observations could be critically compared with ideas and perspectives obtained from questionnaires and interviews. Completing the observations last in the sequence of data gathering had another benefit: the practitioners who took part in the interviews had become familiar with me and with the research itself by the time the observations took place, and this may well have helped to moderate the 'Hawthorne effect' described earlier.

Ethical considerations

As would be expected, a broad range of ethical issues applied to this research. Many of these did not exclusively link to observation itself but underpinned the study and its methodology as a whole. Two, which were particularly relevant to the observations, are highlighted here: informed consent and the involvement of other, non-target children.

The observations were very focused on the six young children, so the informed-consent process also needed to be applied to them (Flick, 2015). Alongside the formal consent given by their 'gatekeepers' (parents and managers of the settings), a less formal procedure was therefore designed for them. This involved introducing myself and explaining in child-friendly and developmentally appropriate ways the reasons for me being there. The absence of a negative response to this was judged to be their passive consent for the observations to take place. Some children seemed rather keen and interested in my intentions and others rather indifferent to them, but none expressed any aversion to what was outlined – perhaps they were already very accustomed to being observed for a variety of reasons. In addition, I sought to monitor the children's behaviour during observation sessions as a way of ensuring that there was no unfavourable impact on their everyday activities.

A second ethical dilemma related to the involvement of other children in the settings. Although they were not the target of my observations, I could envisage that due to the nature of activities they would inevitably interact with the target child whom I was observing. I decided, therefore, that their consent needed to be obtained too, as well as that of their parents. Information about the research was consequently provided to all and the possibility of opting-out was given, but in fact no parents opted their children out and the children themselves raised no objections.

Findings

Data from all sources, including observation, was combined to reach findings which addressed the study's research questions. Overall, shared outlooks were found, often reflecting similarities in parents' and practitioners' backgrounds and experiences. Contrasts were also identified, these often related to perceptions of disability in general and of cerebral palsy in particular. The observations themselves revealed both parallels and differences in the six target children's experiences, enhancing critical understanding of the data as a whole. Pedagogical competence and aspirations for the children seemed to influence the ways in which practitioners interacted with the children in the settings and consequently how children participated in the activities. In interviews parents had expressed a desire for good, all-round support for their child, but this in some instances contradicted the priorities and strategies observed in the settings. Observations also highlighted that, regardless of their age, complexity of difficulties or the kind of provision they received, when the children were motivated and wishing to do something, they without exception showed determination to accomplish it in active ways and were strong in their desire to participate and succeed. This element, supported by both interview and observation data, became a key finding in the research.

Conclusion

Observation can be a highly illuminating data source which produces persuasive and valuable findings in educational research – but only if it is designed, conducted and reflected upon with close concern for methodological, moral and ethical issues. This chapter has outlined some of these and how they can be addressed. Here in summary are some key recommendations which you can apply to your own research:

- The purpose and pragmatics of the method should be carefully selected, planned and piloted.
- Threats to validity and credibility should be closely considered and addressed.
- The observation process should be ethically defensible in relation to those taking part.
- Data collected from observations can be usefully triangulated and combined with data from other sources in a mixed-methods approach.

Recommended reading

This chapter has used three sources in particular: Basit (2010), Papatheodorou *et al.* (2013) and Cohen *et al.* (2018). Closer examination of each of these is well worthwhile. In addition, here are other texts which you will find useful when developing observation as part of methodology for your own research:

Podmore, V.N. and Luff, P. (2012) *Observation: Origins and Approaches.* Maidenhead: Open University Press.

This book explains the historical roots of observational research in childhood and discusses various approaches to observing young children in early-years settings.

Vogt, W.P., Gardner, D.C. and Haeffele, L.M. (2012) *When to Use What Research Design.* New York: Guilford Press.

A systematic, practical and accessible book which is unique in its approach to finding the most appropriate data-gathering methods with which to address a particular research question.

Wragg, E.C. (2012) *An Introduction to Classroom Observation.* Classic edition. Abingdon: Routledge.

First published in 1994, this is a seminal work on observing in the classroom.

References

Baker, L.M. (2006) Observation: A complex research method. *Library Trends*, 55(1), 171–189.
Basit, T.N. (2010) *Conducting Research in Educational Contexts.* London: Continuum.
BERA (2018) *Ethical Guidelines for Educational Research.* Fourth edition. London: British Educational Research Association.
Clough, P. and Nutbrown, C. (2012) *A Student Guide to Methodology.* Third edition. London: Sage.
Cohen, L., Manion, L. and Morrison, K. (2018) *Research Methods in Education.* Eighth edition. Abingdon: Routledge.

Delamont, S. (2016) *Fieldwork in Educational Settings: Methods, Pitfalls and Perspectives*. Third edition. Abingdon: Routledge.

Denscombe, M. (2017) *The Good Research Guide*. Sixth edition. Maidenhead: Open University Press.

Flick, U. (2015) *Introducing Research Methodology: A Beginner's Guide to Doing a Research Project*. Second edition. London: Sage.

McCambridge, J., Witton, J. and Elbourne, D.R. (2014) Systematic review of the Hawthorne effect: New concepts are needed to study research participation effects. *Journal of Clinical Epidemiology*, 67(3), 267–277.

Mukherji, P. and Albon, D. (2017) *Research Methods in Early Childhood: An Introductory Guide*. Second edition. London: Sage.

Papatheodorou, I. and Luff, P. with Gill, J. (2013) *Child Observation for Learning and Research*. Abingdon: Routledge.

Patton, M.Q. (2015) *Qualitative Research and Evaluation Methods: Integrating Theory and Practice*. Fourth edition. London: Sage.

Plowright, D. (2011) *Using Mixed Methods: Frameworks for an Integrated Methodology*. London: Sage.

Robson, C. and McCartan, K. (2016) *Real World Research*. Fourth edition. Chichester: John Wiley.

Rozsahegyi, T. (2014) *A Bio-Ecological Case-Study Investigation into Outlooks on the Development and Learning of Young Children with Cerebral Palsy*. PhD thesis for University of Warwick, UK.

Simons, H. (2009) *Case Study Research in Practice*. London: Sage.

Simpson, M. and Tuson, J. (2003) *Using Observations in Small-Scale Research: A Beginner's Guide*. Revised edition. Glasgow: Scottish Council for Research in Education.

Sylva, K., Roy, C. and Painter, M. (1980) *Childwatching at Playgroup and Nursery School*. London: Grant McIntyre.

Thomas, G. (2017) *How to Do Your Research Project: A Guide for Students*. Third edition. London: Sage.

Chapter 4

Involving children

Mike Lambert

Introduction

The involvement of children in education enquiry has been advocated for many years. This chapter extends discussions by examining issues relating to their effective contribution to data and outcomes in research projects.

Woodhead and Faulkner (2000:31), citing a range of studies, suggested that 'significant knowledge gains result when children's active participation in the research process is deliberately solicited and when their perspectives, views and feelings are accepted as genuine, valid evidence'. Uprichard (2010) has argued that children have valuable perspectives to share about many issues, not just about those directly pertaining to their own childhood lives, and an investigation into early education in Italy by Corsaro and Molinari (2017) shows how children's participation can make essential contributions to longer-lasting, longitudinal research.

We should be careful, nevertheless, not to be carried away by this idea. Despite the growth of inclusive methods which have challenged the practice of doing research *on* children rather than *with* them (Barker and Weller, 2003), as well as moves to help children to carry out participatory research themselves (for example, Kim *et al.*, 2017), almost all research, as Greene and Hill (2005) pointed out early on, is still designed, analysed and disseminated by adults. We can also be cautious about emphasizing how much age can influence data – differences in status, relationships, experience and culture may bring greater variation. There may too be practical problems in relation to the time during their education which children have available to take part in research and the circumstances in which they can do so.

Involving children also raises particular ethical concerns, some of which will be considered later in this chapter. Indeed, it is possible that a more detailed ethical review will be required prior to approval of the research (ESRC, 2015) or that children's involvement may even not be allowed at all, for instance in an investigation undertaken at undergraduate level. If you are doing research of this kind, you should check your institution's guidelines or your course documentation, or simply ask your supervising tutor if you are allowed to include children in your research project. If you are, but your institution has no clear, specific instructions available, it will be worth examining guidance issued by others (examples can be retrieved online), as well as explaining in your study which has been followed in your own investigation.

My research

My own research (Lambert, 2009) examined notions of 'difficulty and challenge' in the curriculum and learning of academically very able children. It was a fairly extensive doctoral study, but the issues which needed to be addressed were similar to those faced by any researchers at any level seeking to gather data from children in their investigation.

The primary rationale for including children in the research was their proximity to the topic. Children are both recipients of educational difficulty and performers of it. They have it set for them (and sometimes seek it for themselves) and must address it in their school work. Excluding children's perspectives, I felt (and as you may also feel in relation to your own research focus), would have ignored a whole set of meaningful perspectives on classroom reality, some of which at least might be different to those of their teachers and other adults. I wanted to take advantage of the competence of children to take part in research, their familiarity with the issue I was investigating, and the potential value of their contributions. In this respect, the approach also met long-established political, social and moral concerns that children's views should be more clearly heard and acted upon (UNICEF, 1989). Currently still, 'children who are capable of forming their own views should be granted the right to express those views freely in all matters affecting them, commensurate with their age and maturity' (BERA, 2018:15).

Involving children

Some aspects of involving children in research are outlined here. What other reasons can you think of for including or not including children in your methodology?

Involvement

The children in the research (the youngest was 6 years old, the oldest 15) were involved in three ways. The greatest number – over 700 in 36 different locations across England – completed a four-page questionnaire, which asked about their attitudes to difficult and easy work in school and in special classes outside of school. In addition, 43 children took part in 13 small-group interviews and 17 observations of classroom practice were made, of which children were, of course, an integral part. All three approaches met with a positive, often enthusiastic response from these participants. This was helped perhaps by the fact that the children taking part (mainly chosen by their teachers) were generally lucid and confident, also that they were contributing data about a subject – curriculum difficulty – which was close to their experience, and perhaps even close to their heart.

Features of their relationship to the investigation became particularly clear in the interviews. These did not follow a consistent, formal, question-and-answer structure but were organized more around themes, exploring experiences and beliefs in an often discussive style. For the most part, the participating children were self-assured enough to take some control over the interview agenda, expressing opinions, spontaneously recollecting memorable occurrences and even setting out new directions for dialogue. Although nothing inappropriate was ever said, the fact that the children were away from their teachers may also have helped to promote active and honest discussion.

The fact that the interviews were carried out in groups of three, four or five children, not individually, seemed to add to the value of the methodology. Children, more than adults, stimulated judgements and reflections in each other: 'Do you remember this?' Their disagreements provided doubt and contradictions from which a single, persuasive perspective sometimes (but not always) emerged. However, groups brought dangers too: 'the impulse to present oneself in a way that is socially acceptable to others' (Greene and Hill, 2005:7), and meant that beliefs and motivations could be difficult to unravel – the small-group context may have sometimes obscured differences in perspective. However, it may also have been an advantage to a few children who had little to say and who could hide embarrassment by expressing agreement with what had been said before – 'I disagree' or 'I don't know' can, for children (and sometimes for adults too), be awkward perspectives to express. The children, overall, seemed 'fortified by the presence of others' (Greene and Hill, 2005:17); the group added to their power, giving them authority in numbers. There were more of them and they said much more than me, the lone researcher.

A lack of uniformity resulted from all of this. For instance, some interviews (those with children with much to say or where time constraints were few) lasted much longer than others, which seemed more an advantage than a deficit in the collection of rich data and a range of perceptions. Some irrelevances also intruded, brought to a halt on occasions by the comments of other children in the interview group, on others by my own further questions and comments.

Ideas and perspectives emerging from all sources of children's data were as varied as those which came from adult sources and on occasions reached areas (social and emotional considerations, for instance) which responses in corresponding adult interviews hardly touched. I had no way of knowing what these grown-ups would have written or said if I had asked them to say what children thought, but I was encouraged by Hill's (2005) suggestion, drawn from examination of research studies, that adult perceptions of what children think or do may differ from what children say themselves. All in all, I felt justified in involving the children directly in the research.

To what extent could I understand the data?

By involving children, however, I could not change the fact that I, the research designer, data collector and data interpreter, was several times older than they were. Indeed, in terms of mutual understanding, the generational gap between the children and myself was not fully eliminated in the study, even after piloting. Both the questionnaire and the interviews indicated that some presumptions and understandings of the researcher-adult did not fully match those of the being-researched children. During interviews and in the questionnaire responses, there were occasions when terms and phrases in the questions were interpreted differently than I had intended in my research design (see Lambert, 2008); examples of children's 'linguistic inventiveness', noted by Greene and Hill (2005:10); evidence of their need to check and repeat language, remarked on by Hill (2005); and in the interviews occasions where meaning had to be left unclear in order to move forward. Similar confusions may indeed have affected the way I interpreted observational data, for these are even more difficult to identify and put right than with data from questionnaires and interviews – the researcher rarely has checks available which might increase confidence that what children are doing and saying in the classroom is explained or interpreted in a similar way to how they themselves would do so.

What helped to ease such difficulties, to some extent at least, was my familiarity, as a former school teacher and teacher trainer, with 'children's routines, timetables and expectations' (Greene and Hill, 2005:11). As Corbin and Strauss (2015:78) have suggested: 'It is [the researchers'] knowledge and experience … that enables them to dig beneath the surface and respond to data'. There was a danger that this could act as an inadvertent inducement for presuming too quickly child participants' intended meaning, but overall, in terms of my approach to data collection and interpretation, a blend of both familiarity and apartness was maintained. As Woods (1981:18) wrote long ago: 'At least we can identify more readily with teacher culture; the road to understanding is a longer one with [children]'.

Understanding children

Think of children you know (professionally or personally) and the way they speak, write and act. Can you think of instances where you may find it difficult to understand fully what they mean? Or where you might presume one understanding, but the children themselves might have another? What implications might these gaps in understanding have in research involving children? How might such gaps be lessened?

What about 'power'?

A further issue in the research was the potential power imbalance between the adult researcher and the child participants, particularly in interviews and particularly when the researcher's role was easily blurred with that of a teacher. Fortunately perhaps, interviews for my research did not seem to suffer too much from this. The children's views did not lack a critical dimension, and many children seemed quite adept at determining what they said and how they expressed it. The immediate link between interviews and observed lessons helped this process. An observation was always followed by a group interview with several children who had been in the lesson, providing shared experiential stimuli for discussion and analysis, also diluting the presumed greater knowledge of the adult (Mayall, 2000). The children had perspectives based on involvement, experience and emotion; I had only those derived from detached seeing and listening to one learning event. This sense of child expertise extended to wider experiences also: to consideration of their schooling as a whole and to more personal issues, such as their emotional responses to difficult work. I, as the researcher, was uninformed, so needed to be informed. My lack of knowledge was ultimately an advantage, serving as an invitation to children to elucidate what I could honestly confess was unclear. It was the adult-researcher who tried to enter the child-interviewee's world of understanding, the researcher's comprehension which was modified through the experience (Mayall, 2000). Children – in this respect at least – had the power, even though I could not get away from the fact that I, the adult, had designed and organized the investigation as a whole.

Power

The view expressed here suggests that to a certain extent 'power' in research can reside with participating children, rather than the researcher. To what extent do you agree or disagree with this? In what ways might the researcher (or other adults), perhaps inadvertently, retain power or superiority in an investigation of this kind? How might this influence the data that are gathered and how the data are interpreted?

And what about ethics?

This brings us to reflections on ethics. These involve the basic idea that 'research should avoid causing harm, distress, anxiety, pain or any other negative feeling to participants' (Oliver, 2010:15), or even that researchers should aspire 'to conduct research that benefits participants in positive ways' (Piper and Simons, 2011:25). Indeed, the unusualness, the specialness, perhaps the 'grown-upness' of the task, especially in the interviews, seemed stimulus and reward enough for the children in this research. The lending of self-esteem, as well as the educational benefits which might ultimately result (albeit unseen to them) from the study and their participation, balanced with the advantages of their involvement to the researcher himself.

Were it all so clear and easy, however. Pring (1984:10) described ethics as a 'foggy area of establishing rights and obligations, where there is not agreement on what these are and where there is no well-established social tradition that can be appealed to' – and the situation may not have wholly improved since then. In my research, I had to argue my need to know, and implementation of that need was conditional on the right of others to have a choice about how they spent their time and effort and to what extent they wished to share their thoughts and experiences. Rubin and Rubin (2012:90) have written vividly: 'Some truths are not worth the pain that they cause; others might be necessary for the pain they prevent'. Ends and means in research may conflict with each other; it is not easy, nor always possible, to achieve good things in good ways.

Such considerations have particular resonance in relation to children, generally regarded as having a degree of vulnerability within adult-oriented society. The building of 'rapport' is often put forward as best practice in any kind of research in which they are involved, most credibly perhaps by Collins *et al.* (2014) in relation to social-work and police investigations. There must too be a greater concern for equality and relationships, with children's best interests as the primary consideration (BERA, 2018). Particular issues may arise in relation to children who are in care or those who have disabilities or special educational needs. Researchers should try to avoid the discriminatory practice of excluding participants (children or adults) from research because of these factors but may have to make special adjustments to facilitate research processes, for instance when asking for informed consent. Some of the complexities are well explored by Davis *et al.* (2017).

Informed consent

A first, prominent issue in the research was indeed the quite usual expectation that participants indicate their 'informed consent' to be involved. The researcher's responsibility is to 'explain the basics of the research project to the participants, in a manner which they can understand' (Oliver, 2010:28), as well as to maintain their 'rolling informed consent' throughout the research (Piper and Simons, 2011:26).

As I myself found, the issue in relation to young participants can be difficult to work out. The principle is clear: for children, as with adults, there should be informed consent, but a situation whereby children did not feel obliged to participate was hard to achieve. Particularly relevant was the need to apply first to one or more people to gain access to children in the schools and centres, to what have become known as their 'gatekeepers' (Oliver, 2010): the headteacher, class teacher or centre coordinator. The difficulty was that having given consent for the research to take place, these custodians may then have assumed that same consent on behalf of the school's or centre's children – after all these are places where children are expected to do as they are asked or told. Indeed, there were indications in some questionnaire returns that participation of children had been presumed and that there may not have been sufficient, conscious opportunity for them to volunteer. Similar issues sometimes related to teacher participation too – once the research was agreed by a headteacher, it could be difficult for these adults to say no, and a sense of professional obligation may in some cases have had to take precedence over any personal anxiety.

Another factor was the extent to which parents or carers needed to be consulted about their children's participation in the research. It is a long-established, general but not indisputable principle that parents have a right to have information about what their child is doing in school, also an obligation to act in the child's interests (Pring, 1984). However, a mature child also has the right to make decisions independently (Masson, 2004). In discussion at that time, Hill (2005) suggested that children aged nine and above could give such informed consent but younger with an individual approach. Masson (2004:39) felt that 'it is children's level of understanding, not their age, which is important', while Lindsay (2000) had suggested an even wider range of considerations: children's age, general cognitive ability, emotional status, knowledge, and also the nature of the task in which they are involved. It was, and still is, all a bit of minefield, with the notion of 'assent', a less complete kind of consent, sometimes applied to children of a very young age (but not always happily so – see Alderson and Morrow, 2011:103). Overall, it can perhaps be agreed that 'it should not be assumed that agreement cannot be sought from children because of their age' (ESRC, 2015:24). In my research it no doubt helped that the participating children were sometimes mature above their years. However, if I had asked for consent from the children without asking their parents as well, it risked creating difficult situations, not just for the parent–child relationship but for the gatekeepers of the school or centre as well.

Whatever the difficulties, my obligation towards all participants was to explain fully the purpose, process and intended outcomes of the research and to seek consent on that basis (Masson, 2004). So, once access to the research venue had been negotiated, letters were written (with research information attached) to all the children – questionnaire respondents, interviewees and to those being observed. The letters presumed their consent unless participants replied that they did not wish to take part – passive, rather than active consent. Choosing discretion ahead of valour, I asked for consent from parents and carers as well. Additional letters were written therefore, offering them the chance to withdraw their child from the research process if they wished. Denial of consent by either child or parent would have been sufficient not to include the child in the research. In the event, to my knowledge at least, none denied this consent.

I took great care to design materials for schools and centres which were clear, concise and well presented, and which showed appreciation of potential difficulties. All the documentation invited direct communication with the researcher in case of query. The formal letter to child participants sought to treat them as responsible for their decisions and actions, but I told them too that their parents were also being informed of the research. The resulting packs – incorporating information for the children, parents and teachers – were bulky, and the procedures of distributing them somewhat onerous, probably not always welcomed by busy schools and centre personnel. Balance between substance and succinctness in this kind of research is not easily achieved.

Ethics of observation

Observation in the classroom raised its own ethical issues, in particular in relation to the researcher's relationship to the context being observed. Oliver's (2010:84) reminder is that the researcher should not challenge the accepted customs and value systems of that context, its 'social ecology', not just for ethical reasons, but also so that data will reflect the real nature of the observed setting. Instead, the researcher should try to merge with these systems. Hill (2005) had similarly advised that the researcher should not disturb the relationship between child and teacher (or, one could add, that between the teacher and his or her manager or headteacher). If, as happened several times in the research, a child seeks the observer-researcher's attention during a lesson, what should the researcher do? What should the researcher do if a child asks for help with a task when the teacher or assistant is busy elsewhere? My experience as a teacher trainer, observing emergent teachers and their classes on a regular basis, suggested two actions in these circumstances. First, one should act as an outsider by wherever possible directing the child in silent but amicable fashion towards whatever has been indicated should be the focus of their current effort or attention. Second, one should act like a human being, offering (albeit at the expense of a moment's research observation) brief, cautious help or advice, if the normal sources within the class are not available.

Confidentiality and anonymity

With many settings involved, I often did not administer the questionnaires myself – it was done by helpful practitioners in the settings on my behalf. In the questionnaire, however, I had to ask the children for their names, in order subsequently (with their consent) to approach schools for their results in national tests. In an attempt at confidentiality, I therefore provided an envelope for each child respondent, with instructions to seal their completed questionnaire inside. Nevertheless, any overly inquisitive professional could fairly easily have found out what had been written and by whom. Because of this possibility, I could not assure children that their responses would be fully confidential, only that 'your teachers have been asked not to look at your completed forms'. This may of course have affected what the children wrote, although some frank comments suggested that it was not a worry for all. Another 'breach' of confidentiality in the research was that interviews were held with groups of children, meaning that while their teachers and assistants had no direct access to the data, the children themselves could not keep comments secret from each other.

Sensitive issues

Any researcher needs to consider the information which an investigation might generate and be prepared in particular to deal with 'unexpected disclosures' (Mooney-Somers and Olsen, 2018:359). In one interview in this study, a child shared personal information about the effect of her school work on circumstances at home. The response of another child to the questionnaire indicated some distress at a particularly difficult piece of school work which had been set. Should I have shared this information with the schools concerned? I decided no – the assurance of confidentiality could not be compromised by doing so. But one can think of other, more serious circumstances where the decision might go the other way. Researchers make sometimes problematic judgements in order to balance promises made to child participants against concern for their well-being and for the responsibilities of their educators, parents or others accountable for their welfare.

Ethics

Four ethical topics relating to involvement of children are reflected upon in this section: informed consent, observations, confidentiality and anonymity, and sensitive issues. Consider the questions below in relation to the situations described in this section:

1. What other responses could have been made by the researcher?
2. What would you have done in the same circumstances?
3. In relation to sensitive issues, what other situations might arise which might cause the researcher to question the promises of confidentiality and anonymity given to participants?

Conclusion

Christensen and James (2017:9) cite the French children's writer, Antoine de Saint-Exupéry, who in *The Little Prince*, first published in 1943, claimed that grown-ups cannot, on their own, understand the world from the child's point of view and therefore need children to explain it to them. Indeed, involving children in educational research recognizes the value which their experiences, perspectives and ideas bring to an investigation. There are issues to address in the organization of data collection, in data interpretation, and of course, in ethics. Many would point out also that it is important not just to 'listen' to children but also to 'hear' what they say (Roberts, 2017), that is to consider closely the implications of their perspectives for research and for educational practice itself. Yet as long as institutional guidelines are followed and the researcher's professional approach (and her or his common sense) is maintained, then addressing those issues is well worthwhile. Here, therefore, are two final recommendations for researchers wishing to involve children in their enquiry:

*   Respect the children, and those who have responsibility for them. As the researcher, you are the 'intruder' and you are the one above all who might need to adjust their plans.
*   At the same time, respect yourself as the researcher. If your investigation is well thought out and has beneficial aims, then your work is valuable too and deserves to be carried out in a good way. Most participants, including children, will understand this and be ready to give you as much cooperation as possible in making a success of your research.

Recommended reading

Christensen, P. and James, A. (Eds.) (2017) *Research with Children: Perspectives and Practices.* Third edition. Abingdon: Routledge.

This collection of articles examines the complexity of contemporary issues, including those relating to children's use of digital and networked technologies, participatory research, disability and diversity, as well as more long-standing ideas about their different 'cultures of communication'.

Online searches will take you to substantial material on the ethics of research, including the International Ethical Research Involving Children (ERIC) project (https://childethics.com), which places responsibility for ethical research firmly on the researcher's attitudes and practice.

References

Alderson, P. and Morrow, V. (2011) *The Ethics of Research with Children and Young People: A Practical Handbook*. London: Sage.

Barker, J. and Weller, S. (2003) 'Is it fun?' Developing children centred research methods. *International Journal of Sociology and Social Policy*, 23(1), 33–58.

BERA (2018) *Ethical Guidelines for Educational Research*. Fourth edition. London: British Educational Research Association.

Christensen, P. and James, A. (2017) Introduction: Researching children and childhood: Cultures of communication. In: P. Christensen and A. James (Eds.) *Research with Children: Perspectives and Practices*. Third edition. Abingdon: Routledge.

Collins, K., Doherty-Sneddon, G. and Doherty, M.J. (2014) Practitioner perspectives on rapport building during child investigative interviews. *Psychology, Crime & Law*, 20(9), 884–901.

Corbin, J. and Strauss, A. (2015) *Basics of Qualitative Research: Techniques and Procedures for Developing Grounded Theory*. Fourth edition. London: Sage.

Corsaro, W.A. and Molinari, L. (2017) Entering and observing in children's worlds: A reflection on a longitudinal ethnography of early education in Italy. In: P. Christensen and A. James (Eds.) *Research with Children: Perspectives and Practices*. Third edition. Abingdon: Routledge.

Davis, J., Watson, N. and Cunningham-Burley, S. (2017) Disabled children, ethnography and unspoken understandings: The collaborative construction of diverse identities. In: P. Christensen and A. James (Eds.) *Research with Children: Perspectives and Practices*. Third edition. Abingdon: Routledge.

ESRC (2015) *ESRC Framework for Research Ethics*. Swindon: Education and Social Research Council. [Online] https://esrc.ukri.org (accessed 4 September 2018).

Greene, S. and Hill, M. (2005) Researching children's experience: Methods and methodological issues. In: S. Greene and D. Hogan (Eds.) *Researching Children's Experience: Approaches and Methods*. London: Sage.

Hill, M. (2005) Ethical considerations in researching children's experiences. In: S. Greene and D. Hogan (Eds.) *Researching Children's Experience: Approaches and Methods*. London: Sage.

Kim, C-Y., Sheehy, K. and Kerawalla, L. (2017) *Developing Children as Researchers: A Practical Guide to Help Children Conduct Social Research*. Abingdon: Routledge.

Lambert, M. (2008) Devil in the detail: Using a pupil questionnaire survey in an evaluation of out-of-school classes for gifted and talented children. *Education 3–13*, 36(1), 69–78.

Lambert, M. (2009) *Difficulty and Challenge in Curriculum, Teaching and Learning: A Contribution to Pedagogy, Using Insights from In-School and Out-of-School Education of Gifted and Talented Pupils*. PhD thesis for University of Warwick, UK.

Lindsay, G. (2000) Researching children's perspectives: Ethical issues. In: A. Lewis and G. Lindsay (Eds.) *Researching Children's Perspectives*. Buckingham: Open University Press.

Masson, J. (2004) The legal context. In: S. Fraser, V. Lewis, S. Ding, M. Kellett and C. Robinson (Eds.) *Doing Research with Children and Young People*. London: Sage.

Mayall, B. (2000) Conversations with children: Working with generational issues. In: P. Christensen and A. James (Eds.) *Research with Children: Perspectives and Practices*. London: Farmer.

Mooney-Somers, J. and Olsen, A. (2018) Role conflict and questions of rigour: Working with community researchers in sexual health. In: R. Iphofen and M. Tolich (Eds.) *The SAGE Handbook of Qualitative Research Ethics*. London: Sage.

Oliver, P. (2010) *The Student's Guide to Research Ethics*. Second edition. Maidenhead: Open University Press.

Piper, H. and Simons, H. (2011) Ethical issues in generating public knowledge. In: B. Somekh and C. Lewin (Eds.) *Theory and Methods in Social Research*. Second edition. London: Sage.

Pring, R. (1984) Confidentiality and the right to know. In: C. Adelman (Ed.) *The Politics and Ethics of Evaluation*. London: Croom Helm.

Roberts, H. (2017) Listening to children: And hearing them. In: P. Christensen and A. James (Eds.) *Research with Children: Perspectives and Practices*. Third edition. Abingdon: Routledge.

Rubin, H.J. and Rubin, I.S. (2012) *Qualitative Interviewing: The Art of Hearing Data*. Third edition. London: Sage.

UNICEF (1989) *The United Nations Convention on the Rights of the Child*. London: UNICEF UK. [Online] www.unicef.org.uk/what-we-do/un-convention-child-rights (accessed 4 September 2018).

Uprichard, E. (2010) Questioning research with children: Discrepancy between theory and practice? *Children & Society*, 24(1), 3–13.

Woodhead, M. and Faulkner, D. (2000) Subjects, objects or participants? Dilemmas of psychological research with children. In: P. Christensen and A. James (Eds.) *Research with Children: Perspectives and Practices*. London: Farmer.

Woods, P. (1981) Understanding through talk. In: C. Adelman (Ed.) *Uttering, Muttering: Collecting, Using and Reporting Talk for Social and Educational Research*. London: Grant McIntyre.

Chapter 5

Using video as data

Marte Blikstad-Balas

Introduction

Many researchers in our field are attempting to study complex social situations as they unfold, for example, in the classroom, playground, library or at home. To make meaningful observations in any of these settings, the researcher must make many choices in advance, many of which are irreversible. Let us imagine, for instance, that we walk into a classroom to observe what is going on and get an impression of typical instructional practices there. Should we keep an eye only on the teacher or should we try to see what the students are doing? Both are important if we are trying to develop insights into normal activity. And how should we write down in our fieldnotes what the students are doing, when it rapidly becomes evident that they are seldom all doing the same thing at the same time? Should we choose a specific group and watch them? If we do, and we at some point discover that they are not the group providing the most interesting data, do we change and observe a different one? But then we will have already lost the opportunity to see the new group at the beginning of the lesson. Even with careful planning and piloting, researchers often encounter dilemmas such as these and we often wish that we could revisit situations that have just occurred.

The use of video data does not solve all of these problems, but it is a game changer for improving rigour and detail in observations of social situations (Heath *et al.*, 2010; Blikstad-Balas, 2017). Janík *et al.* (2009:7) draw a parallel between how natural scientists came to appreciate the microscope and telescope to observe very small and very distant objects, and the way social scientists now see video technology as a tool to 'observe phenomena that are too complex to be noticed by the naked eye'. In this chapter, I elaborate on and discuss some of the benefits and challenges of utilizing video data in educational research, drawing on practical examples from recent studies. In the final section, I provide some practical advice for researchers planning to collect and analyse their own video data. The ambition of the chapter is thus to provide useful information to researchers who are considering using video in their field research and also critical reflection on implications of this type of methodology.

Benefits

The use of video data has become very popular among researchers in education research – and for good reasons. The number-one benefit is that it allows researchers to systematically and repeatedly look for patterns that would be impossible to observe directly *in situ*. The fact that video is a real-time, sequential medium (Jewitt, 2012) makes it possible to capture, at least in part, what is happening in a given situation. In contrast to researchers carrying out direct observations, those who rely on video do not have to deal with the fact that the activities they are watching unfold only once and thereafter are lost forever, without any possibility for repeat observation. It follows from this that video researchers can, to a greater extent than others, separate the data-collection phase in the field and the subsequent data-analysis phase in a calmer environment. We now look in detail at four specific, beneficial uses of video data arising from this.

Multiple review

Complexity reduction is a basic principle in social-science research and with video this is done in two separate steps. First, we include some things by recording them and systematically leave out everything else. Second, when the video is analysed, we emphasize particular aspects through coding. Perhaps the most rewarding aspect of doing research with video is that this second step is reversible – the researcher can always disregard initial analytical choices applied to the material and return to the raw data (Janík *et al.*, 2009). This is the idea of 'multiple review'.

This possibility also means that the same researcher can approach the same set of data with two or more different analytical foci. This has been done in several projects. For example, for the large-scale video study, Linking Instruction and Student Achievement (LISA), led by a pioneer of video research in classroom settings, Professor Kirsti Klette, almost 200 mathematics and 200 Norwegian language-arts lessons have been recorded in Norwegian schools. These lessons have then been analysed by different members of the research team and also made available for Master's students, who have then conducted in-depth studies on smaller subsets of the recordings (Klette *et al.*, 2017). In this way, data from the same classrooms have been approached with diverse analytical foci and perspectives to answer a number of different research questions. Such multiple takes on the same data are particularly fruitful in complex contexts such as naturally occurring classroom instruction.

Detailed analysis

Video also allows detailed analysis in a way that is difficult with direct observation. It is a fine-grained record in which modes such as speech, gestures and movements are recorded simultaneously (Jewitt, 2012). Thus, one is not only able to look at what participants say and do but also investigate 'resources and practices through which participants in interaction build their social activities and how their talk, facial expression, gaze, gesture and body elaborate one another' (2012:6). Put simply, video enables detailed analysis of actions that would be impossible to grasp during real-time interaction. A relevant example here is a study conducted by Simpson *et al.* (2013), in which the authors recorded children using iPads and systematically tracked their interactions with the digital platform. Detailed analysis enabled the researchers to show how the affordances of touch-technology allowed for multimodal, multidirectional reading paths. The level of detail in these analyses would not have been possible without the recordings.

Simultaneous perspectives

Educational settings such as classrooms are rich, situational contexts in which people interact in complex ways. One option on which video researchers sometimes draw is to place several cameras in the same context, thereby obtaining multiple perspectives. In this way, researchers can examine how different temporal sequences unfold simultaneously in a single setting. For example, for the previously mentioned LISA study, we fixed one camera at the back of each classroom to capture the teacher and another in front of the class, capturing the students.

Cameras can also be placed directly on participants' bodies or on helmets that they can wear, thus tracking their every movement. Most commonly used for this seems to be the GoPro camera. These cameras are easy to obtain from sports stores and are relatively inexpensive. They are also becoming increasingly well known, as they are used by news media and on social-media platforms, most frequently to document sporting events. In a study about literacy practices in upper secondary schools (Blikstad-Balas, 2012), I asked four students to wear head-mounted GoPro cameras during 16 lessons and was thus able to obtain four different perspectives on each lesson. The data gave detailed insight into the individualized literacy practices in which the students engaged on their laptops during these lessons, including systematic evidence of how they pursued a range of computer activities of their own choice. For instance, while one student took notes in Microsoft Word, another spent the same time reading newspapers and blogs, and the two others engaged in different online games. The documentation of the students' activities served as a very concrete starting point for separate interviews with them about their use of computers at school. In another study (Bjørkvold and Blikstad-Balas, 2018), the same kind of head-mounted cameras were employed to see how students in the 7th grade (12–13 years old) conducted their own research projects over a period of eight weeks. Here, students were doing all kinds of activities across different settings, including outdoor experiments. The cameras made it possible to follow them, providing nuanced insight into how they reasoned about their science activities as these were taking place.

Discussion of data

A final advantage with video is that it is possible to share the raw data and analyses with peers, enabling discussion and multiple takes on interpretation of the recorded material (Derry *et al.*, 2010). Although this is relevant for all researchers, it may be particularly beneficial for those who do not yet have substantial experience conducting research.

Imagine that you record a complex situation, such as two students discussing a text in a literature lesson, then at some point it becomes difficult to determine whether their interpretation of the text is based on or differs from what the teacher said a few minutes earlier. In a situation such as this, the ability to discuss with relevant others students' competing interpretations as shown on the video is invaluable.

The fact that video is a 'durable, malleable and shareable record' (Jewitt, 2012:6) also makes it possible to increase the validity of your data interpretation in this way. You can see whether other researchers consider your interpretation plausible, or talk to someone who knows the setting well. In the example above, for instance, you could review and discuss the data with a small group of literature teachers. You could even talk with the actual students in the recording to discover how they understand the recorded situations. A good example of video being used this way is Silseth's (2012) study, in which he first recorded how teenagers played a digital game together and then conducted stimulated-recall group interviews, in which they discussed their game play.

It should be noted that the possibility of sharing video depends greatly on the nature of the data, the sensitivity of information contained in the data, and what kind of consent the participants have provided. In most countries, there are particularly strict regulations about disseminating video data, and in some cases the researcher may actually not be able to discuss complete video recordings with a group of peers. To maximize the possibility of using peer debriefing, as described by Creswell and Poth (2017), in order to increase the validity of video research, researchers should think about this possibility when designing consent forms for participants and when making sure the study complies with ethical guidelines.

Benefits

- Summarize the main benefits of video research described in this chapter.
- Can you think of any other benefits which might apply?
- To what extent could these benefits be relevant to your own research project?

Ethics

Research ethics are, of course, important for all researchers, but this importance cannot be overstated with regard to video methodologies. First of all, the benefits discussed so far indicate that video researchers are usually making a detailed, permanent record of social phenomena, in which individual participants can be identified. Close attention to ethics is therefore needed in a variety of areas, including obtaining consent to record, the nature of actual filming, secure storage of the data, and how and when the data should eventually be destroyed. As the rules and regulations for conducting video research vary, it is of paramount importance that the researcher thoroughly understands and complies with all the ethical recommendations which apply in the particular country and context where the recording is being made.

All social research involving individuals should be based on informed and free consent. Ideally, this implies that the researcher does not pressure people into agreeing to participate in a study (Silverman, 2006), although defining and identifying 'pressure' in a given context can be challenging. In most countries, participants have the right to withdraw their consent at any time, which in the case of video data would mean that the recording would have to be deleted. While this is a possibility, my experience after recording a large number of students and teachers is that they rarely, if ever, take up this possibility.

A further complication is that educational researchers tend to record children and young people who, depending on their age and maturity, may not always be able to provide full independent, voluntary and informed consent on their own behalf. Uneven power relations between teachers and students may mean that the wishes of the latter are not properly taken into account. The researcher will often have to ask for the consent of parents of the children being filmed, and this complexity also means that the researcher has to think, in advance, about what to do if a child or student gives consent and the parent does not, or *vice versa*.

The main concern for those who participate in studies which utilize video recording tends to be the extent to which the data will be made available to others. Consent forms should, therefore, be very explicit about the purposes of the recordings and the parameters for who can access them and how. During the actual recording, it is important that those who do not wish to participate have an option to stay outside the camera's scope at all times. In a classroom, this is often done by placing students in a pre-defined 'blind spot', but then it is important, of course, to consider for how long it is reasonable to place one or more students in such a location, as it often greatly limits their ability to get up and move around. My experience with consent and video is that in addition to a formal letter explaining the research process, the researcher needs to talk directly with the participants, and in some cases with their parents or carers too, in order to address all their possible concerns and answer all their questions, perhaps showing them the equipment and reassuring them about how the videos will be used.

Ethics

- What rules and regulations might apply to video recording in your own national or local setting?
- What other ethical concerns would you need to address if using video data in your own research?
- What steps could you take to address these?

Challenges

As well as ethical considerations, there are other methodological issues which need to be understood and addressed when using video in research. Here are some of the most important.

Reactivity

A majority of qualitative researchers want to study naturally occurring situations – normal, even mundane, everyday situations in the lives of those being studied. However, by obtaining prior written consent from participants, by then placing a camera in such settings and by being present ourselves, we might change – and, some might even say, destroy – the 'naturalness' of the situation. This is 'reactivity': the idea that the research triggers changes in participants in ways that affect whatever is being investigated. Reactivity in video studies refers to people changing their behaviour because they know they are being not only watched but also recorded for further analysis. If their 'normal' behaviour is what we wanted to study in the first place, this is, of course, a problem.

The big question is whether reactivity is a greater problem for the researcher who relies on video than for researchers using other methods, as all must deal with it in some way. The discussion, therefore, needs to go beyond whether or not video affects participants, and engage instead in debate about the nature, degree and length of this effect. Furthermore, we need to acknowledge that the cultural norms related to appearing in a video have changed dramatically with the ever-increasing popularity of smartphones. It means that most people now carry a reasonably good camera with them most of the time, and many use it frequently, so the majority of research participants will have a great deal of prior experience recording and being recorded. In view of this, I agree with Heath *et al.* (2010), who argue that the issue of reactivity is often exaggerated when it comes to video research. The goal should perhaps not be to eliminate reactivity in qualitative research but to use it productively (Maxwell, 2013). Indeed, video recordings may be one of the very few ways in which to actually investigate reactivity (and decreased camera awareness) systematically, as it is possible to pay attention to whether participants appear nervous, look for the cameras, address the cameras directly, or talk about being recorded. Among video researchers, there seems to be consensus that the camera effect in most studies rapidly decreases with time (see, for example, Aarsand and Forsberg, 2010; Rusk *et al.*, 2012).

Finally, I should emphasize that no data are – or could ever be – 'natural', as the process of treating something as research data changes our very perception of 'naturalness'. As Goldman and McDermott (2007) elaborate, the behaviour captured on video is not itself data; it becomes data when subjected to our analytical activities. Expecting participants to act as if they were unaware of the camera may be the most unnatural expectation of all: 'The camera is there, and if it was not, there would be no data' (Rusk *et al.*, 2012:74). The camera does not capture some alternative reality but (to the degree it is possible to capture a social situation) a version of whatever happened. As we have seen, by using video, this recorded version may be scrutinized systematically and repeatedly.

Reactivity

- What are your personal experiences of being recorded?
- To what degree do you think you are able to act 'naturally' on camera? Does this change over time?
- How might reactivity be traced in your research project – and to what extent do you believe it might pose a threat to the validity of your study?

Context

In most investigations of social phenomena, deciding on the nature and extent of the research context is crucial, and there has been a shift in the social sciences from studying fairly stable *units* to studying more complex *practices* (Heath *et al.*, 2010). For example, rather than investigating students' reading solely by measuring reading comprehension by means of tests, many literacy researchers today are exploring how children engage in a variety of literacy practices in their everyday lives, both at school and at home. A big challenge for video researchers, therefore, is determining how closely you can follow participants without losing important contextual details. For example, if you are concerned with doing this very closely, you risk obtaining material that is so detailed that the overall context in which these details are situated becomes impossible to understand. Maltese *et al.* (2016), who used head-mounted cameras to study students' activities, underscore also how such data are bound to be limited, because although data from the head-mounted camera 'provide new insights into student activity, it is also somewhat limited in that it can only capture a subset of their visual field, potentially leaving key activities under-documented' (2016:212).

The opposite is equally problematic. If the scope of the data collection is broad, it may provide a general picture of the context but insufficient detail to really understand what is going on. For example, in the LISA study (Klette *et al.*, 2017), the research design aimed to provide an overview of what happened in the classroom through two fixed cameras. At times, this provided less information than was desirable about what each student was doing. So when students were writing and teachers were walking around and providing feedback on individual texts, we were able to see the class as a whole but not the relevant text or the details of that student's facial expression. This meant that we were able to analyse what the teacher had said but not how the student responded. While teachers' discourse was definitely worth investigating (Blikstad-Balas *et al.*, 2018), it was a good example of a situation where the researchers in hindsight wished that they had more detail about what was going on.

So although video data are often described as rich data, they are also inherently partial and limited. Recordings have a certain perspective, and while we systematically observe what happens in the scope of our camera or cameras, we also systematically neglect everything else (Blikstad-Balas, 2017). This is particularly important for video data, because these data tend to deceive us. When we look at a video recording which is taken from a particular angle or perspective, it is easy to think that 'we know what happened there'. It is hard to keep in mind all the possibilities of what might be going on just outside the camera's scope.

Choosing scope

1. What are the advantages and disadvantages of choosing a broad scope for your gathering of video data?
2. What are the advantages and disadvantages of choosing a narrower, closer scope?
3. What kind of approach might be best for your own research?

Magnification

While all research is demanding work, analysing video data is known to be particularly time-consuming (Haw and Hadfield, 2011). The very detailed nature of such data leads to many researchers conducting in-depth analyses of short fragments (Snell, 2011). One of the benefits described above – the fact that video researchers may initially collect data and then decide on the focus of analysis later – can, therefore, also be problematic, and lead to enormous amounts of data being left unanalysed (Barron, 2007). This may seem like a practical issue of 'death by data' for researchers who have more than they can handle, but it is also a serious challenge for the research community as a whole. As Lemke (2007:35) points out, the educational field is filled with thousands of excellent analyses of five-minute episodes from classrooms, but few of these studies have looked at complete lessons and we have almost no analyses of longer timescales, such as whole school days, or whole weeks, or even a whole year in the lives of students or teachers. When we know so little about the longer timescales, how can we judge the relative significance of all the smaller episodes we study?

By systematically choosing only fragments of data (a sampling issue), or by recording only a very limited amount of data in the first place (also a sampling issue), we risk amplifying or magnifying events that are not representative for participants. In other words, we may study events that are insignificant for the participants or in relation to the social practices we wish to know more about. Lemke (2007:45) explains how video researchers may 'magnify small details and minor events out of proportion to the flow of activity on a longer time scale'. The dangers of sampling bias are further magnified when we share rich case materials with an audience, because, as Miller and Zhou (2007:330) also emphasize, 'whether or not the cases are representative of what the researcher saw, they will be representative of what the viewer sees'. This can also apply when we present our findings in scientific articles and, in doing so, share only small fragments of our data.

Sampling issues

1. What difficulties can arise by recording events which may not be representative of participants' normal activity?
2. What sampling measures could you take in your own video research to avoid these difficulties?
3. How can you describe these measures so they are transparent to readers of your research?

Conclusion

To conclude, here are some issues to consider when planning and carrying out video research:

1. Consider carefully how sensitive are the data you are planning to collect and the ethical recommendations for gathering, analysing and storing such data. These issues should be dealt with before you plan data collection in detail.
2. It is fairly easy to place a camera in a setting, but to place it well – in the sense that it provides you with useful, relevant and credible raw data for your analyses – is far harder. It requires careful consideration and piloting, as well as awareness of and attention to your unit of analysis.
3. When analysing video data, take advantage of the opportunity to look systematically for the things that are crucial to your research question. Go back through recordings as many times as needed. Expand or narrow down the analytical focus where necessary, but be systematic when you make any changes in what you are looking for.

Video recordings provide unique opportunities for researchers in education to scrutinize complex learning and social situations. As with any method, use of data from these recordings holds great promise but is also bound to involve some methodological problems. The key to credible video research lies in transparency, not only about the final stages of analysis – clearly outlining what you looked for and how – but also about your sampling: how you choose which data to gather and which data to analyse, and your rationale behind these choices. By following guidelines such as these, you can take advantage of the many benefits the use of video has to offer.

Recommended reading

Blikstad-Balas, M. (2017) Key challenges of using video when investigating social practices in education: Contextualization, magnification, and representation. *International Journal of Research & Method in Education*, 40(5), 511–523.

This article deals in depth with the main methodological challenges of using video to investigate social practices.

Goldman, R., Pea, R., Barron, B. and Derry, S.J. (Eds.) (2007) *Video Research in the Learning Sciences*. New York: Routledge.

This key reference work gathers together seminal articles on video research from a range of different theoretical and thematic perspectives.

Heath, C., Hindmarsh, J. and Luff, P. (2010) *Video in Qualitative Research: Analysing Social Interaction in Everyday Life*. Thousand Oaks, CA: Sage.

A good introductory book for all researchers planning to conduct video research. It covers the different stages of data collection and analysis, and also deals with ethical issues.

References

Aarsand, P. and Forsberg, L. (2010) Producing children's corporeal privacy: Ethnographic video recording as material-discursive practice. *Qualitative Research*, 10(2), 249–268.

Barron, B. (2007) Video as a tool to advance understanding of learning and development in peer, family, and other informal learning contexts. In: R. Goldman, R. Pea, B. Barron and S.J. Derry (Eds.) *Video Research in the Learning Sciences*. New York: Routledge.

Bjørkvold, T. and Blikstad-Balas, M. (2018) Students as researchers: What and why seventh-grade students choose to write when investigating their own research question. *Science Education*, 102(2), 304–341.

Blikstad-Balas, M. (2012) Digital literacy in upper secondary school – What do students use their laptops for during teacher instruction? *Nordic Journal of Digital Literacy*, 7(2), 81–96.

Blikstad-Balas, M. (2017) Key challenges of using video when investigating social practices in education: Contextualization, magnification, and representation. *International Journal of Research & Method in Education*, 40(5), 511–523.

Blikstad-Balas, M., Roe, A. and Klette, K. (2018) Opportunities to write: An exploration of student writing during language arts lessons in Norwegian lower secondary classrooms. *Written Communication*, 35(2), 119–154.

Creswell, J.W. and Poth, C.N. (2017) *Qualitative Inquiry and Research Design: Choosing Among Five Approaches*. Fourth edition. Thousand Oaks, CA: Sage.

Derry, S.J., Pea, R.D., Barron, B., Engle, R.A., Erickson, F., Goldman, R., ... Sherin, B.L. (2010) Conducting video research in the learning sciences: Guidance on selection, analysis, technology, and ethics. *Journal of the Learning Sciences*, 19(1), 3–53.

Goldman, S. and McDermott, R. (2007) Staying the course with video analysis. In: R. Goldman, R. Pea, B. Barron and S.J. Derry (Eds.) *Video Research in the Learning Sciences*. New York: Routledge.

Haw, K. and Hadfield, M. (2011) *Video in Social Science Research: Functions and Forms*. Abingdon: Routledge.

Heath, C., Hindmarsh, J. and Luff, P. (2010) *Video in Qualitative Research: Analysing Social Interaction in Everyday Life*. Thousand Oaks, CA: Sage.

Janík, T., Seidel, T. and Navjar, P. (2009) Introduction: On the power of video studies in investigating teaching and learning. In: T. Janík and T. Seidel (Eds.) *The Power of Video Studies in Investigating Teaching and Learning in the Classroom*. Münster: Waxmann Verlag.

Jewitt, C. (2012) *An Introduction to Using Video for Research*. NCRM Working Paper. National Centre for Research Methods. [Online] http://eprints.ncrm.ac.uk/2259/ (accessed 10 May 2018).

Klette, K., Blikstad-Balas, M. and Roe, A. (2017) Linking instruction and student achievement. A research design for a new generation of classroom studies. *Acta Didactica Norway*, 11(3), Art.10.

Lemke, J. (2007) Video epistemology in-and-outside the box: Traversing attentional spaces. In: R. Goldman, R. Pea, B. Barron and S.J. Derry (Eds.) *Video Research in the Learning Sciences*. New York: Routledge.

Maltese, A.V., Danish, J.A., Bouldin, R.M., Harsh, J.A. and Bryan, B. (2016) What are students doing during lecture? Evidence from new technologies to capture student activity. *International Journal of Research & Method in Education*, 39(2), 208–226.

Maxwell, J.A. (2013) *Qualitative Research Design: An Interactive Approach*. Third edition. Thousand Oaks, CA: Sage.

Miller, K. and Zhou, X. (2007) Learning from classroom video: What makes it compelling and what makes it hard. In: R. Goldman, R. Pea, B. Barron and S.J. Derry (Eds.) *Video Research in the Learning Sciences*. New York: Routledge.

Rusk, F., Pörn, M., Sahlström, F. and Slotte-Lüttge, A. (2012) Everything, everywhere, all the time: Advantages and challenges in the use of extensive video recordings of children. In: *Responsible Research*. Papers from the Fourth Qualitative Research Conference, edited by P. Salo. Vaasa: The Faculty of Education, Åbo Akademi University, Finland.

Silseth, K. (2012) The multivoicedness of game play: Exploring the unfolding of a student's learning trajectory in a gaming context at school. *International Journal of Computer-Supported Collaborative Learning*, 7(1), 63–84.

Silverman, D. (2006) *Interpreting Qualitative Data: Methods for Analyzing Talk, Text and Interaction*. Third edition. Thousand Oaks, CA: Sage.

Simpson, A., Walsh, M. and Rowsell, J. (2013) The digital reading path: Researching modes and multidirectionality with iPads. *Literacy*, 47(3), 123–130.

Snell, J. (2011) Interrogating video data: Systematic quantitative analysis versus micro-ethnographic analysis. *International Journal of Social Research Methodology*, 14(3), 253–258.

Chapter 6

Using quantitative data

Michael Jopling

Introduction

'98 per cent of statistics are made up' (anon.)

If the thought of working with quantitative data frightens you or leaves you cold, this chapter is designed to make you feel more confident. The intention is to demystify quantitative research and give you the basic information you need to understand how it works. While quantitative research is essentially about measurement and using numbers to generate breadth and generalizability (Basit, 2010), the chapter does not call for any quantitative or statistical expertise and contains nothing more than ordinary mathematics. Its focus is on outlining the logic and some of the methods and key terms that lie behind quantitative approaches and the use of quantitative data, with examples taken from real research.

It is important to emphasize that I approach this subject not as a statistician but as someone who has come to recognize the power and value of incorporating quantitative data into educational enquiry. Anyone seeking more detailed consideration of the issues discussed, particularly in relation to data analysis, is referred to the methodological texts cited throughout. They all offer invaluable information and in-depth explanation.

It is still common for researchers working in the education field to regard 'quantitative-qualitative' as a methodological divide, in which they have to choose a side. This chapter rejects this view, taking as its starting point the notion that researchers should view them merely as different types of data and that they therefore need to understand how both are collected, analysed and interpreted. As using the quantitative option can seem particularly problematic, here are three reasons why readers who are nervous of numbers should consider familiarizing themselves with quantitative data processes:

- Having some understanding of quantitative data will improve your ability to assess investigations which use quantitative approaches, particularly if you are new to research.
- Being able to incorporate quantitative data into your own research could strengthen its impact, particularly if you are interested in influencing aspects of education practice or policy. Although they often use them carelessly and unreflectively, policymakers like numbers.
- Having an improved understanding of quantitative data and research will put you in a better position to evaluate or conduct mixed-methods investigations.

What is quantitative research? What are quantitative data?

The application of quantitative methods in social-science research derives from interest in the 19th century in experimental investigation in the natural sciences. This sought to understand the processes of cause and effect through manipulation and controlled testing. However, it became clear that many of the issues explored in social sciences, such as education, do not lend themselves well to experimental approaches, so researchers began from the 1950s to apply them to what became known as 'quasi-experimental' and 'non-experimental' situations – these approaches are considered in more detail later in the chapter.

Provocatively, Berliner (2002:19) has described what social scientists, and particularly educational researchers, do as the 'hardest to do science [...] because humans in schools are embedded in complex and changing networks of social interaction'. It is engaging with this social complexity that makes the application of experimental research to education so challenging (Hadfield and Jopling, 2018), and it is partly as a consequence of the need to address this complexity and the limitations of the persistent quantitative-qualitative divide, manifested in the so-called 'paradigm wars', that mixed-methods research design (Tashakkori and Teddlie, 1998) gained ground in the 1990s.

There are also many definitions of quantitative research. Aliaga and Gunderson (2000, cited in Muijs, 2011:1) describe it as 'explaining phenomena by collecting numerical data that are analysed using mathematically based methods (in particular statistics)'. Punch and Oancea (2014:264) state that quantitative research essentially does three things: it conceptualizes reality in terms of variables, measures these variables, and studies relationships between these variables. But what are 'variables'?

Variables: Understanding cause and effect

Quantitative research is essentially concerned with cause and effect, and this is expressed in terms of variables. A *variable* is simply a construct or characteristic which a researcher is interested in observing, measuring or manipulating. Age, ethnicity and experience are all possible variables.

Quantitative research distinguishes between independent and dependent variables. The *independent variable* is also known as the input, treatment or predictor variable. It is often a stimulus, intervention or treatment, like a new teaching approach, that causes a specific outcome. A *dependent variable* is the outcome or criterion variable and can be regarded as the effect or consequence of the use of the independent variable.

Control is a central concept in quantitative research design. It refers to attempts to minimize the effects of variables, other than that of the independent variable. As researchers, we want to control these *extraneous variables* to prevent them affecting the results of the experiment. In experimental research therefore, participants are assigned randomly, either to the group which has the intervention (the *experimental group*) or the group which does not (the *control group*), so that there are no systematic differences between them. Or they are matched purposefully on a number of characteristics, so that the two groups are as similar as possible when the experiment begins. In quasi-experimental research, which is research where such randomization or matching is not possible, the researcher uses statistical methods to control (or remove) the effects of other variables which may influence their results.

If variables are not controlled, or cannot be controlled, they become confounding variables. A *confounding variable* is a kind of extraneous variable, separate from independent and dependent variables, which may influence those variables and the relationships between them. An *intervening variable* (also known as the control or mediating variable, or covariate) is another kind of extraneous variable, one which helps explain the relationship between the dependent and independent variables. For example, research has found a relation between an individual's level of education and their level of income, but this is not a direct cause-and-effect relationship – intervening variables, such as type of occupation, also play a part.

Here is a fuller example of the above notions. If we were interested in comparing the resilience levels of girls and boys, that is, their respective capacity to cope with adversity, resilience (however measured) would be the dependent variable and gender would be the independent variable. Extraneous variables could include the time of day when the research was conducted or the participants' ages. We would wish to take steps to control these extraneous variables, for example, by ensuring that participants were all tested at the same time on the same day or that they were all within a certain age range. If this was part of research into the effectiveness of an intervention designed to increase their resilience, we would want to measure the young people's resilience levels before and after the intervention.

Using quantitative data

From your reading of the first part of this chapter, as well as drawing on your own ideas:

1. What kinds of research issues might you want to explore where quantitative data could play a part?
2. How might you determine the aims, schedules and even the costs involved in such a project?
3. What kinds of data would you need to collect and how might you translate your data into variables?

Three types of quantitative design

As seen earlier, there are different ways to categorize quantitative research design, each referring to the extent to which they are experimental. The categories usually used are experiments, quasi-experiments and non-experiments.

Experiments

Experiment is used here as a precise technical term, defined as 'a test under controlled conditions that is made to demonstrate a known truth or examine the validity of a hypothesis' (Muijs, 2011:11). Scott and Usher (2011:61) state that 'the experimental researcher attempts to explicate causal relationships between phenomena by intervening in the natural setting and controlling the relevant variables'. True experiments also involve randomizing participation and controlling variables, as considered above.

The concepts of internal and external validity (Campbell and Stanley, 1963) are relevant in this context. *Internal validity* refers to the extent to which researchers can be sure that the effects they ascribe to the interventions under examination are not caused by other factors. In education contexts, such factors could include participants' maturation or socio-economic status, alongside broader issues, such as sampling and the reliability of the test itself. *External validity* refers to the extent to which findings can be generalized to larger populations.

Until recently, much experimental research in education was really quasi-experimental (considered below). This changed once randomized controlled trials (RCTs) started to be promoted and funded by governments in England and elsewhere as a 'gold standard'. Imported from medical research, RCTs involve randomization and pre- and post-testing (Connolly *et al.*, 2017). They are typically large-scale and expensive. Although you would not always think so from the evangelical terms in which RCTs are often described, a number of limitations have been identified. Goldacre (2013:13), an advocate of applying RCTs to educational issues, was clear that 'randomised trials are very good at showing *that* something works; they're not always so helpful for understanding *why* it worked' (italics in original), a constraint which is more likely to be addressed by using qualitative methods. Morrison (2001) and Wrigley (2018) have criticized RCTs for taking a restricted view of causality and neglecting the contexts and complexity of the phenomena being researched.

One of the most commonly heard objections to the use of RCTs in education research is that it is unethical to exclude students through randomization. Goldacre's (2013) fairly robust response was that RCTs are about deciding whether an intervention works before implementing it, and that successful interventions can and should subsequently be offered to 'non-treated' participants. Hanley *et al.* (2016) argue that viewing RCTs as the gold standard has obscured the value of integrating the use of other, more implementation-specific measures. All of this suggests that you need to be aware of the ethical and pragmatic issues involved when planning an RCT and should never assume that social research of any kind is value-free.

The Educational Endowment Foundation (EEF), established in 2010, has created a Teaching and Learning Toolkit (Higgins *et al.*, 2016) which summarizes the international evidence on teaching in the compulsory phases. This is a good source of examples of experimental research and, at the time of writing, featured reports on 90 intervention projects. The most highly rated project in terms of effectiveness was one which used an approach called 'Self-Regulated Strategy Development' to help struggling writers in the final year of primary school and the first year of secondary school in England. The evaluation of this approach (Torgerson and Torgerson, 2014) involved 23 West Yorkshire primary schools, randomly allocated to the intervention. Schools assigned to the control group were offered the intervention training at the end of the trial. The evaluation found that the approach had a strong positive effect on the writing outcomes of low-attaining students, particularly those from low-income families and therefore eligible for free school meals.

Quasi-experiments

As already indicated, quasi-experimental research is used when randomization is not possible and therefore extraneous variables cannot be controlled physically. Quasi-experimental research compares groups and tries to assess and extract the variance between them through statistical procedures. The advantages are that you can investigate and compare naturally occurring groups, for example, within a school or between different schools, which are already representative of aspects of the real world, although this requires you to think carefully about issues of validity and generalizability. One major limitation is related to the possibility of selection bias, which is why it is crucial for anyone using quasi-experiments to justify sampling procedures in detail in the study's research design.

In our study of practice leadership in the early years (Hadfield *et al.*, 2015), we used structured observations of interactions between adults and children in early-years settings to evaluate practitioners' impact on children's learning and development. Adopting a mixed-methods approach, we undertook multiple sets of two types of observation: rating of the pre-school environment and observations of interactions between adults and children. With these we assessed the quality of provision and the impact of improvement interventions over three years. We used correlation analysis, which quantifies how closely variables are related, to investigate impact and to construct from the data 'improvement trajectories' for the 25 case-study settings, which were not randomized. The challenges involved included ensuring observational reliability in a large research team and maintaining participants' engagement and involvement in the investigation. We tried to address the latter by sharing initial analysis of the quantitative data with them in order to stimulate reflections and explanations in the qualitative elements of the research, for example, in relation to changes in the kinds of interactions between adults and children that had been observed.

Non-experiments

If you are a relatively inexperienced researcher, survey or correlational research is likely to be the most common form of quantitative investigation you undertake. Such research is described as non-experimental, because there is no randomization or experimental manipulation and, therefore, no attempt to identify cause-and-effect relationships. Instead, it examines *correlations* between variables – how and how much the variables are related to each other (covered in a little more detail in the next section). Surveys are particularly good for capturing the attitudes or characteristics of a population, for example, individuals' beliefs, opinions or behaviours. However, surveys often do this without acknowledging the messiness and complexity of social reality, represented not least by the fact that people interpret questions in different ways. This suggests that findings from surveys need to be very clearly described and heavily caveated.

Questionnaire surveys can be conducted face-to-face or by telephone, but here I focus predominantly on those that are completed in writing, either online or in hard copy. Essentially, there are two types: cross-sectional and longitudinal (Creswell, 2018). *Cross-sectional* questionnaire surveys give you a snapshot of views at a single point in time; *longitudinal* surveys are repeated and enable you to see developing trends. Both are relatively quick and inexpensive ways to get a breadth of views. Online questionnaires, which are increasingly popular, have advantages in terms of accessibility and sample size, but also create challenges in authenticating respondents and ensuring that samples are representative. There are also large, regular, national surveys, such as the Millennium Cohort Study (MCS) and the British Social Attitudes (BSA) survey, that can be mined to inform your research. Surveys of all kinds need careful planning and piloting to ensure that key factors, such as form, content, language, sequencing and length, are appropriate. See Oppenheim (1992) or Hartas' (2010:266) checklist of common problems for guidance.

Design

1. What benefits do you see in undertaking experimental, quasi-experimental or non-experimental research?
2. What challenges are associated with each and how might these be addressed?
3. Which approach might be most appropriate for quantitative research you are intending to carry out yourself?

Analysing quantitative data

As indicated at the beginning of the chapter, there is not sufficient scope here to offer more than a brief introduction to some of the issues involved in quantitative data analysis. Therefore, this section can be regarded as a kind of extended glossary, which introduces some of the key terms you will need in order to understand other people's quantitative research and to think about conducting your own.

In order to collect quantitative data, as in all kinds of research, you need to be clear about what you want to find out. Your methods and analysis will be derived from your hypotheses or research questions, as part of your research design. One of the key issues to understand is the notion of measurement itself. Punch and Oancea (2014:287) define it as 'the process of using numbers to link concepts to indicators, where there is a continuum involved', that is, assigning numerical values to ideas. They identify six main steps in constructing a measuring instrument, which include defining what you are planning to measure, selecting a measuring technique (such as a Likert scale – see below), and generating items – statements or questions – to use. You also need to decide whether to construct a new instrument, adopt an existing one, or use a combination of the two. In the practice leadership study (Hadfield *et al.*, 2015) described above, we used validated rating scales for evaluating the pre-school setting environments and devised a new observation tool, based on findings from relevant research, to assess the interactions between adults and children. Using these tools in combination enabled us to create the quantitative baseline and progress measures for the case studies we developed.

Levels of measurement

In quantitative research, there are four levels of measurement: nominal, ordinal, interval and ratio. It is important to understand these levels, as they determine the kinds of analysis you can apply to your data.

Nominal scales assign numerical values arbitrarily. Gender is a good example of this: female may be assigned the value '1', and male the value '2'. They are mutually exclusive categories and have no logical order or ranking in relation to each other. Being labelled '2' does not make an individual greater, better or worse than being labelled '1', and *vice versa*.

In *ordinal scales*, characteristics are assigned numerical values which allow researchers to rank survey responses on a continuum, for example, in relation to their frequency or importance. Political orientation – left, right and points between – can be measured on an ordinal scale. A Likert scale, commonly used in questionnaire surveys, is probably the most common example of an ordinal scale – respondents are asked to select from a range of responses, such as 'Strongly agree', 'Agree', 'Neither agree nor disagree', 'Disagree' and 'Strongly disagree'. These responses have a logical order, but the intervals between them are not equal, and, like nominal scales, they are mutually exclusive categories.

As with ordinal scales, the points in *interval scales* are mutually exclusive and logically ordered, but they differ in that they are continuous and the intervals between them are assumed to be equal. However, they do not have a true zero point corresponding to the absence of the quality being measured. Time of day on a 12-hour clock is an example of an interval scale, as are numerical scales for measuring opinions or attitudes, for instance running from 1 to 10.

Ratio scales also have equal distances between their units, but they do have an absolute zero point. Weight and height are examples of ratio variables measured with ratio scales, as the difference between 45kg and 50kg, for example, is the same as the difference between 55kg and 60kg. 24-hour time, where midnight = 0, is another ratio scale.

Interval and ratio scales create *parametric* (or continuous) data. Nominal and ordinal scales create *non-parametric* (categorical or non-continuous) data. This is important, because as we move through these levels from nominal to ratio, the procedures we can use in statistical analysis become less restricted. Parametric data can be analysed using a wide range of techniques, including regression and factor analysis (see below). Non-parametric data can be analysed only by using a narrower set of analytical tools. Parametric data are regarded as more robust than non-parametric data. Hartas (2010:350) has another good checklist you can refer to in order to establish what kinds of tests can be used with what kinds of variables and data.

Most quantitative data analysis is undertaken with statistical software, the most commonly used of which is SPSS Statistics, produced by IBM. A number of excellent guides to this exist, relating both to social science in general (Field, 2018) and to education more specifically (Muijs, 2011). Microsoft Excel can also be used for many analytical tasks. However, before you begin, you need to know what kind of analysis is appropriate for your data, for answering your research questions or for testing your hypothesis. The two main types, descriptive and inferential, are covered now.

Descriptive statistics

Analysis usually starts with descriptive statistics, which summarize your data. Nominal and ordinal data are described in terms of frequencies, percentages or cross-tabulations. Interval and ratio data allow centrality and dispersion to be identified – discussed below. Such statistics are an essential part of quantitative analysis and can take you a long way, particularly in mixed-methods research. Indeed, depending on your research design, a descriptive analysis may be all you need, especially in a small-scale or pilot project, and the analysis can be done using software, such as SPSS.

Central tendency: Mean, mode and median

Central tendency is a way of describing what is typical in a dataset. It has three main measures: mean, mode and median. The *mean* is a hypothetical value, colloquially referred to as the 'average', calculated by dividing the total of all the values in a dataset by the number of values in that set. While the mean is often calculated for ordinal variables, it makes most sense for continuous data (interval and ratio variables). The *mode* is simply the value which occurs most frequently in a dataset and therefore applies to nominal, ordinal, interval and ratio variables. The *median* is the middle category in a distribution of values, arranged by ordering them from high to low. For example, in a dataset of ages which runs 28, 27, 25, 25, 23, 22, 20, the median age is 25 (the mode is also 25; the mean is 24).

Dispersion: Range and variance (standard deviation)

Dispersion indicates how the values are spread around the central tendency. The two most common measures of dispersion are range and variance. The *range* is calculated simply by subtracting the lowest from the highest value in a distribution of values from an interval or ratio variable. For example, in the dataset for which the median was calculated above, the range is 8 (28–20). *Variance* is the measure of the spread and indicates how close or how far the observed scores or values are from the mean. A large variance suggests that the mean is not a good representation of the data. A small variance indicates that the mean is a good representation, as the data cluster around it. In this connection, you will often find reference to the *standard deviation* (SD). SD is the square root of the variance and is considered to be a more accurate description of dispersion than the range between extreme scores (known as *outliers*). SD is an important concept to understand, because parametric data are assumed to come from a population which is normally distributed. This is an idealized or standard distribution with a 'bell-curve' shape, which assumes a mean of 0 and a standard deviation of 1. SD is included in SPSS outputs and data tables.

Inferential statistics

Before outlining some of the methods that you can employ in inferential statistics, it is crucial to introduce two key ideas which you will almost always come across when you read research reports with quantitative findings: statistical significance and effect size.

Statistical significance

Statistical significance simply refers to the probability that a relationship or difference between variables occurred by chance (Creswell, 2018). Conventionally, the threshold or critical value for the significance level is set at 0.05 (5 in 100 or 1 in 20). A high level of statistical significance would be 0.01 (1 in 100). It is usually represented as a p-value. Statistically significant results are more likely to be found with large sample sizes. In recent years, statistical significance has been increasingly criticized for shortcomings, such as its arbitrary cut-off points, and more emphasis has been placed on measuring effect sizes (Muijs, 2011).

Effect size

Effect sizes have become increasingly prominent since the publication of Hattie's (2009) *Visible Learning*, which is a synthesis of over 800 meta-analyses of education research. Hattie used the effect size of quantitative studies to aggregate information about a range of interventions and to rate their effectiveness. Effect size is the size of the difference between groups or of the relationships between variables. Whereas statistical significance only tells you the likelihood of an outcome occurring by chance, effect size helps to identify the strength of the conclusions of a research study. While there are different ways to calculate effect sizes, the output value ranges between 1 and –1. Usually an effect size of greater than 0.5 is considered a strong effect; between 0.3 and 0.5 is a moderate effect; 0.1–0.3 is a modest effect; and 0–0.1 is a weak effect. As you would imagine, negative effect sizes identify negative effects.

Alongside estimations of the strength of the evidence associated with an educational intervention or teaching approach, and of its cost, the EEF Teaching and Learning Toolkit, mentioned earlier, translates effect sizes into additional months' progress in learning that students can make as a result of that particular teaching approach being used. In the 'Self-Regulated Strategy Development' project, used as an example above, the overall effect size of the intervention was 0.74, which was translated in the Toolkit into an additional nine months' progress for the school students involved. The effect size was higher for those eligible for free school meals. While the Toolkit offers useful summary guidance for practitioners, there is criticism that findings from very different studies and contexts are collated into a single, potentially misleading, headline progress figure (Wrigley, 2018).

Tests of difference and variance

The *chi-square* test examines association or, more usually, difference. It measures the variance between a result that is expected statistically and the actual result, to determine whether it is significant. The *t-test* determines if there is a significant difference between the means of two randomly selected groups with a normal distribution of scores. You will also often find reference to ANOVA – analysis of variance. Whereas t-tests focus on two groups, two variables or two timepoints, ANOVA is used to compare and examine differences between more than two groups, all of which have been randomly selected and have normal distribution. Equivalent tests have been created to use with non-parametric data. Available in software like SPSS, the Mann-Whitney U and Wilcoxon tests are alternatives to the t-test; the Kruskal-Wallis and Friedman tests are the non-parametric equivalents to ANOVA.

Correlations

Correlations are used to test hypotheses about the relationships between variables. They measure the extent to which change in the value of one variable is accompanied by a change in the value of another variable. They are calculated as a *correlation coefficient*, expressed as a score between +1 and –1. +1 is a perfect positive relationship; –1 is a perfect negative relationship; and 0 is no relationship. The closer the score is to +1, the stronger the relationship. For example, in research into effective university teaching (Allan *et al.*, 2009), we found that the strongest correlation in a 32-item questionnaire, with a correlation coefficient of 0.829, was between lecturers' enthusiasm about learning and their respecting of students' opinions. It cannot be emphasized enough that while correlation identifies a relationship between variables, even a very strong correlation never implies causation.

Factor analysis

Factor analysis uses correlation to reduce the number of variables in a dataset. By factor-analysing the correlations between variables, it creates a smaller number of derived variables, referred to as *factors*. For example, test results from a range of subjects, such as physics, chemistry, sociology and psychology, can be reduced to two groups: sciences and social sciences (depending on where you see the dividing line) in order to simplify analysis.

Regression analysis

Regression analysis, or more accurately multiple linear regression, is used when you want to study the relationship between a dependent variable and a number of independent variables. Punch and Oancea (2014:279) use the example of school achievement as the dependent variable, in relation to which the effect of independent variables, such as socio-economic status, motivation and levels of homework, can be investigated using regression analysis.

Presenting quantitative data

Although they invariably contain examples, most research-method guides devote much more space to the analysis of data than they do to how to present those data and their analysis. While journal articles generally contain data tables, it is still all too common to see standard Excel or SPSS charts exported without modification into student assignments, research reports or conference presentations. Graphs and charts can be a very effective way of conveying complex findings to an audience, but you need to ensure that they are not overly complicated, that you can explain them either verbally or in writing, and that they are appropriate for the audience towards which they are targeted. Testing graphs with colleagues, or getting input from information designers, will help.

Analysis and presentation

1. How confident are you about using descriptive analysis in your quantitative research? What planning do you need to do?
2. If you are thinking about using a more sophisticated approach, such as inferential statistics, what kind of analysis do you need to do and, more importantly, who are you going to ask to help you?
3. How are you going to present your quantitative data and its analysis?

Conclusion

Scott and Usher (2011) conclude their overview of experimental and correlational research with two points that are worth reiterating here. The first is that the open systems in which we operate in social-science research make accurate prediction impossible. The second is that attempts to model school processes mathematically are necessarily reductive of the complexity of these systems and fail to incorporate the effects of individuals' intentions, beliefs and attitudes. This is not to delegitimize the role of quantitative data in areas like education, but to acknowledge the importance of recognizing that determining 'what works' in quantitative terms is only part of the story. Equally, however, if researchers and practitioners, open to the idea of evidence-informed practice, are reluctant or unwilling to engage with the procedures or findings of quantitative research, they are closing themselves off from evidence, approaches and ideas which may be of benefit. Researchers, therefore, need to be able to draw on multiple research methods, in which a knowledge of quantitative data is necessary but not sufficient. As Berliner (2002:20) emphasized: 'A single method is not what the government should be promoting for educational researchers. It would do better by promoting argument, discourse, and discussion.'

To conclude, do not be afraid of quantitative research or quantitative data. If you are drawing on the investigations and findings of others to inform your learning or your teaching, an understanding of the basic tenets of quantitative research design will enable you to evaluate the value of the reports you encounter more effectively. If, however, you are doing your own research, start with your research issue, questions or hypothesis, and think about what kinds of data you need to collect. Descriptive analysis can take you a long way, but work with more expert colleagues if you want to go further and move into inferential analysis. Finally, think carefully about how you present your data. A bad graph may lose you your audience; a good graph can convey your findings powerfully and more quickly than a lengthy description.

Recommended reading

Punch and Oancea's (2014) *Introduction to Research Methods in Education* has three chapters on quantitative research and is an excellent overview. Muijs's (2011) *Doing Quantitative Research in Education with SPSS* is a relatively brief guide and a good introduction to inferential analysis. Field's (2018) *Discovering Statistics Using IBM SPSS Statistics* is the canonical text, which includes all the explanations (and the mathematics) you will need and the kind of user-friendly design you will either love or hate.

References

Allan, J., Clarke, K. and Jopling, M. (2009) Effective teaching in higher education: Perceptions of first year undergraduates. *International Journal of Teaching and Learning in Higher Education*, 21(3), 362–372.

Basit, T.N. (2010) *Conducting Research in Educational Contexts*. London: Continuum.

Berliner, D.C. (2002) Comment: Educational research: The hardest science of all. *Educational Researcher*, 31(8), 18–20.

Campbell, D.T. and Stanley, J.C. (1963) Experimental and quasi-experimental designs for research. In: N.L. Gage (Ed.) *Handbook of Research on Teaching*. Chicago, IL: Rand McNally.

Connolly, P., Biggart, A., Miller, S., O'Hare, L. and Thurston, A. (2017) *Using Randomised Controlled Trials in Education*. London: Sage.

Creswell, J.W. (2018) *Educational Research: Planning, Conducting, and Evaluating Quantitative and Qualitative Research*. Sixth edition. London: Pearson.

Field, A. (2018) *Discovering Statistics Using IBM SPSS Statistics*. Fifth edition. London: Sage.

Goldacre, B. (2013) *Building Evidence into Education*. London: Department for Education. [Online] http://media.education.gov.uk/assets/files/pdf/b/ben%20goldacre%20paper.pdf (accessed 9 July 2018).

Hadfield, M. and Jopling, M. (2018) Case study as a means of evaluating the impact of early year leaders: Steps paths and routes. *Evaluation and Program Planning*, 67, 167–176.

Hadfield, M., Jopling, M. and Needham, M. (2015) *Practice Leadership in the Early Years: Becoming, Being and Developing as a Leader*. Maidenhead: Open University Press.

Hanley, P., Chambers, B. and Haslam, J. (2016) Reassessing RCTs as the 'gold standard': Synergy not separatism in evaluation designs. *International Journal of Research and Methods in Education*, 39(3), 287–298.

Hartas, D. (Ed.) (2010) *Educational Research and Inquiry: Qualitative and Quantitative Approaches*. London: Continuum.

Hattie, J. (2009) *Visible Learning: A Synthesis of Over 800 Meta-Analyses Relating to Achievement*. London: Routledge.

Higgins, S., Katsipataki, M., Villanueva-Aguilera, A.B., Coleman, R., Henderson, P., Major, L.E., Coe, R. and Mason, D. (2016) *The Sutton Trust-Education Endowment Foundation Teaching and Learning Toolkit*. London: Education Endowment Foundation.

Morrison, K. (2001) Randomised controlled trials for evidence-based education: Some problems in judging 'what works'. *Evaluation & Research in Education*, 15(2), 69–83, DOI: 10.1080/09500790108666984.

Muijs, D. (2011) *Doing Quantitative Research in Education with SPSS*. Second edition. London: Sage.

Oppenheim, A.N. (1992) *Questionnaire Design, Interviewing and Attitude Measurement*. Second edition. Reprint. London: Continuum, 1998.

Punch, K.F. and Oancea, A. (2014) *Introduction to Research Methods in Education*. Second edition. London: Sage.

Scott, D. and Usher, R. (2011) *Researching Education: Data, Methods and Theory in Educational Enquiry*. Second edition. London: Continuum.

Tashakkori, A., and Teddlie, C. (1998) *Mixed Methodology: Combining Qualitative and Quantitative Approaches*. Thousand Oaks, CA: Sage.

Torgerson, D. and Torgerson, C. (2014) *Improving Writing Quality: Evaluation Report and Executive Summary*. London: Education Endowment Foundation.

Wrigley, T. (2018) The power of 'evidence': Reliable science or a set of blunt tools? *British Educational Research Journal*, 44(3), 359–376.

Chapter 7

Document analysis

Jane O'Connor

Introduction

This chapter provides a discussion of document analysis as a method for social and educational enquiry. It begins with an overview of the definition and use of this approach as part of the larger notion of 'discourse analysis', and goes on to explain how it was employed by the author in a research project which explored how gifted and talented children are portrayed in the British press. Processes around data collection and analysis are carefully considered and explained, interpretation of findings are discussed, and the final section provides guidance on how to decide if document analysis might be a suitable method to use in your research project.

Discourse and document analysis

Document analysis is part of a raft of methodological approaches which come under the umbrella term of 'discourse analysis'. The aim of discourse analysis is to investigate the social meanings inherent in spoken language, images and text. Methods range from micro-analysis of every utterance, pause and intonation in spoken language, using the specific techniques of conversation analysis (see Sidnell, 2010), to document analysis itself, which focuses on illuminating the themes and ideologies which give meaning to pieces of writing, such as newspaper articles, company websites or policy documents. The fundamental theoretical concept of all discourse analysis, however, is that the surface level of language, in whatever way it is presented, is the 'tip of the iceberg' and that this hides a vast array of socially constructed and culturally shared information and knowledge which give the spoken language, images or text meaning to the audience to which it is addressed.

By giving us strategies for unpicking the underlying, socially constructed knowledge which informs the content and form of the language we use to communicate, both formally and informally, discourse analysis allows us to analyse texts, images and speech acts critically, in order to challenge the assumed, often biased or unjust assumptions and the 'common-sense', shared ideologies which inform them. In this sense the key questions to ask when approaching data from any discourse-analysis perspective are these:

- Why are these words or images being used and not others?
- What is being assumed or implied about the subject in this discourse material?
- What shared cultural or social knowledge is allowing me to understand and make meaning from it?

- How are individuals or groups of people being positioned in this material?

Discourse analysis, and specifically document analysis, have often been usefully employed as tools for highlighting and uncovering social issues. For example, van Dijk (2016) reviewed use of the discourse-analysis approach in studying racism, including investigating the role of the Dutch media in the reproduction of racism; analysis of everyday conversations and storytelling about immigrants; and the representation of immigrants and third-world peoples in Dutch social-science textbooks. Baker (2014) used document analysis to explore gender and sexuality in a case study of a British newspaper article about the death of the boy-band singer, Stephen Gately, in 2009. Baker's analysis, both of the newspaper report and of the online responses to it, critically examined features of sexual-identity discourse in the British media at that time. Fealy and McNamara (2009) used a similar approach in their analysis of two daily newspapers over a key period in Irish politics, when in 2008 the Irish Government withdrew automatic entitlement to free medical care for people aged 70 and over. They identified in these media particular ways of naming and referencing older people and also revealed distinct and discernible constructions of ageing and of age identities. Their research demonstrated the ways in which older people are positioned in discourses and how these resultant identities have consequences for their behaviour and for the way that other individuals and society behave towards them.

These examples show how discourse and document analysis can be used for highlighting dominant, often unjust discourses which underpin governmental policy, media and other material around important issues in education, health and social equality. Such discourses are frequently invisible or well hidden within rhetoric and euphemistic language. The following section outlines how document analysis was used in a piece of education-studies research (O'Connor, 2012), which explored how the concept of childhood 'giftedness' was constructed and written about in the British press in 2006–2008, and how this related to the educational practice of labelling certain children as 'gifted' or 'talented' in English schools, which was current policy at that time.

Using document analysis in a research project: Is it good to be gifted?

This research project was carried out in the context of a new educational policy initiative in England in the 2000s, which required schools to identify up to 10 per cent of children as either gifted academically or talented in sports or the arts, then to provide them with specialized support and opportunities to extend and enrich their learning (DCSF, 2009). It is worth noting here that this distinction between 'gifted' and 'talented', which was made in government documents, tended not to be used more widely. Indeed, in the media the term 'gifted' was and still is often applied to those who excel in any area.

As a childhood-studies expert, I had previously investigated the stigmatizing experience that being labelled as extraordinary in any field could have on children (O'Connor, 2008). Therefore, in this subsequent research study I was concerned about the way in which being labelled as gifted or talented may be perceived by the general public and about the unintended adverse outcomes that such a practice may have on the well-being of a potentially large number of children. This was reinforced when I reviewed associated research in this field and discovered that socially negative perceptions around exceptionally able children were a particular problem in other countries, which had already established a similar educational policy around classifying children as gifted or talented. For example, Geake and Gross (2008) conducted research with trainee teachers in Australia and found that negative attitudes towards students labelled in this way were prevalent.

I reflected on how best to explore this issue in England and decided that it would be interesting and useful to look from a social perspective at how the media conceptualizes and presents children by employing such terms, as this is one way in which any associated stigma might be reinforced and circulated. That is not to say that other approaches, such as a study of individual experiences or a survey of parental or practitioner responses to this policy, would not also have been important ways to investigate this topic. With the document-analysis approach, however, I wanted to achieve a different, wider way of seeing the issue, one which was not situated in specific schools or families or professional groups, but one which recognized the practice of labelling as a powerful social act, part of a broader process in which we, as a society, construct childhood in certain bounded ways, and which might show how we understand and use related categories, such as giftedness. The concept of childhood as being socially constructed underpinned the research theoretically and allowed me to explore giftedness as an 'invented', rather than a 'natural' category, which in turn allowed me to critically examine its use in educational policy in England.

The social construction of childhood

Within the dominant discourse that is recognized as characterizing contemporary Western constructs, childhood is understood as being separate from adulthood, and children as less knowledgeable and skilful than adults (Hockey and James, 1993). As Archard (1993:30) states: 'Childhood is defined as that which lacks the capabilities, skills and powers of adulthood.' This clear distinction not only legitimizes unequal power relations but also validates the long period of compulsory education that characterizes the increasingly global definition of how children should spend their time. In this sense, the child who is academically gifted upsets these normalized relations and can be seen to be transgressing the boundaries between childhood and adulthood which have been so carefully constructed in Western society over the last 300 years (Ariès, 1996). Such children also challenge the developmental 'ages and stages' approach to organizing education systems, based on the work of Piaget, that structures the vast majority of schooling across Europe and the Western world (Bentham, 2002).

Find and read a newspaper article about a child or children. Then use the ideas presented in the review above to inform your responses to the following questions:

1. What assumptions or shared ideologies about childhood are evident in the newspaper report you have chosen? For example, it might assume that readers agree that childhood is a time of innocence, or that children should be protected, or that teenagers are dangerous.
2. What specific words (for example, 'angels' or 'hoodies') are used to describe children in the article? How might these labels influence or reinforce readers' behaviour and attitudes towards children and young people?
3. Think about the wider context of the newspaper article you have found. How might the same story have been written 20 years ago? Or 100 years ago? Or in a different country or culture?

Data collection

The first step in my research was to identify and collate a data set with which I would explore my chosen issue. I decided to use articles from a range of British broadsheet and tabloid newspapers from a two-year period between March 2006 to December 2008. The data was collected via the free (at that time) newspaper database, Proquest, using the search terms 'child prodigy', 'gifted child' and 'talented child'. In all, 187 stories were found, many being about the same children. Of these stories, 17 related to academic giftedness, 15 to high ability in sport and 13 to high ability in music: 45 relevant reports in total. 28 of these were about boys, 17 were about girls. The stories were about British children and other high-profile, exceptional children from across the world.

One advantage of using document analysis is the convenience of being able to collect data from publicly available, web-based databases, which saves both time and resources at this early stage of the research. It is important to define your search terms, also to be flexible in adjusting them to obtain the stories which cover the area you are interested in, as you become more familiar with the kind of language used around the topic. For example, in my initial search I did not use the term, 'child prodigy', as I perceived it as too unusual and rarely used. But when I did include it, many extra articles came up, as this is actually a common way for British journalists to refer to any child of above-average ability, especially in tabloid newspapers.

There is also the opportunity to be flexible in relation to your search period. For example, if a search over a one-year period does not yield many results, then it can be extended to two years, and so on, until you have collected a critical mass of stories. It is important, however, to provide some rationale for the range of material and the time period you are using. For example, in my research I purposefully chose a period of time when government policy was developing in the area of gifted-and-talented provision.

There is no definitive way of knowing when you have enough data, as the number of documents available on different topics varies immensely. It also depends on your research design and aims. For example, if you are investigating formulation of a government policy, then the main policy document alone could be your data set. However, where there is a large amount of potential data, I tend to use the grounded-theory concept of 'saturation' (Charmaz, 2014) to know when I have collected enough documents. Saturation refers to the point when the same themes, narratives and language keep coming up again and again, and nothing novel seems to be contributed to the data by adding more material. That is generally the point when I can begin unpicking the deeper discourses that are informing the stories and start to identify the underlying themes and assumptions that are supporting and giving meaning to the texts.

So it is important that you are both flexible and systematic in your data collection and are able to explain clearly the provenance and scope of your final data set. This will lend trustworthiness and validity to your research and give you the basis to address, in the methodology or other section of your written project, two important questions: Have I gathered enough data to make a convincing case that my findings are trustworthy? Have I gathered it in a transparent way that could be replicated by another researcher? It is important to show that you did not 'cherry-pick' only the articles that fitted your assumptions about the research questions and discard any that did not.

Another positive aspect of undertaking document analysis is that the absence of human subjects means there are fewer ethical considerations to take into account. It is not necessary to obtain permission to use databases which contain public-domain material that has already been published, such as newspaper articles (although some publications charge a fee to access their archives). There is also no need normally to obtain consent from the individual journalists or subjects of the stories, although all sources do need to be referenced in your research paper, just like academic texts. Document analysis involving personal information (such as diaries) or confidential material (such as health and education records) would, however, necessitate permission for access from the individuals involved and stringent ethical approval on several issues, including informed consent, anonymity and storage of data (BERA, 2018). If in doubt about whether to seek permission to scrutinize a particular document in your research (as might be the case, for instance, with material coming from a school), you may wish simply to inform those responsible for the document about what you are doing, and keep details of its origin confidential in your written project report.

Planning your research

1. What kind of documents could you analyse in order to investigate your research topic?
2. How would you access these documents? What challenges, if any, might be involved?
3. What ethical issues would you need to consider? What steps would you need to take to address these issues?

Analysis and findings

To analyse and interpret the textual data collected for the gifted study, a qualitative approach was taken. This involved carefully reading all the newspaper articles in the sample and coding them according to categories which related to how the children were described. This was done by printing out the stories and using coloured highlighter pens to identify extracts or quotes with similar themes (this process of 'coding' can also be undertaken using specially designed software, such as NVivo). Common themes and patterns were identified in the discourses and terminology was noted. For example, articles using the term 'boffin' were found to be generally less positive about childhood giftedness than those using the term, 'genius'. The portrayal of the three types of giftedness – academic, sport, music – were also compared in order to highlight any differences in the way each was represented. Finally, the texts were analysed in relation to dominant social constructions of childhood as a time of learning and of children being less knowledgeable and skilful than adults, as shown earlier. This was done in order to identify the potential stigmatizing effects of labelling children as gifted.

Themes identified in the analysis included 'gifted children as deviant', 'having a normal or abnormal childhood' and 'attribution of ability' – for example, was the child described as being born with a gift or working hard to achieve it? These formed the structure for presentation of the analysis of findings in the final journal article (O'Connor, 2012). It is important to note that document analysis can also include a quantitative approach to texts, whereby, for example, instances of the use of certain words or phrases pertinent to the research topic are counted and their frequencies analysed and discussed. This detailed scrutiny of language and word frequency was employed in Fealy and McNamara's (2009) examination of newspaper reactions to changes to medical care in Ireland, described earlier in the chapter.

From my data analysis, I found that newspaper stories about academically gifted children tended to be constructed to highlight differences between the 'normal' and the 'gifted' child, and in doing so, reinforced and naturalized an idealized image of the child as occupying a temporal, cognitive space of pre-adult understanding and knowing. The construction of the academically gifted child as a passive pawn of adult manipulation was a common theme in stories in which the prodigy had encountered misfortune or disaster, reflecting the way in which the press standardize a certain idea of the 'proper child' as one who is not pushed beyond an intellectual stage, socially agreed as appropriate for their years.

The difficulty of striking a balance between being 'pushy' and being 'encouraging' was particularly pronounced in the stories about the parents of academic prodigies, with many commenting on the 'problem' of their child's gift and the burden of responsibility for organizing the best provision for his or her needs. It was also evident from the data that the dangers of academically precocious children being seen as strange were compounded by the tendency of newspaper stories to depict them as oddly different from 'normal' children.

Another key finding was that children who were identified as gifted in music or sport did not appear to be subject to the same negativity in the newspaper stories as those who were said to be gifted academically. Indeed, the stories seemed much less hostile towards young musicians and sports stars than towards their academic counterparts, and a more admiring, proud tone often prevailed when they were described. In the article I theorize that this difference in tone can be explained from a 'social-constructionist' perspective, with children who are exceptional in the fields of music and sport 'constructed' in the newspapers in a largely different way from the academically gifted. This variation seems to emanate from different paradigms of giftedness – children gifted musically or athletically are seen as manifestations of different aspects of childhood 'atypicality' to those showing academic giftedness, and those aspects have more positive connotations in Western culture because of the wider discourses that inform them.

Discussion

It is important to acknowledge the limitations of the document research reported in this chapter, in terms of its relatively small sample of stories and the subjective interpretation of selected data. For these reasons, it was not possible for findings to be generalized to other cultural and social contexts, as they described only how exceptionally able children were being portrayed in the British press at a specific point in time. The value of the study was derived from the way in which it demonstrated the socially constructed nature of childhood giftedness and how public responses to such children appeared to be moulded and constrained by wider social and cultural, normative understandings around childhood more generally. This was only possible through adopting a document-analysis approach to the data. However, even a small-scale study such as this succeeded in providing evidence of differences in social and cultural constructions of these children, and formed part of a critical academic response to the practice of labelling them as 'gifted' or 'talented' in English schools at that time.

As has been seen, my analysis of documents showed that academically gifted children were subjected to the majority of negative attitudes, stigma and cautionary tales in the newspaper stories. They were portrayed as being outside the 'normal' parameters of childhood ability, as 'swots' or 'geeks', for example, sometimes with the additional assumption that their parents were somewhat deviant as well. Relating this finding to dominant discourses on childhood, it seemed that the academically gifted child transgressed the boundaries between adulthood and childhood by 'knowing too much, too soon', and also challenged traditional educational structures regarding incremental exposure to appropriate knowledge at certain ages, as decided by adults.

I extended this thinking further, again by combining findings from the document data with wider social discourses, and again relating them in particular to views on academically gifted children. I concluded that these children can be viewed as being non-compliant and subversive of accepted norms of the teacher–student, or more general adult–child binaries. They also challenge the ideal of childhood innocence by being 'precocious' in their intellect, an unwelcome trait in much of Western society, where children are more often valued for their association with naivety and vulnerability than for their accelerated pace of academic learning. The historical associations between premature sexuality and the overly advanced child still appeared to inform the general distaste for the precocious child (or 'brat'), which was – and probably still is – evident, sometimes quite overtly, in media stories about intellectually able children. The implication from the study was that due to contemporary dominant ideologies of childhood in English society, children labelled as exceptionally able in academic fields could be perceived as challenging adult authority and the received social order around their 'proper' place. On a broader level, the findings suggested that it would be socially desirable to move on from such constraining definitions of what is 'normal' and what is not, and who is 'gifted' and who is not, which may permeate both institutional and cultural discourses on childhood and which ultimately serve to limit the individuality and creativity on which innovation and progress thrive.

Reaching wider conclusions

1. In your view, to what extent and in what ways was document analysis a useful approach to investigating the research issue in this project?
2. What are your thoughts about the way in which the document analysis was used in the study to reach wider conclusions about education, society and the media?
3. What did the use of document analysis add to the debate that other methods may not have contributed?

Conclusion

Techniques of document analysis are developing all the time, and the quantity and range of potential material to analyse proliferates daily, thanks mainly to the Internet and digital technology. Some researchers use specially designed software and linguistic programs to analyse large data sets of text, a process called 'corpus linguistic analysis'. Another term, 'text mining', is often given to the process of deriving high-quality information from large amounts of online text through the identification of patterns and trends. The overarching aim of such approaches is to turn text into data for analysis (see Ignatow and Mihalcea, 2017). In terms of the wider concept of discourse analysis, other researchers have developed innovative techniques for analysing television dialogue (Bednarek and Caple, 2017) and modern 'pop culture' (Werner, 2018), with the aim of critically exploring the meanings behind spoken language and images, as well as written texts.

The document analysis method discussed here demonstrates the availability and accessibility of an extensive range of text material for analysis, opening up the possibility of research into many aspects of education and other social issues. However, there are, of course, limitations in the approach, especially if it is not carried out well. For instance, as has been seen, it is important to report on your data collection in a transparent manner, so that readers of your research understand the processes you went through. It may also be necessary to dig down deeper into issues by combining document analysis with other methods, such as interviews, so that your analysis of the documents is not overly subjective or left open to alternative readings. This also places responsibility on the researcher to gather trustworthy and persuasive evidence, to seek 'saturation' of data, to be cautious in the conclusions drawn and to acknowledge the limits of generalizing findings. It is also important to be familiar with the cultural and social context from which the documents to be analysed arise, as well as with the language in which they are written, as most interpretations will depend on an understanding of the wider and deeper meaning of the texts. Indeed, document analysis of material from an unfamiliar culture can be very difficult, and in such cases a different methodological approach, or the help of a culturally situated research partner, would be advised.

The question of whether document analysis is right for your research project comes down to what you want to explore, what data is available, and whether you are interested in social discourses as evident in documents, or in exploring what people think, say and do – aspects which might be better investigated through other methods. If you are a student, doing your investigation as part of a course of study, there may indeed be a requirement for you to engage in human contact, rather than documents, for your research project and you may need to check this beforehand with your supervising tutor. However, even if it is not used as your main method, document analysis can be combined with other methods, thereby triangulating your research design, and the findings it produces can complement those from other types of data collection. If you are intrigued by how the wider culture that we live in influences how we understand the world and interact with each other, and you are interested in the often concealed power of language and discourse, then document analysis could well be a method worth using in your research.

To summarize this chapter:

- Document analysis is a form of discourse analysis that uses written texts as its data source.
- It is a useful method for exploring discourses and ideologies that inform official and cultural material.
- It can be used to critically analyse policy documents and identify hidden social inequality and stereotyping.
- Many documents are freely available online and this can simplify data collection, especially if time for a project is limited.

Recommended reading

Bowen, G.A. (2009) Document analysis as a qualitative research method. *Qualitative Research Journal*, 9(2), 27–40.

Targeted at early researchers, this article takes a 'nuts-and-bolts' approach to document analysis.

Rapley, T. (2008) *Doing Conversation, Discourse and Document Analysis*. London: Sage.

This book provides an overview of the particular challenges involved in collecting and analysing data, as well as clear guidance for each stage of your project.

Strauss, S. and Feiz, P. (2014) *Discourse Analysis: Putting Our Worlds into Words*. Abingdon: Routledge.

This is another useful resource for understanding the broader techniques and uses of discourse analysis.

References

Archard, D. (1993) *Children: Rights and Childhood*. London: Routledge.

Ariès, P. (1996) *Centuries of Childhood*. London: Pimlico.

Baker, P. (2014) Considering context when analysing representations of gender and sexuality: A case study. In: J. Flowerdew (Ed.) *Discourse in Context: Contemporary Applied Linguistics Volume 3*. New York: Bloomsbury.

Bednarek, M. and Caple, H. (2017) *The Discourse of News Values: How News Organizations Create Newsworthiness*. New York: Oxford University Press.

Bentham, S. (2002) *Psychology and Education*. Hove: Routledge.

BERA (2018) *Ethical Guidelines for Educational Research*. Fourth edition. London: British Educational Research Association.

Charmaz, K. (2014) *Constructing Grounded Theory*. Second edition. London: Sage.

DCSF (2009) *Standards Site: Gifted and Talented*. [Online] www.standards.dfes.gov.uk/giftedandtalented (accessed 12 January 2010).

Fealy, G. and McNamara, M. (2009) *Constructing Ageing and Age Identity: A Case Study of Newspaper Discourses*. Dublin: National Centre for the Protection of Older People.

Geake, J.G. and Gross, M.U.M. (2008) Teachers' negative affect toward academically gifted students: An evolutionary psychological study. *Gifted Child Quarterly*, 52(3), 217–231.

Hockey, J. and James, A. (1993) *Growing Up and Growing Old: Ageing and Dependency in the Life Course*. London: Sage.

Ignatow, G. and Mihalcea, R.F. (2017) *Text Mining: A Guidebook for the Social Sciences*. London: Sage.

O'Connor, J. (2008) *The Cultural Significance of the Child Star*. Abingdon: Routledge.

O'Connor, J. (2012) Is it good to be gifted? The social construction of the gifted child. *Children and Society*, 26(4), 293–303.

Sidnell, J. (2010) *Conversation Analysis: An Introduction*. Chichester: Wiley-Blackwell.

Van Dijk, T.A. (2016) Discourse analysis of racism. In: J.H. Stanfield (Ed.) *Rethinking Race and Ethnicity in Research Methods*. Abingdon: Routledge.

Werner, V. (2018) *The Language of Pop Culture*. Abingdon: Routledge.

Chapter 8

'Doing text'
Madness in the methods

Julian McDougall

Introduction

In research, the term 'text' is often used to mean written texts: documents, newspaper articles and so on. A wider view is to see text as any cultural product we wish to examine, print or audio-visual, including film, song, dramatic production and other types of social, creative or artistic activity (see Bennett and McDougall, 2017), what here I call 'media texts'. This broader perspective is the basis for this chapter, which examines approaches to educational research as forms of 'performative social science' (Jones, 2015).

These approaches embody a fluid approach to epistemology and expertise, reaching what can be termed a 'third space', a strategic intersection of educational research, practice and method (see Potter and McDougall, 2017). They aim to disrupt or 'trouble' what we think about when talking about method and data. The drivers for such disruptions arise from a desire for redistributive social-justice outcomes, beyond methodological naval-gazing towards a deeper consideration of the ethical and material conditions for 'voice' as both process and value (Couldry, 2010).

The chapter also describes and discusses several research projects which explore the lived experience of students, educators and researchers (and often people wearing more than one of those 'hats'). These projects mix traditional social-science research methods with media texts from arts and the humanities, including narrative, storytelling and metaphor, visual ethnography and the generation of 'live data' – data that emerges from people's actual and current activity. In this way, researchers are able to examine 'identity' – how people see themselves in their everyday lives – and how this perception is mediated by, for instance, printed or audio-visual agencies. After setting out the broader approach and sharing examples, the chapter finally focuses on the mediated negotiation of educational-researcher and participator identities and explores the value of putting creative methods to work in our research.

The intention is to challenge ways of thinking about research design and data collection. I do this both to preach to the converted and more seasoned travellers, by introducing the use of media texts as a 'plug-in', and to encourage readers who may be new to, or sceptical about, creative methods of this kind to consider their inclusion in their enquiry so as to reflect a different perspective, whereby 'recognition of the visual and sensory nature of the world includes a widening of research methods to signal what counts as data and why' (Flewitt *et al.*, 2015:2).

There are three ideas underpinning this chapter as a whole:

1. Social-science research is richer when we get up close and personal to people's life narratives.
2. Creative methods work well for this, better than other approaches, and usefully bring ethical tensions to the surface. However …
3. … everything is mediated, and we give meaning to media texts by putting them working together in so-called 'assemblages'. As such, we *are* texts, so research and researchers need to 'do text'.

Ways of seeing research

The kinds of creative and visual methods declared above are used to 'hear the noise of everyday life' (Pahl, 2014:134). Employing media texts as a stimulus for this relates to the affective or emotional mediation of our experiences in contemporary popular culture as a 'societal container', offering a therapeutic function (Richards, 2018), and thus not only standing in for ideas about our experiences and situated practices (for example, in education) but also holding us together, socially. To ignore the role of media texts in our negotiation of self-identity and the identities of others is to miss something important in our research. But as researchers, our understanding of 'mediation' is rhizomatic (Deleuze and Guattari, 1987:16), allowing participants to react to developing circumstances with redefinition of the task in hand. As such, we resist the idea of 'The Media' as a powerful 'Big Other' (see Bennett *et al.*, 2011), the notion that media texts straightforwardly represent the reality of people in education, one step removed. Rather we are interested in how thinking about education through texts works in flow and in the affective nature of this thinking, as the one, to use a term from the French philosopher, Gilles Deleuze, is 'plugged into' the other in an assemblage.

But what about method 'as a thing'? Law (2004) argues that our conventional academic methods of inquiry from the social sciences are unable to account for the texture of the world, as they mean we see agency as cognitive, rather than embodied and emotive. Writing about more quiet, modest, slow research, which uses assemblages of images and metaphor to embrace uncertainty, he asks why it is not widely acknowledged that methods *produce* the reality they seek to understand and are therefore imperialist by nature. So there is a deeply political impulse to the use of methods which deconstruct their own conditions of possibility – that is, methods which explore their own impacts on data – and as such, ideas, including those of Law, deserve to be taken seriously.

The third (research) space?

The notion of a 'third space' has its origins in the work of Bhabha (1994) and has been of interest in the design of pedagogy for equity and social justice and in researching the distance travelled towards such objectives (see Potter and McDougall, 2017). The concept is most well known from Gutiérrez (2008), who offered the third space as a way to resist the standard binaries of home and school and instead to incorporate 'shifting practices and communities' into pedagogical design (2008:149). Gutiérrez discussed ways in which the resources of participants' own lives could take on the creation of a new knowledge as, ultimately, a new social history in the setting.

Put simply, the first space is home and community, the 'lifeworld', and the second space is school, college, university or work, the 'systemworld'. As we get older, the boundaries between these blur more and more. So whereas school students, teachers and even parents work hard to preserve the boundaries between the first and second spaces (see Livingstone and Sefton-Green, 2016), students and teachers in post-compulsory education work 'out of hours' and in more flexibile, potentially more 'third-space' ways. Indeed, in this sector currently there is a great deal of interest in working with students as partners on co-creation or co-production projects, and these have overlaps with the third-space concept (see, for example, Kehler *et al.*, 2017; Mercer-Mapstone *et al.*, 2017).

Many people do research which *observes* this third space through non-participant observation or case study, in effect regarding it as 'a thing' and then 'researching that thing'. But in this act, the third space becomes a second space, and this is precisely what in recent research collaborations we have been trying to avoid. From our perspective, the third space can create a more agentive system by recognizing the social and connected nature of learning, similar to the concept of the zone of proximal development from Vygotsky (see Daniels, 2001). The third space then becomes a site for subverting power relations, and as such we are interested in 'affects' out of assemblages – how the practices we engage in change our thinking patterns (from Deleuze, see Harper and Savat, 2016:7). And in the question too, that if data is constructed by research participants 'live', can we subvert boundaries between research setting, life and educational or professional setting, so the research setting itself *becomes* a third space?

Creative visual methods

In 2014, Ivan Sigal walked the 43-kilometre length of the Karachi Circular Railway in Pakistan. He captured his experiences (see Sigal, 2018) in drone footage, still and moving images, writing and field recordings and then represented them, as research, through non-linear narratives:

> The result is a kaleidoscopic impression of fluidity and complexity, a visual subversion of the standard narrative – indeed of almost any narrative – one might try to apply to the place. The ghostly lines of the defunct railway are overlapped by the vibrant life of the city it was meant to serve. The images and the way of life they reveal are not consistent with the headlines that shape many people's impression of this conflicted metropolis.
>
> (Bierand, 2018)

This is one of many examples we could draw on. It combines artistic practice with ethnography, but what draws our interest might be the choice of data collection and means of presentation, together with the intense reflexivity at work behind these choices, relating to experience, perception and counter-narrative representation. Educational research is very well known for its reflexivity and first-person identity negotiation (or another person's 'navel-gazing'), but, as this chapter documents, we are seeing more creative and visual methods for data collection and an emerging body of work which also presents or represents educational research through visual, artistic or performative modes. So what might be an application of Sigal's approach to research in an educational setting?

Creative and visual approaches to research accumulate to represent a far broader, now well-established methodological field than we can do justice to in a contextual section of a chapter such as this. In the research of Sarah Pink (who is influential in visual ethnography), edited work and collaborations, visual ethics, auto-ethno-cartography, body arts and digital ethnography are collectively understood as 'the multiple routes that are developing and the way that they constitute visual methodology as a field of scholarship' (2012:7). So we are encouraged to see the strands of creative visual methodology here as an area of scholarship in itself, as opposed to (or rather, as well as) a 'toolkit' for use across fields. In Pink's research with Akama and Moline, design ethnography is used to conduct participative research 'where uncertainty and the "not-yet-made" is at the centre of inquiry' (Akama *et al.*, 2017:2). Their research workshops combine reflections on practice and uncertainty, cooking, automation and future design. Groups generate themes – empathy, privilege, temporarility – and, combined with the activities, produce images, video and writings to evoke 'ways of collaborating, inspired by the environment as well as one another' (2017:40).

What is emerging here is the importance of various new or previously untapped forms of participation, meeting with creative visual methods and some form of social-justice or positive-change purpose. In their collection of methodologies with these objectives, Mitchell *et al.* (2017) cite digitial storytelling initiatives for HIV-prevention activism and participatory video research on sexual violence on South African campuses. For the former, seven elements were required: point of view, dramatic questioning, emotion, voice, soundtrack, economy and pacing. For the latter, the young female participants made cellphilms (cellphone videos) and policy posters. In both:

> A participatory visual research study designed with the end in mind builds in appropriate methodological opportunities to explore the social issues under study and to enable different facets to be made visible and multiple voices to be heard ... The self-created visual artefacts are critical resources that can be used in the process of dialogue, and to ensure that policy makers can see close up what the social realities that need to be changed, actually look like.
>
> (Mitchell *et al.*, 2017:45)

Creative methods, converged with digital affordances such as virtual learning environments, digital video, online platforms, social media and gaming, also provide rich connecting opportunities over time and distance in virtual third spaces (see Potter and McDougall, 2017) and between generations. For example, Botturi and Rega (2014) conducted a digital twinning project between a primary school in an affluent area of Italy and an after-school centre in a disadvantaged community in Brazil. The intercultural encounters were facilitated by methods which combined very longstanding storytelling traditions with creative, new, digital-media contexts:

> First and foremost, connecting generations in a (digital) storytelling project means creating a space where value is given both to the elders – the source of memory and of wise stories – and to younger 'natural born' digital artists ... Digital storytelling can [also] be a powerful method to investigate how children perceive adults, allowing educators to work on intergenerational relations and on the issue of trust; while, at the same time, opening a window on other cultural perspectives.
>
> (Botturi and Rega, 2014:229 and 235).

This was a social-development activity with lifelong learning objectives. So, if creative and visual methods are now an established field of scholarship, as the work of Pink observes, then their application to educational research is a sub-field. See, for instance, Yamada-Rice and Stirling's (2015) edited collection, in which professionals from the visual industries offer perspectives on working methodologically with children and young people. Crucially, working with arts-based approaches in this way situates production as research, so that the act of taking apart and putting back together locates the work in culture. This all said, as we move rapidly through a series of 'cases' below for the purpose of a chapter overview, we must pause to acknowledge the ethical gravity of such arts-based work with children, best articulated by Nutbrown:

> I suggest that whilst researchers who involve children in their studies continue to trouble over issues of consent, the questions of whether and how we use photographs of children in our research go almost without comment in the literature. Prosser (2000) identifies visual methods as having 'no established history of ethical protocols' and for Pink (2007) ethical practices are culturally defined and collaborative research designs are more likely to be ethically sensitive than those that treat participants as 'objects' (Pink, 2009).
>
> (Nutbrown, 2011:6)

Parry (2013) suggests, in agreement with Pink, that creativity forms common ground between academics and practitioners. On this, research can be re-imagined, as both parties see their work as being about reworking and re-interpreting, as opposed to neutrally observing. The challenge is to take this approach into social science more broadly and to design research to facilitate it (see Potter, 2016). For example, when using drawing as a research method, it is combined with talking or writing about meaning-making, capturing in language something from the drawing which initially evaded it (see Mitchell *et al.*, 2011). Sometimes personally 'therapeutic', sometimes community-facing, it enables participants to identify issues and imagine solutions, rather than just answer questions:

> Drawing as a participatory visual methodology offers researchers ... a rich entry point for engaging participants in issues that are important to them, for studying the act of representation itself, for reaching multiple audiences, and ultimately, for social action.
>
> (Mitchell *et al.*, 2011:34)

The same can be achieved with modelling, for example with Lego Serious Play. This is a methodology created by the Lego group, which aims to foster creative thinking and team-work using Lego bricks (see Gauntlett, 2011). When combined with participation, again, the outcome is to 'double-loop' new knowledge of the social world with its representation, both in the way the research represents its findings and in the way it represents itself, for the outside world, but captured live, in the moment.

Going even further, the idea of 'data' itself is now increasingly at risk, and the possibility of post-anthropocentric methodology taking its place, as researchers – informed again by Deleuze's ways of thinking about thinking (Deleuze and Guattari, 1987) – look for ways of getting beyond or outside of the constraints of understanding data as 'a thing'. Instead, 'data and descriptions of data encounters are rethought as conceptual, theoretical, philo-sophical, ethical, material, performative, practical and spatial projects' (Koro-Ljungberg *et al.*, 2017:3). This is to do with the very difficult challenge of moving beyond human rationality as the lens for generating and analysing data to a position of 'subscribing to an ontological approach according to which our existence does not precede our encounters with other beings or things' (2017:23).

As seen earlier, the key Deleuzian idea informing such work is to 'plug in' theoretical concepts to problematize and rethink social practices – plugging one machine (research, academic writing) into another, like working with a toolbox. Working in this way, Kendall *et al.*'s research with further-education practitioners

> opened up and expanded definitions of what might be 'counted' as data and the curatorial, productive role of the researcher as an agent of, rather than conduit or receptacle for, meaning-making and taking. We would, we suggested, make objects; tell stories; listen to stories; discuss our object and storymaking; curate and share symbolic objects; take pictures and audio recordings; and discuss our thoughts and feelings uninhibited by research conventions, interviews, structure or systematisation along the way. We would 'count' all of this as empirical *stuff*, material openings for our grappling with our own entanglement.
>
> (Kendall *et al.*, 2016:119, italics in original)

On the one hand, the visual methods were established: identity boxes, curation of objects, reflexive discussions, storytelling workshops and a blog. But the 'researcher as agent', as described in the quote, resisted the forcing of the generated 'stuff' into the constraining metaphysics of presence, assumed by the idea of data to be written up. There is not the space here to do this justice, but this goes to another level, drawing again on Deleuze's assemblages, with post-human research that bears witness to 'thing-power':

> The relevant point for thinking about thing-power is this: a material body always resides within some assemblage or other, and its thing-power is *a function of that grouping*. A thing has power by virtue of its operating *in conjunction* with other things.
>
> (Bennett, 2004:353–4, italics in original)

Crucially, we must keep our sights on the core objective of all this being a shared interest in opening up spaces for matters to be seen, heard and told that were not being included in social science before. These 'new thinkables' lead to new possibilities for social action. There is method in the madness of the methods.

The next part of this chapter will be a tour through some experiences with these creative methods, as a participant and researcher, and both at the same time.

We need to talk about Maggie

A few years ago I took part in a workshop run by Kip Jones (see Jones, 2015):

> You are invited to contribute to our on-going experiment. Look through that box in the wardrobe with bits and pieces that you are unable to throw away because they represent you and your past. Bring one or two of them along to share with a stranger. By doing this, we learn what it feels like to reveal one's often most private self to an unfamiliar person.

Over two days, we worked in pairs, telling each other about the objects we had brought from home, listening to each other, asking for more detail on certain aspects and then performing (not presenting) our partner's story to the group through a creative approach. I do not consider myself especially creative or emotional in work situations, but the way Kip facilitated this activity helped me to be both. I was working with Maggie, and I decided to write postcards as if they came from – and were addressed to – characters, pets, objects and places from her 'back-story':

> Imagine if you could bring together people from your past and present to talk to each other from their pasts, presents and futures?
> Talking about you, not to you.
> To talk about each others' influences on your life.
> To share things with one another that you might not have had the chance to pass on.
> A bit like a funeral whilst you're still alive but with the luxury of time travel for the audience. And the added value of not being dead.
> On September 5th 2014 this happened to Maggie for five minutes only.
> The guests were teleported through time and space to be there and asked to exchange postcards about each other.
> About each other and Maggie.
> Here's what happened.

Participating in Kip's event opened my eyes to something important. I had worked with mixed-methods, digital and media, and broadly speaking 'creative' approaches before, but I had not paid sufficient attention to the way that working in these ways brings to the surface the ethical issues associated with asking research participants to share their stories. I realized that the educational research I had been doing had often given me access to deeply personal narratives, which maybe I had been working too hard to systematize, or to relate to macro-social themes, or to skew to fit my research questions, instead of giving them life on their own terms.

Wiring the audience

This was a project about television in the era of 'Media 2.0' about fragmented audiences and about educational identities. I was trying to revisit, and test out in the download age, a classic theory from David Morley's study of the BBC current-affairs programme, *Nationwide* (see Morley, 1981). Morley had worked with different socio-occupational groups to account for their preferred, negotiated or oppositional readings of the programme. I wanted to see if the same methodology could work with the crime drama from the HBO television network, *The Wire*, but I added a mixed-methods element. I asked trainee teachers, media teachers working at Master's level, drama academics and youth workers to watch a particular season of the drama, which is set in a school, and I added online fans and critics as my fifth 'data set'. Each group had a different method to work with: blogs, interviews, film-making, drawing or visual equivalents. When I analysed the data, I had two conceptual frames: one, called the 'Return to Morley', focused on the extent to which in the data there was manifestation of Morley's ideas; the other examined the influence of respective methods on the data and findings produced. I found that a preferred reading – a secondary encoding of *The Wire* as authentic – could be identified as consistent across the groups, but that each group situated themselves differently in relation to this, both politically and professionally. I found also that the mode of address, essentially the method used, influenced the responses on axes of respect, hope, despair, anger or more neutral intertextual engagement (see McDougall, 2010).

Digital transformations

This project (Berger and McDougall, 2013) was a digital ethnography, for which the video game *L.A. Noire* was used by teachers and students as literature within the orthodox framing of the English-literature curriculum in further and higher education. Four groups of teachers and students in three locations first contributed to a gameplay blog. Then the students taught the teachers to play the game, worked together with a series of study resources, locating the game firmly as a literary text, and made film posters and 'genre tube maps' to locate it in terms of genre categories, finding a partial reframing of the extent to which 'expert literacy' can adapt for gameplay and what this says about knowledge. Our key finding was that there was no problem with *L.A Noire* being studied as literature, but that plenty of identity politics around English as a subject might have needed unpacking first. The data collated and analysed was formed out of the blog posts, interview transcripts, posters, tube maps and observations of the study resources in use. But fundamentally we were observing the playing of a video game as an act of reading, hence the creative digital transformation of what we think it means to be a reader.

(Negatively) Benefits Street

This was part of a larger project, called 'Hard Times Today', which explored the representation of austerity in popular culture. Returning to *The Wire* project described above, I worked with three groups, recording a book-club discussion on a weekday evening with the first, using a blog with another, and community film-making again with the third. Here I was drawing out responses to a controversial British Channel 4 television documentary series, *Benefits Street*, from local residents, but in different socio-economic and occupational contexts, again mixing up the groups and the methods to see what difference the representation of response would make. As had been the case with the 'Wiring the audience' project, open-brief film-making elicited the boldest and most forthright, opinionated data, the book group operating as more of a middle-class 'safe space' and the blog yielding a more academic tone (see McDougall, 2017b).

Hunger by the Sea

This was a collaboration between university researchers from media practice and education backgrounds, two media-production students from related but distinct disciplines, and the users and providers of a food bank. The research was co-authored by the students and researchers, and the food-bank users' voices are heard in the project's outcome: the animated film *Hunger by the Sea* (Sudbury, 2017). In bringing together academics, students and community participants in a challenging but rich space, the project enabled exchanges of expertise and new, boundary-crossing 'ways of being' in education, which could be discussed as third-space interactions. However, we made no dubious or potentially exploitative claims for the food bank itself as a third space – the research was restricted to a focus on the experiences of students and academics in partnership and on the research outputs themselves, as existing in a third space across and between the written-up article (Han *et al.*, 2018) and the visual media it speaks to.

By asking people who use a food bank to participate in the production of an animated film – sharing experiences from their everyday lives but adding the distance of anonymity and diverting from the original intention for them to make the film – this ethnography sought to provide users with opportunities to speak directly to policymakers and politicians. In doing so, they could self-represent, in a similar way to the work cited earlier from Mitchell *et al.* (2011), a process expressed well by one of the student co-authors:

> It's a great idea – participatory filmmaking for a misunderstood demographic. It's not really been done before … but it could be ethically challenging to involve them. They either have addiction or mental-health issues. People don't want to be filmed. That's okay. I get it. Nor would I.
>
> (Han *et al.*, 2018)

Comrades and curators

My current research with the Bill Douglas Museum in Exeter (see McDougall, 2017a) concerns Douglas' film *Comrades* which represents the story of the Tolpuddle Martyrs (six English labourers who in the 19th century were convicted and exiled for swearing a secret oath to an agricultural society), with a magic lanternist character telling the story. My angle on this is to combine physical locations – museums – and ways of seeing and thinking about learning, history and politics, through and with film. I am exploring the 'in-between' relationship between four things. First, *Comrades* as a film. Second, the curation of the director's collection of magic lanterns and other optical artifacts at the museum in Exeter. Third, the role of the magic-lanternist character as pivotal to the representation of social history in the film. And fourth, the educational curation of this social history in two other museums: the Martyrs' Museum in Tolpuddle itself and the Shire Hall Living History project in Dorchester. I have made visits to the museums and spent time with the pre-cinema devices, interviewed curators and run a workshop at the Tolpuddle Festival with the Radical Film Network, during which participants drew 'maps' of each other's engagements with films, history and politics, in the same way as I am doing with *Comrades*. Getting people to draw maps or other visual representations of the connections they make helps us understand how our interpretations of films can bring history, politics and our own personal stories to life. Again, this is about local and particular connections, when the film, museums, festival, historical discourse, political discourse and people form assemblages. This cannot really be 'got to' through interviews alone.

For me, *Comrades* sits in a space between my own political views and trade unionism, some deeply personal things, my working life, and then the connection between all of those. When I ask people to choose a film with political and historical meaning for them and then to think about similar connections, usually they come up with rich, deep and personal stories. I use some distancing techniques, putting people together in pairs and then groups, so that by the time they share their stories, they are combined into themes arising from several people. Then, with their consent, I photograph the maps and use them as data for the research. As with all of the projects I have shared here, the devil is more in the detail of the 'messing about' with visual methods.

Doing text

'Doing text' in research is, therefore, about understanding our lives as texts and using media as stimulus for getting into the detail (going back again to Deleuze) of these 'folded-over' aspects of social practices, including education. The projects are about creating new connections and flows of thinking 'after the media' (Bennett *et al.*, 2011; Bennett and McDougall, 2017), as a consequence of the examination of media texts as part of everyday life, also (again from Deleuze) to 'think about media in terms of "affects", how the media machines we engage with change our unconscious thinking patterns, shift our intensities and thus alter the domain of our possible actions' (Harper and Savat, 2016:7).

Working in these ways, the process is usually non-linear. We are looking for emergent alignments and disconnections between the deskwork, the texts, artefacts and the live data – stories in our ears and in our heads and pictures on the researcher's phone. We are asking people to bring stuff from the first space of home and community, so we can work up an assemblage of our research situations and share stories from our textual lives that impact on how we think about research. Ultimately, perhaps we might seem to be more interested in troubling methods than in the 'stuff' we are finding out. But that is not the case: we have some very serious social-justice objectives and often find that we get to the heart of what we think we mean when we talk about 'the truth' by working in these messy ways.

Disruption and redistribution

Diane Reay's recent work on the enduring injustices of education and class privilege in the UK reminds us that, still, 'social mobility is often presented as a straightforward linear process from one occupational category to another, but when we look at the lived experience of social mobility it is full of doublings-back, loops and curves, cul-de-sacs and divisions' (Reay, 2017:102).

Consider how the 'madness in the methods' described in this chapter might contribute to closer and more effective disruption of standard methodology and the pursuit of redistributive, social-justice outcomes for research.

Wrapping up

In a nutshell, I have taken some established ways of working with creative methods in social science and added mediation to the mix. So, the key argument this chapter makes is that creative and visual methods of data collection (notwithstanding the issues discussed about the very *idea* of data), representation of our research through visual or creative modes, and the use of texts as affective symbols for the mediated assemblage of our educational identities are more than just novel, inclusive or innovative alternatives to numbers and words on pages in books and articles or on slides at conferences. Instead, such ways of doing text enable us to see and hear differences and contingencies, and to be more agentive, participative and expansive in our research, so that ultimately we can understand education better.

Recommended reading

'Methodology matters', the short editorial 'think-piece' in *Literacy* by Flewitt *et al.* (2015), offers an accessible but convincing argument for the use of arts-based research methods in the social sciences, including education.

The Location of Culture (Bhabha, 1994) is an important reference point for the concept of the the 'third space' which informs this chapter. Its ideas about identity, power and agency come out of the post-colonial approach to texts. The implication of this work is that the second space of education, but also of research, often silences the first-space experiences of marginalized groups.

Jones (2015) reports on an experiment that the author of this chapter participated in and was greatly influenced by. This was a workshop in arts-led interviewing techniques, using ephemera to elicit life stories and then reporting narrative accounts back, using creative means of presentation. The conclusion is drawn that researchers yearn to express the more emotive connections generated by listening to the stories of participants.

References

Akama, Y., Moline, K. and Pink, S. (2017) Disruptive interventions with mobile media through Design+Ethnography+Futures. In: L. Hjorth, H. Horst, A. Galloway and G. Bell (Eds.) *The Routledge Companion to Digital Ethnography*. New York: Routledge.

Bennett, J. (2004) The force of things: Steps toward an ecology of matter. *Political Theory*, 32(3), 347–372.

Bennett, P., Kendall, A. and McDougall, J. (2011) *After the Media: Culture and Identity in the 21st Century*. Abingdon: Routledge.

Bennett, P. and McDougall, J. (Eds.) (2017) *Doing Text: Media After the Subject*. Leighton Buzzard: Auteur.

Berger, R. and McDougall, J. (2013) Reading videogames as (authorless) literature. *Literacy*, 47(3), 142–149.

Bhabha, H.K. (1994) *The Location of Culture*. London: Routledge.

Bierand, D. (2018) *Seeing Karachi through its Abandoned Public Railway System: An Interview with Ivan Sigal*. Vantage. [Online] https://medium.com/vantage/seeing-karachi-through-its-abandoned-railway-78d276fe41b5 (accessed 13 February 2018).

Botturi, L. and Rega, I. (2014) Intergenerational digital storytelling: Four racconti of a new approach. *Formazione & Insegnamento*, 12(2), 225–236.

Couldry, N. (2010) *Why Voice Matters: Culture and Politics After Neoliberalism*. London: Sage.

Daniels, H. (2001) *Vygotsky and Pedagogy*. Abingdon: RoutledgeFalmer.

Deleuze, G. and Guattari, F. (1987) *A Thousand Plateaus: Capitalism and Schizophrenia*. Minneapolis, MN: University of Minneapolis Press.

Flewitt, R., Pahl, K. and Smith, A. (2015) Methodology matters. *Literacy*, 49(1), 1–2.

Gauntlett, D. (2011) *Making is Connecting: The Social Meaning of Creativity from DIY and Knitting to YouTube and Web 2.0*. Cambridge: Polity Press.

Gutiérrez, K.D. (2008) Developing a sociocritical literacy in the third space. *Reading Research Quarterly*, 43(2), 148–164.

Han, X., McDougall, J., Mott, C. and Sudbury, S. (2018) Hunger by the Sea: Partnerships in the Brave Third Space. *International Journal for Students as Partners*, 2(2), 71–84. DOI: 10.15173/ijsap.v2i2.3493.

Harper, T. and Savat, D. (2016) *Media after Deleuze*. London: Bloomsbury.

Jones, K. (2015) A report on an arts-led, emotive experiment in interviewing and storytelling. *The Qualitative Report*, 20(2), 86–92.

Kehler, A., Verwood, R. and Smith, H. (2017) We are the process: Reflections on the underestimation of power in students as partners in practice. *International Journal for Students as Partners*, 1(1).

Kendall, A., Gibson, M., Himsworth, C., Palmer, K. and Perkins, H. (2016) Listening to old wives' tales: Small stories and the (re)making and (re)telling of research in HE/FE practitioner education. *Research in Post-Compulsory Education*, 21(1–2), 116–136.

Koro-Ljungberg, M., Löytönen, T. and Tesar, M. (2017) *Disrupting Data in Qualitative Inquiry: Entanglements with the Post-Critical and Post-Anthropocentric*. New York: Peter Lang.

Law, J. (2004) *After Method: Mess in Social Science Research*. Abingdon: Routledge.

Livingstone, S. and Sefton-Green, J. (2016) *The Class: Living and Learning in the Digital Age*. New York: New York University Press.

McDougall, J. (2010) Wiring the audience. *Participations*, 7(1), 73–101.

McDougall, J. (2017a) *Comrades and Curators*. University of Exeter. [Online] www.bdcmuseum. org.uk/news/comrades-and-curators-by-professor-julian-mcdougall (accessed 13 February 2018).

McDougall, J. (2017b) (Negatively) Benefits Street: The return of naked ideology. In: P. Bennett and J. McDougall (Eds.) *Popular Culture and the Austerity Myth: Hard Times Today*. New York: Routledge.

Mercer-Mapstone, L., Dvorakova, S.L., Matthews, K.E., Abbot, S., Cheng, B., Felten, P., Knorr, K., Marquis, E., Shammas, R., and Swaim, K. (2017) A systematic literature review of students as partners in higher education. *International Journal for Students as Partners*, 1(1).

Mitchell, C., De Lange, N. and Moletsane, R. (2017) *Participatory Visual Methodologies: Social Change, Community and Policy*. London: Sage.

Mitchell, C., Theron, L., Stuart, J., Smith, A. and Campbell, Z. (2011) Drawings as research method. In: L. Theron, C. Mitchell, A. Smith and J. Stuart (Eds.) *Picturing Research: Drawing as Visual Methodology*. Rotterdam: Sense Publishers.

Morley, D. (1981) The 'Nationwide' audience: A critical postscript. *Screen Education*, 39, 3–14.

Nutbrown, C. (2011) Naked by the pool? Blurring the image? Ethical issues in the portrayal of young children in arts-based educational research. *Qualitative Inquiry*, 17(1), 3–14.

Pahl, K. (2014) *Materializing Literacies in Communities: The Uses of Literacy Revisited*. London: Bloomsbury.

Parry, B. (2013) *Children, Film and Literacy*. London: Palgrave MacMillan.

Pink, S. (2012) *Advances in Visual Methodology*. London: Sage.

Potter, J. (2016) Review of *Visual Methods with Children and Young People*, E. Stirling and D. Yamada-Rice (Eds.) (2015) *Media Education Research Journal*, 6(2), 75–77.

Potter, J. and McDougall, J. (2017) *Digital Media, Culture and Education: Theorising Third Space Literacies*. London: Palgrave MacMillan.

Reay, D. (2017) *Miseducation: Inequality, Education and the Working Classes*. Bristol: Policy Press.

Richards, B. (2018) *What Holds Us Together: Popular Culture and Social Cohesion*. London: Karnac Books.

Sigal, I. (2018) *Karachi Circular Railway*. Ryerson Image Centre. [Online] https://vimeo. com/251851955 (accessed 18 July 2018).

Sudbury, S. (2017) *Hunger by the Sea*. [Online] https://vimeo.com/234840520 (accessed 18 July 2018).

Yamada-Rice, D. and Stirling, E. (Eds.) (2015) *Visual Methods with Children and Young People*. London: Palgrave MacMillan.

Chapter 9

Q-methodology
A science of subjectivity

Gavin Rhoades and Zeta Brown

Introduction

Other chapters in this book have covered a range of practical research methods, some of which produce qualitative data, others quantitative. This chapter discusses an approach which combines both types: Q-methodology, often known simply as 'Q'.

We start by introducing Q, discussing its main characteristics and how it developed. We then examine the process of actually conducting a Q study and the importance of the researcher's position when taking up this approach. A former student reflects on her experiences of using Q in her final-year undergraduate dissertation, and the chapter concludes by reviewing a recent Q-based study and considering what this tells us about use of this methodology. It is impossible to discuss everything there is to know about Q in just one book chapter, so we therefore advise readers to see this text as an initial introduction and take up our suggestions in the 'Recommended reading' section at the end to pursue interest further.

What is Q-methodology?

Not all research tools are well suited to investigating people's attitudes. 'Attitudes are concealed and not directly observable in themselves, but they cause actions and behaviours that are observable' (Cross, 2005:207). This relationship between behaviour and attitudes is complex and can be impacted by a range of factors, for example, different social situations (Erwin, 2001). Therefore, 'observing behaviour as an indicator of attitude alone ... is pointless' (Cross, 2005:208). Another problem for research in this area is that the mere act of asking participants about their attitudes and why they hold them has been shown to lead to a change in those attitudes (Wilson and Schooler, 1991).

Q-methodology is a useful tool for exploring opinions, perspectives and attitudes, without directly requiring participants to expressly state (or even understand) their overall position on a topic. It involves participants placing statements (typically printed on cards) onto a grid, which is shaped as an inverted pyramid. Participants sort these cards based on their perspectives on each statement. In order to do this, they have to compare the statements and work out the extent to which they agree or disagree with each one, without there being any 'right' or 'wrong' responses – it is the individual's perspective that Q-methodology is seeking to capture. A participant's completed card-sort configuration is known as a 'Q-sort'.

Analysis of all the resulting Q-sorts involves grouping them together in their shared positions (Brown, 2016) and is normally done using specific factor-analysis software. These positions, or 'communalities', become 'factors' in the analysis. In this way, Q-methodology investigates the complexity of participants' judgements on a given subject, where differences of opinion are expected (Combes *et al.*, 2004).

Q-methodology was originally developed by Stephenson (1935) and has been used in research since that time. Stephenson, a psychologist, was concerned about the dominant focus on positivist research that tested a hypothesis on a selection of participants (Watts and Stenner, 2012). He wanted, instead, to investigate subjectivity, to look at 'life as lived from the standpoint of the person living it' (Cross, 2005:208). Differences between subjectivity (in Q) and objectivity (in more positivist research) are not only prevalent in the participants' roles during the data collection but also in how the factor-analysis process is implemented.

Developing a Q study

Q offers great flexibility: researchers are able to develop a design that relates to the way they think about research and to what is appropriate for their study. You too will find yourself drawn to certain ways of analysing and understanding your data and the perspectives produced. Nevertheless, conducting a typical study will normally involve several steps. Before going through these steps, here are explanations of the main terms used:

- The *concourse* is the complete range of views that people or society have on the topic being researched.
- The *Q-set* is the collection of statements chosen by the researcher from this concourse.
- The *distribution grid* is a pyramid-shaped set of boxes, on which participants place their Q-set statements, either in positive positions (if they agree) or negative positions (if they disagree).
- The *Q-sort* is the configuration which results from each participant placing the statements on the grid.

The broad Q-methodology process for the researcher is, therefore, as follows:

1. Explore the concourse of views relating to the area to be researched.
2. From this concourse, develop and refine the Q-set. Each statement in the Q-set should be given a unique number.
3. Design a distribution grid which can accommodate all of the statements. This involves also formulating the *condition of instruction*, which tells the participants what they should be considering when they are completing their Q-sort.
4. Ask the participants to complete their Q-sorts. This can be done one at a time or (providing there are sufficient copies of the distribution grid and Q-set statements) by a group of participants, all working individually on their own Q-sort.
5. Record the completed Q-sorts in some way. As each of the statements in the Q-set has a unique number, one way is to write these numbers in their corresponding positions on a blank copy of the distribution grid. Another approach is to photograph each completed Q-sort, including the unique numbers.
6. Enter all the Q-sort data (the different ways in which the statements have been placed by the participants on the grid) into a computer for factor analysis.

7. Work out what factors have been produced. Typically, these will be given a descriptive name that instantly tells people what the factor is saying. For example, in a study about student attitudes towards university study, the first factor derived from the data might be summarized as: 'Factor 1: I've paid my money, where is my degree?'.

8. Often but not always, there is then some sort of follow-up data collection, such as a questionnaire survey or interviews. The latter could take place with a sub-set of the participants, usually chosen because their Q-sorts strongly match or correlate with a particular factor, known as *loading* on a factor, although they would sometimes be carried out immediately after the Q-sort before those data are analysed. The purpose of this extra stage is to explore the factors in more detail and further develop understanding of the participants' positions.

9. The final step is to combine data from both the Q-sort factor analysis and the follow-up interviews or survey, so they can be analysed together and conclusions drawn.

Elements of Q

It is worth now examining some of the key elements of Q in a more detailed way, so you can apply this understanding to your own research.

The concourse

The first step in the Q process is to explore the concourse relating to the particular issue or topic which will be researched. This involves collecting opinions and views from a wide range of sources. Any source available that is about the issue being investigated can be used for this, including academic literature, popular culture, laws, organizational information, the media, or even 'common sense'. Note that exploring the concourse is not the same process as developing an academic literature review. Any view might be valid and therefore a wide net must be cast into a churning sea of competing ideas and perspectives.

Statements

The next steps involve developing a selection of statements to be sorted, the Q-set. As well as using ideas from the concourse, these can also include extra perspectives and themes generated by interviews, surveys or focus groups conducted with typical participants. The final statements in the Q-set can, therefore, be 'opinions, plans, questions, options or strategies' (Eden *et al.*, 2005:416). For example, in a study about attitudes towards arranged marriage, the statements might include: 'Arranged marriages are appropriate for most people' and 'I would like to have an arranged marriage'. They should be expressed in a positive way, so that participants can agree or disagree. Negatively phrased statements, such as 'I do not wish to have an arranged marriage', should normally be avoided, as it can be confusing for participants to figure out on which side of the grid – positive or negative – they should place them.

The size of the Q-set is determined by the scope and scale of the subject matter, but most studies have between 40 and 80 statements (Watts and Stenner, 2012). For example, Brown (2016) investigated primary-school teachers' perspectives on the simultaneous implementation in schools of an 'inclusion' agenda, which promotes equal access and opportunities for all children, and a 'standards' agenda, which promotes the raising of academic achievement levels. There were 48 statements in the Q-set for that study, covering participants' potential positions on both agendas, drawn from scrutiny of the literature.

Whatever approaches are used, and whatever kind of statements are included, the finished Q-set must be 'broadly representative' of the concourse of opinions about the issue being investigated (Watts and Stenner, 2012:75). This is very important if participants in the research are to be able to genuinely express their views when sorting the statements on the distribution grid. The Q-set that is produced should also cover all aspects of the research questions but not stray into unrelated areas that would detract from the focus of the study.

Statements

Examine these statements from the concourse in Brown's (2016) study which is described in this section:

- 'My position on the inclusion agenda has changed through practical experience'.
- 'I should focus more attention on the children who could achieve the "national average"'.
- 'It is necessary for the school to be accountable to external inspection and the assessment process'.

What might have been the sources of these statements? What range of views do they represent? Have a go at designing statements for a research topic of your own. You could draw ideas from your literature review, borrow concepts from the media, or even conduct a small focus group to generate perspectives.

Distribution grid and condition of instruction

The distribution grid is designed by the researcher so that all the Q-set statements can be placed on it. When doing their Q-sorts, participants can choose a position for each statement, ranging from the most negative to the most positive possible position, and a series of positions in between. Watts and Stenner (2012) advise using an 11–13 point scale for this, ranging either from –5 to +5 or –6 to +6. Smaller grids, –4 to +4 or even –3 to +3, can also be used very successfully.

Figure 9.1 shows an example of a –5 to +5 grid, currently being used in Rhoades (in preparation), a doctoral Q-methodology study into student satisfaction in higher education.

The 'Not bothered' heading in the middle does not usually appear on distribution grids but, after a pilot for the study, was found to be more easily understood by the participants than the more commonly used label, 'Neutral'. Note the condition of instruction at the bottom of the grid, which is there to remind the participants about what they should be considering while Q-sorting the statements (the instruction can also be shared with participants verbally before they start their Q-sort). Different conditions of instruction will elicit different Q-sorts from participants. For example, in Brown's (2016) agenda study,

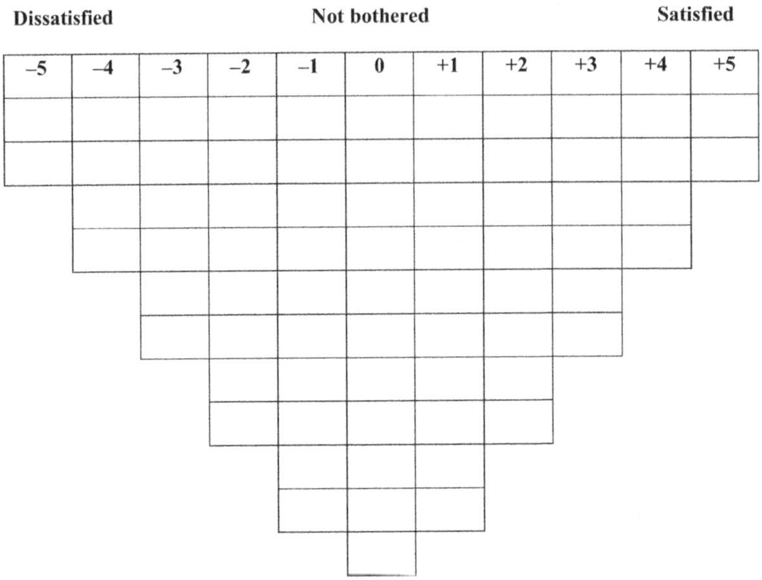

Dissatisfied					Not bothered					Satisfied
−5	−4	−3	−2	−1	0	+1	+2	+3	+4	+5

To what extent does this issue make you feel satisfied or dissatisfied with your course at the university?

Figure 9.1 Example of a forced-distribution grid with condition of instruction

instructions to place the statements 'according to your position on the *inclusion* agenda' and 'according to your position on the *standards* agenda' produced two different Q-sorts, as participants had different views on each.

The Q-sort

To complete their Q-sort, participants order the Q-set statements onto the empty grid in a way which reflects their views on the condition of instruction. This process is known as *forced distribution*, because participants are only allowed to place a small number of statements in the extreme positions. You can see this in Figure 9.1 – there are only two spaces at the extreme ends (−5 and +5) where statements might be placed. It means participants have to think very carefully about each issue, especially about those on which they have the strongest opinions.

Stainton Rogers (1995) indicates that Q studies usually have 40–60 participants, while Watts and Stenner (2012) suggest having half the number of participants doing Q-sorts as there are statements in the Q-set. The grid in Figure 9.1 has room for 71 statements, so this would indicate a participant sample of at least 36. However, the nature of Q means that using a smaller number of participants can also be satisfactory. In fact, Q studies can investigate just one participant's perspectives on a subject area – Watts and Stenner (2012:50) examine this possibility. Having fewer participants in your study means that each individual Q-sort will form a greater proportion of each of the factors produced (if there is only one participant, it will form 100 per cent) and that more detail from participants' individual perspectives will appear in them.

Factor analysis

As indicated earlier, the extent to which any individual Q-sort correlates with an overall factor is known as that Q-sort loading on that factor. Factor loadings are expressed in the analysis as a decimal between 0 and 1, where 0 represents complete disagreement with a factor and 1 represents complete agreement. An individual Q-sort with a factor loading of 0.83 therefore corresponds much more closely to that factor than one with a 0.27 loading. Most Q researchers use specifically designed computer programs to do this kind of analysis – PQMethod, for example, is popular and can be downloaded for free. It is also possible to analyse the data manually, as pre-computer Q researchers had to do, but this can be a tedious, error-prone and lengthy process.

Some of the participants will have agreed to some extent with other participants about the relative placement of some of the statements, but others will have shown widely varying and distinctive views. This is called *variance*, the overall differences of opinion as expressed across all of the Q-sorts. The amount of variance in the data is influenced by a wide range of issues, including the nature of the topic being investigated (a study where everyone has similar views will have low variance; a study on a contentious or disputed topic will have high variance). Each factor will then explain part of the overall variance in the study – so Factor 1 might explain 25 per cent of the overall variance and Factor 2 might explain 10 per cent. Understanding how much variance a factor accounts for helps to understand the relative importance of the factor.

The number of factors extracted from the data for analysis can differ between studies, but it is advisable to start by isolating seven (this is the standard option in PQMethod), then running the program to see how many of these are 'statistically significant', a calculation which indicates whether a relationship between variables in the data is likely to have occurred by chance or because that relationship really does exist or occur more widely. The number can then be further reduced by re-running the analysis until only those that have what is known as an *eigenvalue* of 1.00 or higher are included. Any factor with an eigenvalue below 1.00 explains very little of the overall variance and would therefore typically be discarded, unless the researcher felt that it demonstrated a unique perspective that should be retained to add qualitative breadth to the findings.

Ideal Q-sorts, representing each factor, are established by the computer process or by manual data handling. These are represented as *factor arrays* in a table, allowing comparison of relative statement positions between factors. They can then be analysed qualitatively to describe the participants' communalities of perspectives in each factor.

Table 9.2, shown later in this chapter, shows factor-arrays output by PQMethod for a project called 'Explore University'. Each factor array is presented in a separate column and shows the position that each factor has allocated to each statement. If you were to place each statement onto the distribution grid according to the numbers in the Factor 1 column, you would produce the ideal Q-sort that represented Factor 1's shared position. This is just one of the many data tables that the PQMethod produces, but it is a common starting point for factor interpretations.

Additional research methods

As we have seen, Q-methodology can be complemented with additional methods to inform either the development of the Q-set or to validate the Q-analysis (Eden *et al.*, 2005).

Many Q researchers carry out interviews, for example, either straight after the Q-sort or after data analysis. There is also the option, with agreement, to record what participants say as they place their statement cards onto the distribution grid.

Brown (2016) created brief summaries of her factor interpretations and used these in later interviews. Participants were asked to look at the summaries and decide which best represented their perspectives. Interestingly, most participants selected the same factor interpretation that had been assigned to them by the Q analysis. Those that picked a different factor interpretation stated that they did so because their perspectives had changed since completing their Q-sort (a reminder that research is often time-specific and not representative of permanent or long-standing views).

Use in an undergraduate dissertation

Q-methodology gives the flexibility to design a study that is appropriate to the topic under investigation and to the researcher's position on research. In this section, an undergraduate student reflects with her project supervisor on how she used Q-methodology in her final-year project.

Hannah Sheares recently graduated from the University of Wolverhampton with first-class Honours. For her final-year dissertation (Sheares, 2017), she investigated teachers' attitudes towards the National Curriculum (NC) in England, contrasting the views of teachers who taught in schools before it was implemented (in 1988) with those of more recently qualified teachers who have never known schools without it. There were 22 participants in total.

In terms of methodology, what were you thinking of doing before we discussed Q?

I was originally going to do a case-study design and use two forms of data collection: semi-structured interviews as a primary source and then observations. But I realized that observations of behaviour aren't necessarily an accurate indicator of attitude and that was what I really wanted to explore. So, where Q was really good was that I was able to dig in further and explore those attitudes.

What did you think you might find out before you started your research?

Initially, I thought I'd get two clean, opposing attitudes towards the NC. I thought that all of the people who taught before the NC was implemented would hate it, and that all of the people who went into teaching later would love it. Further into my research, I realized that it was not so black and white.

How did you go about constructing your Q-set?

I decided to have 30 statements in my Q-set. I did a little focus group to pick up on 'buzz' words to help create these and also took ideas from my literature review. It was definitely an iterative process of gradual improvement, weaving the statements all together so they were short and sweet and so that participants could agree or disagree with them. The statements have to be worded so specifically and carefully, otherwise your participants' responses could be unintentionally skewed. I opted to allow just one statement to be placed at either end of the forced-distribution grid, so as to encourage the participants to think really strongly about their answers. In hindsight, this was probably a bit too brave and I could have done with maybe allowing two each side, because in the actual data-collection process I could hear participants complaining 'I could put five on the strongly agree end', and I had to say 'Well, you have to choose just one', and they said 'But I believe so strongly about all of these', and I had to say 'Well, the grid only has space for one'.

How did you address validity in your study?

Due to my interpretivist position, I tried to aim for 'moments of authenticity' in my study, rather than a more positivist approach, because by their very nature my results would not be widely generalizable. I did, however, pilot my interviews and also asked participants to check my interpretation of their data, it's called 'participant validation'. Also, the participants had to sort all of the statements without having seen them previously, then I did the interviews afterwards. If I had done the interviews first, they may have then given me answers in the Q-sorts that they thought I wanted. By doing them afterwards, I could purposefully select which participants to interview based on their Q-sort results to gain further understanding of specific issues, and also ask questions as to why they had sorted certain statements in the way that they had.

Did you have any issues using Q when you were in the field collecting your data?

No, it was so easy! I think the main thing is to be super organized. I did A3-sized print-outs of my distribution grid, got them and my statements laminated, and put them into poly-pockets for giving to the participants. The Q-sorts were completed individually, some in person and some by post. I photographed them, so it was easy to input the data into the PQMethod software. People might worry about all of the numbers and all of the grids which is what I initially thought, but no, it was fine.

What results did you get?

I thought I'd have two factors, it turned out I had three. I had my 'Anti-NC' group (teachers who did not want or feel they needed the NC), which was Factor 1. Then Factor 2 was my 'NC Dependents', people who relied on the NC as a kind of life-jacket and would be reluctant to plan lessons without it. Factors 1 and 2 were oppositional, which is what you would expect in Q. But then I also found I had a 'Pro-NC' group as Factor 3, teachers who recognized the potential benefits of the NC for teachers generally, whilst not actually being keen about using it too much themselves. I wasn't expecting this group, it was in a grey area between the first two factors, and in my write-up I had to go over the results section quite a few times to really understand it. It was pretty tricky, but I just had to gather everything from the statements in that factor and work out how they related and how they were valued by the participants.

I used PQMethod for my analysis. My preferred approach was to look at the statements that scored highly for their factor, both positively and negatively, and try to understand what they were collectively telling me. That was really the longest part of the process.

I couldn't have got these results with simple interviews though, because I wouldn't have asked questions that could have explored these views and get attitudes I wasn't expecting.

Is there anything you would do differently were you to repeat the study?

Yes, I would definitely have two boxes at each end of the distribution grid after the participants' struggle choosing one statement to go at each end! I would also have done the research with either primary-school or secondary-school teachers but not with both, because I just felt it complicated things when I was trying to take participants' background into account.

Would you recommend using Q to other students?

Absolutely. Especially because many are interested in finding out what teachers think about issues. With Q, participants express their opinions and attitudes through their Q-sort, which makes it easier to then explore them further with interviews. It's a science of subjectivity!

The 'Explore University' Q evaluation

During the 2016–2017 academic year, we were asked to evaluate a project that endeavoured to inspire young people to go to university (we would like to thank our colleagues, Dr Neil Duncan, Dr Matt Smith and Dr David Thompson, who also worked on this evaluation). In an attempt to address social inequalities in university-level education in England, government policy developed initiatives which encouraged and supported more applications to university from school students with less traditional backgrounds, for instance, those from lower socio-economic households. An outcome of this was the National Networks for Collaborative Outreach scheme (www.hefce.ac.uk/sas/nnco/find). One of the 34 networks was led by the University of Wolverhampton in collaboration with Harper Adams, Keele and Staffordshire Universities and Telford College of Arts and Technology. These institutions were tasked with coordinating their outreach activity to local schools via a single point of contact. Called 'Explore University', the programme sought to raise awareness, provide information and organize experiences for those who might find value in going on to study in higher education. Activities included campus visits, subject-taster days and advice sessions in schools and summer schools. Further details of the project are at https://exploreuni.co.uk.

The evaluation study investigated the views of the young people who were participating in the Explore University interventions. Its objectives were to identify their perspectives towards applying to university, to evaluate if Explore University had influenced or supported these perspectives and to analyse expectations and the strength of commitment to apply to university. We decided to use Q-methodology in this evaluation study (Brown et al., 2018).

Q-methodology is not ordinarily used as an evaluation tool, but we felt that it would enable us to investigate complexities in perspectives and find communalities that may not become apparent if we used traditional data-collection methods. Ethically, we were also aware that attending university could be a sensitive subject for young people to discuss face-to-face. The participants knew we were working with Explore University, but we wanted to ensure that they could disclose their perspectives honestly and retain anonymity, even from us as the researcher-evaluators. We therefore created a web-based, Q-sort program that enabled them to sort the cards anonymously and with minimal assistance.

A Q-set with 36 statements was developed by considering relevant literature. These statements were piloted for validity purposes with a small group of young people within the age demographic. In the evaluation itself, 46 secondary-school students, aged 14–16 years, sorted the statements onto an online distribution grid with a seven-point scale from –3 to +3. Table 9.1 is an example of a Q-sort completed on this grid.

Immediately after completing their Q-sorts, participants were asked to respond, also online, to a small selection of open-ended questions. These asked how the Explore University programme could be improved, whether the participants had a career in mind, and if so, how long they had considered that career. This meant that a mixed-methods approach was used in the study: criteria of quantitative analysis were used to justify using or excluding statements and factors as a basis for qualitative analysis, and the subsequent open-ended questions were also scrutinized qualitatively.

Participants' Q-sort data were analysed using PQMethod, focusing on four factors that had an eigenvalue of 1.00 or higher. The result is shown in Table 9.2.

In the interpretation for each factor which follows, Q-sort statements are accompanied by their unique number and the strength of agreement or disagreement in the Q-sorts. This is an indication of how you might report Q-data findings in your own research.

Factor 1: *I am confident about attending university. Explore Uni has not changed my perspective.*

This factor represented 22 per cent of the overall variance and had an eigenvalue of 10.1905, which is over ten times the amount needed to be a significant factor. In total, 15 participants placed the Q-sort statements in similar places on the distribution grid and therefore revealed communalities in their perspectives. Factor 1 students held a positive perspective of themselves as secondary-school learners: for instance, they believed that teachers thought highly of them at school (26:+2) and that they were pretty good at school work (25:+2). This confidence was also apparent in their aspirations to attend higher education: they were not surprised that people thought they could go to university (14:–2) and did not think university was too big for them (27:+2).

They placed three statements related to their wish to attend university in the most extreme positive column of the distribution grid, including the idea that university was the best option (35:+3) and a good idea for them (15:+2). They disagreed with the idea that university was good for many people but not for themselves (7:–3) and they believed that university would give them good job prospects (23:+3). Due to these strong positions, they did not believe that the Explore University programme had encouraged them to consider going to university (31:–2) – they would have considered university without it (32:–3).

Factor 2: *Explore Uni has supported me in thinking about attending uni, but I need more information before I decide whether or not I will attend.*

The amount of variance accounted for was 10 per cent and its eigenvalue 4.699, which was over four times the value needed to be a significant factor. In total, seven students held these communalities. In the same way as in Factor 1, they held positive perspectives of themselves as secondary-school learners: they believed that they were pretty good at school work (25:+2) and were not surprised that people thought that they could go to university

Table 9.1 Example of an Explore University Q-sort

-3	-2	-1	0	+1	+2	+3
11. My family would be really proud if I went to uni	2. I would like to go to uni but stay close to my home	6. I can't wait to start uni	10. My family really wants me to go to uni	7. Uni is good for lots of people but not in my case	5. I have found the Explore Uni taster sessions helpful	1. I am much more positive about uni than I was before Explore Uni
20. I like school a lot	3. I would definitely still keep in touch with all my friends if I went to uni	9. I would have gone to uni regardless of Explore Uni	15. Uni seems a good idea for me	8. The amount of support available in uni sounds great	12. I could easily cope with going to uni	27. I would not find uni too big for me
	4. I would feel better about myself if I went to uni	21. Uni is nothing like school	16. Most of my friends will go to uni	13. Uni seems a more friendly place than I used to think	17. I think I will fit right into uni	
	19. Being at uni would be just like being at school	24. I would be just as clever as the other students at uni	18. If I went to uni, I would not be worried about keeping up with the work	14. I was surprised that people think I could go to uni	22. I'd make lots of new friends at uni	
	36. Even though I am a bit nervous, I am looking forward to going to uni	26. The teachers think highly of me at my school	25. I am pretty good at my school work	23. I'd get a good job by going through uni	34. I have learned lots about uni that I never imagined	
		30. I have changed my mind about my future	31. Explore Uni has encouraged me to consider uni	28. There are more choices to study what I want at uni than at school		
		35. Uni seems like the best option for me now	32. I would never have thought about uni if it was not for Explore Uni	29. I always knew what job I wanted		
			33. I want to know more about uni before I make my mind up			

(14:–2). However, they were less convinced than Factor 1 respondents that their teachers thought highly of them (26:+1).

These school students placed conflicting statements about attending university in the most extreme columns of the distribution grid. On the one hand, they did not believe that university at this time was the best option for them (35:–2) and they had not changed their mind about their future as a result of the Explore University programme (30:–3). They disagreed with statements that suggested a wish to attend university (2:–3, 6:–2) and believed that university was good for many people but not in their case (7:+2). On the other hand, they also believed that there were benefits to attending university. They stated that there were more choices at university to study what they were interested in (28:+3), that they would make new friends (22:+3) and that the amount of support available sounded great (8:+2). Importantly, they needed to know more about university before they made up their minds about it (33:+2).

Factor 3: *I am still a bit nervous about going to university, but I want to attend. I am more positive after attending the Explore Uni programme.*

The amount of variance accounted for was 6 per cent and its eigenvalue was 2.5311. In total, 12 participants held communalities in this factor. In contrast to Factors 1 and 2, these school students did not hold a strong perspective of themselves as secondary-school learners: they did not like school (20:–3) and placed statements about this issue in the more neutral columns of the distribution grid. They did not agree that they were good at their schoolwork (25:–1) and did not believe that teachers thought highly of them at school (26:0).

These participants believed that university was good for many people, including themselves (7:–2). They had not always known what job they wanted to do (29:–2). However, even though they were a bit nervous, they were looking forward to going to university (36:+2). Similarly to Factor 2, they believed that the Explore University programme had helped them to be more positive about university (1:+3). They clearly differentiated the experiences of being at school and university (19:–3) and believed that university was nothing like school (21:+2).

Factor 4: *Explore Uni has encouraged me to consider university and its benefits. I believe that I am a good learner at school but understand that university is a different experience.*

The amount of variance accounted for in Factor 4 was 5 per cent and the eigenvalue was 2.4812. In total, seven participants held communalities in this factor. Similarly to Factors 1 and 2, these school students had good perspectives of themselves as secondary-school learners. They believed that they were pretty good at school work (25:+2) and that teachers thought highly of them (26:+2). They were also not surprised that people thought that they would attend university (14:–2). They also felt they had been encouraged to consider university by attending the Explore University programme (31:+2), believing that they had learned a great deal about university that they never imagined (34:+2) and would not have thought of going to university without attending the programme (9:–2). They had not always known what job they would like to do (29:–3), but they disagreed with the idea that university was good for many people but not right for them (7:–2). For these students, the benefits of attending university included having more choice to study what they wanted (28:+3) and getting a good job (23:+3). However, just as in Factor 2, these school students wanted to know more about university before they made up their minds (33:+2).

Table 9.2 Factor Q-sort values for each statement in the Explore University analysis

No.	Statement	1	2	3	4
1	I am much more positive about uni than I was before Explore Uni	−1	0	+3	0
2	I would like to go to uni but stay close to my home	−2	−3	−2	−1
3	I would definitely keep in touch with all my friends if I went to uni	+1	0	+2	0
4	I would feel better about myself if I went to uni	0	0	−1	0
5	I have found the Explore Uni taster sessions helpful	−1	0	+1	+1
6	I can't wait to start uni	+1	−2	−1	0
7	University is good for lots of people but not in my case	−3	+2	−2	−2
8	The amount of support available in uni sounds great	0	+2	+1	0
9	I would have gone to uni regardless of the Explore Uni programme	+1	−2	0	−2
10	My family really wants me to go to uni	+1	−2	+1	0
11	My family would be really proud if I went to uni	+1	−1	+1	+1
12	I could easily cope with going to uni	0	+1	−1	−2
13	Uni seems a more friendly place than I used to think	0	0	0	+1
14	I was surprised that people think I could go to uni	−2	−2	−1	−2
15	Uni seems a good idea for me	+2	−1	+1	+1
16	Most of my friends will go to uni	0	0	0	−2
17	I think I will fit right into uni	+1	+1	0	−1
18	If I went to uni, I would not be worried about keeping up with the work	−2	−1	−2	0
19	Being at uni would be just like being at school	−2	−1	−3	−1
20	I like school a lot	−1	−1	−3	1
21	Uni is nothing like school	0	−1	+2	−3
22	I'd make lots of new friends at uni	0	+3	+2	0
23	I'd get a good job by going through uni	+3	+1	+2	+3
24	I would be just as clever as the other students at uni	−1	0	−2	−1
25	I am pretty good at my school work	+2	+2	−1	+2
26	The teachers think highly of me at my school	+2	+1	0	+2
27	I would not find uni too big for me	+2	+1	−1	−1
28	There are more choices to study what I want at uni than at school	+2	+3	+3	+3
29	I always knew what job I wanted	0	+1	−2	−3
30	I have changed my mind about my future	−1	−3	0	−1
31	The Explore Uni programme has encouraged me to consider uni	−2	+2	0	+2
32	I would never have thought about uni if it was not for Explore Uni	−3	0	−1	+1
33	I want to know more about uni before I make my mind up	−1	+2	0	+2
34	I have learned lots about uni that I never imagined	−1	+1	+1	+2
35	Uni seems like the best option for me now	+3	−2	+1	−1
36	Even though I am a bit nervous, I am looking forward to going to uni	+1	−1	+2	1

Overall, the evaluation study found that 26 of the 41 participants who loaded on Factors 2, 3 and 4 believed that the Explore University programme had positively helped them to consider university as an option. The other participants, those in Factor 1, held a strong and already longstanding perspective that they would attend university. As can be seen, the use of Q-methodology for this evaluation study enabled us to see complexity in participants' perspectives, rather than merely finding out whether they did or did not consider university before or after attending the Explore University programme.

Many of the participants completed the Q-sort without asking for any assistance. Some, however, completed it very quickly, which may have meant that they had not thoroughly compared and contrasted all of the statements. Furthermore, the open-ended questions after the Q-sort were rarely answered or had minimal comments included. This meant that we were unable to generate more qualitative data from these responses. The study may have benefited from the researchers going back and interviewing some of the participants in some way, in order to check that they were happy with our interpretation of their data and to try and obtain more qualitative data. Whatever additional approaches had been chosen, the ethical concerns about directly accessing perspectives from these young people would have still applied.

Conclusion

Q-methodology has been around for much longer than many people think and it occupies a distinct and important niche in the continuum of research methodologies. It can be used across a wide range of research subjects and contexts and offers the researcher who is interested in exploring the attitudes and perspectives of individuals and groups a unique and very flexible tool to achieve their aims in a detailed way. Its initial, apparent complexity is soon overcome, although understanding and interpreting the analysed data produced by the software tools can take some time.

In summary, here are some final considerations:

- Although Q is predominantly thought of in terms of Master's or doctoral research, competent final-year undergraduates can, like Hannah, also use it very effectively (although having an experienced mentor to help with factor interpretation is strongly advised).
- It is worth investing time in the exploration of the concourse and the subsequent creation of the Q-set, as the quality of both is a crucial factor in the validity of your Q study.
- Remember that Q-methodology produces a wealth of analysed data and that you might find some of the software tools easier to work with than others. It is worth taking time choosing which to use.
- Despite its challenges, the possibilities that Q-methodology offers to researchers to investigate topics in new and deeper ways can be very exciting and rewarding.

Recommended reading

Brown, S.R. (1997) *The History and Principles of Q Methodology in Psychology and the Social Sciences*. Kent, OH: Kent State University.

This text provides a thorough overview of Q-methodology. It is available at www.scribd.com/document/92246042/History-and-Principles-of-Q-Steven-Brown.

Watts, S. and Stenner, P. (2012) *Doing Q Methodological Research: Theory, Method and Interpretation*. London: Sage.

This excellent, comprehensive introduction to Q will enable you to complete your own research projects using this approach.

http://schmolck.userweb.mwn.de/qmethod/pqmanual.htm

This page hosts the PQMethod manual and provides important information on using this invaluable online tool.

References

Brown, Z. (2016) 'We just have to get on with it'. Inclusive teaching in a standards driven system: The design decisions of a Q-methodological study. *Operant Subjectivity*, 38(1), 1–14.

Brown, Z., Rhoades, G. and Smith, M. (2018) Aspiring to higher education? The complex views of secondary students. Paper to *British Education Studies Association Conference: Internationalisation and Collaboration: Values and Value in Globalised Education*, 28–29 June 2018. [Online] https://educationstudies.org.uk/?p=9101 (accessed 3 September 2018).

Combes, H., Hardy, G. and Buchan, L. (2004) Using Q-methodology to involve people with intellectual disability in evaluating person-centred planning. *Journal of Applied Research in Intellectual Disabilities*, 17(3), 149–159.

Cross, R.M. (2005) Exploring attitudes: The case for Q methodology. *Health Education Research*, 20(2), 206–213.

Eden, S., Donaldson, A. and Walker, G. (2005) Structuring subjectivities? Using Q methodology in human geography. *Area*, 37(4), 413–422.

Erwin, P. (2001) *Attitudes and Persuasion*. Hove: Psychology Press.

Rhoades, G. (in preparation) *Exploring Students' Experiences and Conceptions of 'Student Satisfaction' as a Measure of Quality in Higher Education: A Q-Methodology Study*. Doctoral thesis for the University of Wolverhampton, UK.

Sheares, H. (2017) *The National Curriculum: Straight-Jacket or Life-Jacket?* Undergraduate dissertation for the University of Wolverhampton, UK.

Stainton Rogers, R. (1995) Q methodology. In: J.A. Smith, R. Harré and L. Van Langenhove (Eds.) *Rethinking Methods in Psychology*. London: Sage.

Stephenson, W. (1935) Technique of factor analysis. *Nature*, 136, 297.

Watts, S. and Stenner, P. (2012) *Doing Q Methodological Research: Theory, Method and Interpretation*. London: Sage.

Wilson, T.D. and Schooler, J.W. (1991) Thinking too much: Introspection can reduce the quality of preferences and decisions. *Journal of Personality and Social Psychology*, 60(2), 181–192.

Chapter 10

Mosaic

Participatory research in the early years

Helen Lyndon

Introduction

One of the most influential participatory methodologies used both for early-childhood research and for evaluation and development of professional practice in the UK is the 'Mosaic' approach. Mosaic was first outlined by Clark and Moss (2001), has been further developed in subsequent key texts (for example, Clark and Moss, 2011; Clark, 2017), and is discussed and cited by many more. The approach reflects a growing research body which has embraced the new sociology of childhood (see James and Prout, 1997) and is a response to a previous, more adult-centred research and improvement discourse.

Epistemologically, the Mosaic approach offers a participatory paradigm, underpinned by socio-cultural theory: children are not *objects* of investigation, they are its *active participants* through collaboration with adults and peers. It also sets out a particular view of knowledge, not one which seeks a single truth, but one which recognizes the complexities of human lives. Mosaic provides a process through which meaning is created and greater understanding gained.

In practical terms, it has several stages. First, children and adults (researcher, practitioners, parents and others) gather evidence, then this information is pieced together for dialogue and reflection. Patterns – known as 'mosaics' – begin to develop, indicating, for example, a child's interest in role play or their lack of engagement in mark-making. Children and other participants then get the opportunity to reflect further upon these findings and participate in interpretation. The importance of the final stage is paramount, not just hearing what has been said, but purposeful listening as a pre-requisite for 'deciding areas of continuity and change' (Clarke, 2005:33).

Clark and Moss, in their various publications, have usefully set out the perspectives on childhood which accompany this paradigm and on which the Mosaic approach itself is based. Firstly, children are viewed as experts in their own lives, able to offer their own unique outlooks. They are skilful communicators, a view which emphasizes not only the competency of young children but also the role of adults in facilitating this communication through rich, well-resourced environments. Children are also rights-holders – indeed, the Mosaic approach is underpinned by Articles 12 and 13 of the United Nations Convention on the Rights of the Child (OHCHR, 1989), which state that children have the right to express their views through a range of media and have these taken into account when decisions that affect them are being made. Finally, children are meaning-makers and participants in their own learning, active in constructing their own knowledge and understandings.

This view of childhood and of children's competencies supports what Clark and Moss (2011) call a 'framework for listening' within the Mosaic approach. This involves a recognition that children communicate through both verbal and visual ways and that therefore a range of different ways of 'listening' to a child should be used. Verbal methods include discussions, known as 'conferencing'; 'tours' of the day-care setting given by children themselves and through which they can express their preferences; and shared discussions which review relevant pedagogic documentation, such as planning or observation reports, allowing children to reflect on their learning opportunities and achievements. Visual methods include children engaging in free drawing and photography, thereby allowing communication on a symbolic level, with the results then becoming prompts for further reflection and verbal discussion.

Within the Mosaic approach, children as well as practitioners, parents, researchers and perhaps other adults participate in the interpretation of the evidence gathered. Purposeful listening guides in particular how the needs and wishes of the youngest children are interpreted and used – indeed, there is an ethical purpose behind the intent to listen to all the children, so that professional action and potential improvement can follow.

Importantly, the framework for listening offers adaptability, recognizing that each child's lived experiences differ and that a Mosaic approach can be used in different ways to suit each context. For example, for one child, photographs might provide the basis for fruitful discussion, whilst for another, a conference with a sibling might give a valuable, different perspective. If evaluation of professional practice is the purpose, children might discuss a setting's outdoor provision during a tour, explaining what they enjoy, which areas they like to access and why. There is also acknowledgement that interpretations of findings will vary amongst participants, giving rise to further opportunities for reflection.

Overall, therefore, the Mosaic approach offers a variety of complementary methods, which allow integration of verbal and visual information from children, together with separate evidence from parents, practitioners and others. Any or all of these can be used to build up a broad, deep picture of a child's experiences and preferences – a multi-faceted, personal mosaic, drawn from the many perspectives gained and interpretations made, and likely to be very different for one child to that of another. Clark and Moss (2011) also highlight the importance in this process of being open to the unexpected, bringing a child's priorities and concerns to the fore. It was this adaptability, as well as a desire to embed a listening approach within a particular early-years setting, that led to use of a Mosaic approach in the research project which is used to illustrate methodological issues in the rest of this chapter.

Principles and advantages

Reread this first section and identify the key principles underlying the Mosaic approach. What advantages does such an approach offer:

- For a research project?
- To support evaluation and improvement in an early-years educational setting?

Using Mosaic

The project (Lyndon, 2012) took place in a small, private, pre-school setting. This had just over 30 children registered for full-day care and 30 others for sessional care. The motivation for the study stemmed from a desire to work alongside practitioners at the setting to explore how the Mosaic approach could facilitate better listening to children and so enhance its early-years practice. It offered a participatory methodology in which children's involvement was paramount and practitioners could learn from children's perspectives.

Additionally motivating was a desire to make the setting's pedagogic documentation more meaningful. A key collection of such material in UK systems is a child's 'learning journey', which is used to track development against the seven areas of learning and the three characteristics of effective learning, defined for practitioners in England in the Early Years Foundation Stage curriculum guidance, known as the EYFS (Department for Education, 2017), and related advice (Early Education, 2012). While these learning journeys might ordinarily stay in a cupboard or on a high shelf, in this project they would be used to provide prompts for further discussions involving children. The project also gave an opportunity for learning to be documented with children, rather than by others on their behalf. A key consideration was that any recommendations for changes to practice which emerged from the project should be manageable and efficient: the private provider had struggled with issues of sustainability and did not have the luxury of supernumerary staffing.

My own role with this setting was long established. As an advisory early-years teacher within the locality, I had been working with these practitioners for some time and had developed respectful and trusting relationships with them. This not only meant that we had mutual aims for best professional practice, but it also formed the basis for a shared desire to explore participatory methodologies in developing practice. This approach could be seen as part of an emerging paradigm of praxeology, the study of human action, which offers a mix of 'phronesis [practical wisdom], praxis, ethics and power' (Pascal and Bertram, 2009:477). It is a reflective approach, which emphasizes the importance of practice-led enquiry and in which ethics are fundamental; by balancing power, it provides a truly democratic approach to research. In the case of this project, researcher, children, practitioners and parents all contributed to the development and interpretation of the data within each mosaic, thereby pursuing an adaptable process through which the views of the children in particular could be explored and then better integrated into practice through the staged approach.

Stage 1: Children and adults gather evidence

An initial meeting of practitioners served as a focus group to discuss how the project could be developed and to establish a benchmark of current practices. Areas of concern were highlighted, including a lack of children's input into pedagogical documentation and issues with planning and observations. There was a desire to better understand the children's views of their nursery experience, with particular reference to differences between full-time and part-time children. Parents were consulted about the project and consent was sought from them for their children's participation. In fact, parents were keen for their children to be involved and open to the idea of greater partnership with practitioners at the setting. Finally, a focus-group discussion was conducted with the children, in which they talked about why they came to nursery, what they enjoyed about it and what they thought grown-ups should do there.

The notion of 'assent' applies where participants are under a legal age of consent. It can be recognized with early-years children through observation of their body language, as well as through discussion. Children in this project were invited to participate in the activities and were able to opt in or out, allowing them to respond to the moment, rather than contemplating their assent. In gauging this, practitioners could draw upon their intimate knowledge of the children and their longstanding relationships, which allowed them to judge whether or not a child was comfortable and contributing voluntarily in a discussion or activity.

Six children were selected, representing both genders and with an age range from two to four. They broadly reflected the diverse, ethnic nature of the setting and its wider locality and also represented both full-time and part-time attendance. Mosaics were developed around these children using observations, conferencing (parent, practitioner and child) and photography – multiple, combined methods which provided a range of data around each child. Whilst the process very much related to the six children and to the research project, the practitioners wished to go on to embed these Mosaic techniques into their wider practice, seeking to benefit all children within the setting. This usefully addressed the ethical dilemma, raised by previous researchers, that selecting a few children for research can marginalize others (Harcourt and Einarsdottir, 2011).

Observations: Narrative and coded

Observations for the project involved several prolonged periods of watching interactions, interests and responses of the children, focused largely on two questions: 'What is it like to be here?' and 'Am I listened to?' They were initially recorded in written, narrative form, as was common practice within the setting, and typically produced vast quantities of qualitative information. As a result, the task of interpretation became daunting for practitioners, striving to embed elements of Mosaic into their wider developmental practice.

The practitioners therefore collaborated in a revision of their usual observation form, using examples from Early Effective Learning (Bertram and Pascal, 2004). This programme uses observation coding, whereby activity is assigned in terms of particular elements: involvement (see also Laevers, 2003), social interaction, initiative and area of learning. Such coding enables some elements of analysis to be carried out at the point of observation and therefore reduces the need for long, written narratives. As practitioners began to use this new recording format, they found not only that it reduced the amount they were writing, but also that they could see how much more information was gathered by the coding. For instance, it was clear when children had been deeply engaged in play, when they had led activity amongst peers, and when they had preferred one particular area of learning above others. The coding also offered a succinct way of sharing the outcomes of observations with children themselves, as key points could be easily be extracted, for example: 'I saw how long you spent playing pirates in the garden, Gabriella. Am I right that this was your idea? It looked like you were leading the game.'

Conferencing: Parent, practitioner and child

As well as providing pieces of the mosaics, observations also offered prompts for subsequent conferencing opportunities with parents, practitioners and children themselves. The semi-structured nature of these conferences enabled deeper probing into certain issues, whilst similarity in questions not only determined some broad themes which reflected perceptions of a child's interests and development but also facilitated interpretive analysis of the data, as described by Mukherji and Albon (2015).

Aside from the expected problem of scheduling conferences with busy working parents, this element was very successful. Parents readily agreed to take part, indeed they were keen to discuss their child's interests and experiences at nursery. Their conferences lasted, on average, at least twice as long as practitioner or child conferences and all the parents interviewed expressed a desire for the opportunity to become a regular occurrence.

With practitioner conferences, a decision was taken that these should take place away from children, so that the participants could talk freely. However, this caused scheduling difficulties and even a sense of being rather rushed, as correct adult-to-child ratios needed always to be maintained in the classroom.

Conferences with children (who relished the opportunity for discussion) took place within the setting environment. An important factor here was their already established relationship with myself within the nursery context – they were already familiar with my presence, leading group work. The semi-structured conferences offered space within which the children could demonstrate their perspectives (Formosinho and Araújo, 2006). Clark and Moss (2011) cite the use of older siblings as an area for methodological study and, on a small scale, this was facilitated here as well, with some offering perspectives on the preferences of their younger, pre-verbal brothers or sisters. The views of the oldest children in nursery were also sought in order to explore and interpret further the experiences of the younger children who were the focus of the research.

To further extend these conferences, interpretations of children's learning, as documented in their learning journeys, were also discussed. For this, children and practitioners sat together and reviewed entries in the journals, with the children given the opportunity to reflect upon the evidence collected. The dialogue proved an invaluable participatory approach, especially as children's past successes could be revisited. In some instances, the interpretation of the practitioner became questioned when a child offered a unique insight. For example, a practitioner had documented one child's love of creative activities, but the child indicated that her real motivation was engaging in the same activity as her friends. This participatory element is central to the design of the Mosaic approach and highlights the importance of including the children in the exploration and interpretation of data.

Photography

Photography and visual imagery, such as map-making and book-making, play a central role in methods commonly used in a Mosaic approach (Clark and Moss, 2011), as these can provide valuable representation of children's views. Typically, children take photographs of the setting and use these to compile their own 'map' with which, in effect, they can give practitioners or researchers a 'tour' of the setting and indicate their preferences. Similarly, children can make their own books which reflect such preferences, using their photographs as a central feature. In having this control over the discussion through their photography, children can show increased communicational competence (Formosinho and Araújo, 2006).

However, as indicated earlier, the practitioners were ultimately seeking to embed Mosaic into practice for all children. Natural curiosity around the digital camera would mean that all the children would then wish to participate, and indeed ethically they would have been entitled to do so. However, developing the maps and books from the pictures required a great deal of time and one-to-one attention and practitioners therefore decided that these would not be workable for everyday practice. So instead, A3-sized 'photo-boards' were used, providing a more time-efficient process. For these, all the children took photographs in response to the prompt: 'What do you enjoy about being here?'. The images were printed and given back to the children, who then worked collaboratively with practitioners to develop photo-boards of those which the children selected. The pictures could be annotated or not, depending upon each child's preference. The longest time lapse between taking photographs and the creation of a photo-board was three days, the shortest was one day.

The photo-boards then became a focus for further discussion between children and practitioners. The children were able to talk readily about their pictures and why they had taken them. Practitioners found themselves surprised, not only by the child's competence using the technology but also by their competence in articulating their images. Some of the children organized their photographs around themes, such as 'Friends' or 'Playing outside'. The children could also share their boards with their parents or carers as further opportunity for discussion.

However, the use of visual imagery in Mosaic is not without ethical tension, particularly over ownership of digital, photographic images. In the UK, these have been increasingly used by practitioners to document children's progress through their early years. The growing 'data shadow' that builds around each child has been criticized (Roberts-Holmes and Bradbury, 2016), and the early-years sector is now having to consider the impact of the vast quantity of data which it holds. The security needed for storage and analysis is particularly problematic. Legally, images taken by children remain their own property, as copyright laws are not affected by age (*Copyright, Designs and Patents Act 1988*). However, such images invariably depict multiple children and practitioners from the settings and so permissions are not straightforward (Menter *et al.*, 2011). In this research, the images remained the property of the setting, as happens for photographs taken by practitioners as part of documenting EYFS practice, and their use was thus governed and restricted by setting policy.

Methods

Stage 1 of the project described here used three methods to explore children's perspectives in verbal and visual ways: observation, 'conferencing' and photography. What other methods could have been used in this project to elicit children's preferences and experiences? What methods could be used in a Mosaic research project of your own?

Stage 2: Dialogue, reflection, interpretation

In the Mosaic approach, research methods used in Stage 1 prompt dialogue, reflection and interpretation in Stage 2, joining together the individual pieces of information to develop greater understanding of the priorities of the child (Clark, 2017). Whilst this can take place as a further, formally scheduled conferencing event, practice within early-years settings affords more regular opportunities for such dialogue and reflection, mostly on an informal basis. This approach suited the small community-based setting where the project was carried out. For instance, parents and carers were happy to engage in dialogue with practitioners as they collected their children at the end of their day, sharing their interpretations on the compilation of data gathered. Children also engaged in natural dialogue with practitioners and the use of social time facilitated this, for example during lunch.

The subsequent process of interpretation is best illustrated by a case study of 'Gabriella', who attended the full day-care element of the setting on a full-time basis and who had just turned four years of age at the time of the research. Her parents were relatively new to the UK, having migrated from eastern Europe, and English (in which she was rapidly becoming proficient) was her second language.

During collection of data, Gabriella and I developed quite a bond, and her willingness to participate in everything made it easy to gather evidence of her perspectives. Observations were made and recorded, using the coded format described earlier. Her resulting mosaic consisted of nine separate elements, including a strong bond with practitioners and equally strong engagement in social play. Indeed, relationships were a key element in her mosaic and she often sought out adults to talk to. Her interest in what adults were doing was common in both home and setting environments and came through in both the parent and practitioner conferences. The photo-board that Gabriella created mainly contained images of staff she liked and of friends; there were also a few images she took which demonstrated resources or specific activities.

Gabriella loved role play – this was evident in the observations, as well as in her child conferencing. Not only did she enjoy and participate in this, she was instrumental in initiating such play and supported other children in organizing their own imaginative activities. Neither the parent or practitioner conference had highlighted this interest, nor was it evident in her learning-journey documentation. Instead, these other sources had concluded that Gabriella had a preference for art-and-design activities, even though this was never expressed by Gabriella directly. Reflection on her differing perspectives enabled practitioners to consider whether what they had judged to be Gabriella's personal preference might instead have been evidence of compliance, and to decide to offer her further opportunities to engage in and shape role-play activities instead. What resulted was an understanding that Gabriella liked creative activities when engaging in solitary play, but that her preference was for social activity, specifically that involving role play.

Stage 3: Deciding areas of continuity and change

In creating more participatory practice through the Mosaic approach, stakeholders need to believe that children have the ability to co-construct knowledge relating to their developmental and educational experiences. During the research project, the early focus-group discussions increased practitioner awareness of the different ways of actively listening to children. Indeed, a change was noted immediately, as staff began to check their interpretations of children's speech and actions. It is this ethos within a setting, characteristic of a Mosaic approach, which facilitates a listening culture.

In fact, children not only participated in the building of their mosaics by responding to questions but also influenced design of the research itself. For example, their perspectives directly influenced development of the photo-boards: they decided how these would look, what they would contain and how they could be used. Furthermore, practitioners were also able to see how the 'voice' of even the youngest, pre-verbal children could be analysed, and the children in general started to be viewed as experts in their own lives and experiences, as described in Clark (2017).

As in previous Mosaic research (for example, Clark and Moss, 2005), the target children expressed through this investigation the importance of friendship and the outdoor environment. In line with the idea of purposeful listening, this finding was used to encourage further development of the setting's use of outdoors for children's play and learning, as well as prompting further staff development on the use of 'communication spaces', areas of the setting which specifically encouraged children to engage in discussion. One unlikely example of such a space was the pirate ship in the garden area, originally designed and placed to encourage physical development, with steps and a slide. As a result of the Mosaic project, its use was developed further as a 'den' space in which children could sit and talk. Furthermore, the children had not discussed or documented more adult-led activities, such as early phonics and mathematics, but parents did express interest in such nursery activity and some requested more feedback about them, which they could consolidate in their home environment.

Indeed, the desire of both parents and children to have strong communicative links between home and nursery was generally apparent in this research. Practitioners saw themselves as facilitators of this and a key change following the research was in how they approached it, offering parents choices about what information was disseminated and giving the children physical prompts – a piece of work or an artefact – to take home, so these could become a focus for dialogue with parents and others.

Time itself also became a facilitator of more participatory practice – it was allocated for practitioners to engage in the research process and in reflection. This was not easy to arrange, as staff in busy, private, full-day care settings do not always have the luxury of time, nor often the mechanisms through which reflection can be encouraged. The EYFS (Department for Education, 2017) may offer one such opportunity for reflection through its statutory requirement for supervision of staff, involving support, coaching and training. With such time set aside, as well as an agenda for reflective practice, this and other settings should have further opportunity to consider and act upon what children have to say.

The practitioners' enthusiasm for the project also facilitated the participatory approach, although there was some initial hesitation. Their early perspective was that research was for the researcher and they themselves were mere observers of this. Staff often did not even see themselves as experts within their own field, exemplifying the low status often experienced by early-years workers (Aubrey, 2011). The researcher was seen as the point of knowledge, reflecting perhaps a traditional 'banking' model of education (Freire, 1996), whereby learners (the practitioners, in this case) are viewed as vessels, which educators (the researcher) must fill. It took encouragement and trust to develop a more participatory process in which practitioners could see themselves as 'co-researchers'. Children and parents, however, did not demonstrate this same level of reticence and showed confidence and capacity to take part in the research from the onset. I believed this to be reflective of a welcoming ethos, created by the nursery, as well as the child-centred approach underpinned by the EYFS.

During the research, established processes were challenged, as practitioners were guided away from being solely responsible for recording every element of a child's life and encouraged to adopt different ways of listening and focus on more participatory and efficient ways of gathering information. The research project ended with the staff's prior perception of a child's learning journey as documentation put together by practitioners being altered to that of a shared resource, which included the child's, parents' and practitioners' perceptions. An instance of this was that children's ownership of digital cameras as a mechanism for voice remained post-project and children began to make regular use of cameras to document their own learning. Practical ways were also sought in which the documents could be accessed jointly within the setting.

Strengths and limitations

The research project, with its use of a Mosaic approach, provided a private, full day-care setting with the opportunity to improve children's participation. This succeeded and practice altered. The changes served also as discussion points for other practitioners in other local settings through network meetings, illustrating the study's transferability through the 'thick descriptions' (Geertz, 1973) it offered of participatory processes.

A further strength of the Mosaic approach was the way in which it empowered staff to take on researcher roles and to value their own contribution to the processes of investigation. Knowledge creation was seen as a collaborative effort: staff helped to educate the researcher and *vice versa* (Freire, 1996). This change in mind-set impacted on the setting as a whole, with staff then embarking upon their own participatory initiatives, for example a springtime gardening initiative.

One purpose of the research project was to harness the adaptability that Mosaic offers and to apply it to the development of professional practice and associated documentation within the setting. The multi-modal design offered more than simple triangulation, as it was built on the premise that each piece of each mosaic would add a different perspective regarding the preferences and experiences of a child. Only by gathering information in a variety of ways could a child's true nature be understood. However, a Mosaic approach takes time. The project's original research design recognized this and there was an implicit understanding that mosaics could not be created around every child to the same depth simultaneously.

There is some criticism of participatory approaches, such as Mosaic, for taking advantage of children's 'schooled docility' (Gallacher and Gallagher, 2008:506). Are children like Gabriella conforming to wider norms through their willingness to participate? Do practitioners simply select methods for participation that children are familiar with due to their setting experience? Indeed, participation does not necessarily result in free choice, as practitioners and their settings still operate within the parameters of an adult-designed, professionally dominated, statutory system. It should also be noted that our wider legal system places parental consent above the assent of children in participating in such a project. Practitioners developing mosaics must also be careful that the methods do not resort to tokenism (Hart, 1992) and that continuity and change can result following interpretation of the data.

Insider perspective

As seen in this chapter, the Mosaic approach blurs the lines between research and educational practice. In this respect, it requires understanding of the setting and of the researcher's relationships with those involved, as well as an ability to affect change. All these elements are possible, especially for the practitioner-researcher who is undertaking their research from an insider perspective, that is in a setting where they have practitioner or other involvement already. Nevertheless, key questions apply:

- In what ways does this insider perspective strengthen the research?
- In what ways might it weaken or invalidate it?
- What steps might be taken to avoid or address potential problems?

Conclusion

This chapter has outlined a participatory approach to research, Mosaic, which can be embedded into practice within early-years settings. There is no definitive list of actual methods which can be used for this approach, but Mosaic itself offers both a set of values and guidance for those wishing to undertake research or practice evaluation of this kind. Its adaptability is ultimately a strength for those who recognize the need for context-based methodologies. Ethical concerns, of course, remain at the fore, as seen in the project described, in which consent, assent and the dilemma of an increasing digital shadow created around children had all to be navigated. Some might regard a participatory approach like Mosaic as problematically blurring the lines between research and practice, but others see it as representing an exciting opportunity to develop early-years provision in robust, transparent and research-based ways within existing statutory frameworks.

Recommended reading

Clark, A. (2017) *Listening to Young Children: A Guide to Understanding and Using the Mosaic Approach*. Third edition. London: Jessica Kingsley.

Alison Clark examines further development of the Mosaic approach and cites international case studies to exemplify key points. Ethical and other methodological elements are discussed in relation to its possible use with older children and with adults.

Murray, J. and Gray, C. (Eds.) (2017) Perspectives from young children on the margins. *European Early Childhood Education Research Journal*, 25(2).

This special edition of the EECERJ, with an editorial from Jane Murray and Colette Gray, brings together ten research articles which explore the perceptions of children on the margins of society. The international collection shows how children's perspectives are elicited on issues such as poverty, racial tension and immigration through a variety of methods.

References

Aubrey, C. (2011) *Leading and Managing in the Early Years*. Second edition. London: Sage.

Bertram, T. and Pascal, C. (2004) *Effective Early Learning Programme*. Birmingham: Amber Publishing.

Clark, A. (2005) Ways of seeing: Using the Mosaic approach to listen to young children's perspectives. In: A. Clark, A.T. Kjørholt and P. Moss (Eds.) *Beyond Listening: Children's Perspectives on Early Childhood Services*. Bristol: The Policy Press.

Clark, A. (2017) *Listening to Young Children: A Guide to Understanding and Using the Mosaic Approach*. Third edition. London: Jessica Kingsley.

Clark, A. and Moss, P. (2001) *Listening to Young Children: The Mosaic Approach*. London: National Children's Bureau.

Clark, A. and Moss, P. (2005) *Spaces to Play: More Listening to Young Children Using the Mosaic Approach*. London: National Children's Bureau.

Clark, A. and Moss, P. (2011) *Listening to Young Children: The Mosaic Approach*. Second edition. London: National Children's Bureau.

Copyright, Designs and Patents Act 1988 c.48. [Online] www.legislation.gov.uk/ukpga/1988/48/contents (accessed 8 June 2017).

Department for Education (2017) *Statutory Framework for the Early Years Foundation Stage*. [Online] www.gov.uk/government/uploads/system/uploads/attachment_data/file/596629/EYFS_STATUTORY_FRAMEWORK_2017.pdf (accessed 4 December 2017).

Early Education (2012) *Development Matters in the Early Years Foundation Stage (EYFS)*. London: Early Education.

Formosinho, J. and Araújo, S.B. (2006) Listening to children as a way to reconstruct knowledge about children: Some methodological implications. *European Early Childhood Education Research Journal*, 14(1), 21–31.

Freire, P. (1996) *Pedagogy of the Oppressed*. Translated by Myra Bergman Ramos. London: Penguin.

Gallacher, L-A. and Gallagher, M. (2008) Methodological immaturity in childhood research? Thinking through 'participatory methods'. *Childhood*, 15(4), 499–516.

Geertz, C. (1973) *The Interpretation of Cultures*. New York: Basic books.

Harcourt, D. and Einarsdottir, J. (2011) Introducing children's perspectives and participation in research. *European Early Childhood Education Research Journal*, 19(3), 301–307.

Hart, R. (1992) *Children's Participation: From Tokenism to Citizenship*. Innocenti Essay No.4. Florence: UNICEF. [Online] www.unicef-irc.org/publications/pdf/childrens_participation.pdf (accessed 7 December 2017).

James, A. and Prout, A. (Eds.) (1997) *Constructing and Reconstructing Childhood: Contemporary Issues in the Sociological Study of Childhood*. Second edition. Abingdon: Routledge.

Laevers, F. (2003) Making care and education more effective through well being and involvement. In: F. Laevers and L. Heylen (Eds.) *Involvement of Children and Teacher Style: Insights from an International Study on Experiential Education*. Leuven: Leuven University Press.

Lyndon, H. (2012) *Creating a More Participatory Practice for Children in Early Years: An Action Research Project*. MA Dissertation for Birmingham City University, UK.

Menter, I., Elliot, D., Hulme, M., Lewin, J. and Lowden, K. (2011) *A Guide to Practitioner Research in Education*. London: Sage.

Mukherji, P. and Albon, D. (2015) *Research Methods in Early Childhood: An Introductory Guide*. Second edition. London: Sage.

OHCHR (1989) *Convention on the Rights of the Child*. Geneva: Office of the United Nations High Commissioner for Human Rights. [Online] www.ohchr.org/EN/ProfessionalInterest/Pages/CRC.aspx (accessed 30 January 2018).

Pascal, C. and Bertram, T. (2009) Listening to young citizens: The struggle to make real a participatory paradigm in research with young children. *European Early Childhood Education Research Journal*, 17(2), 249–262.

Roberts-Holmes, G. and Bradbury, A. (2016) Governance, accountability and the datafication of early years education in England. *British Educational Research Journal*, 42(4), 600–613.

Chapter 11

Ethnography

Joke Dewilde

Introduction

Each year a number of young students with refugee backgrounds start in Norwegian schools. Some have full schooling from their home countries, others have received little or no formal instruction prior to their arrival in Norway. All face the daunting task of learning the Norwegian language and catching up or keeping up with their studies in a new environment.

In my recent research, I have been concerned with how these young people develop their writing skills in their new language. Previous research on this matter has tended to focus on the texts written in school and comparing these with texts written by Norwegian peers. To a lesser extent, researchers have also addressed more contextual issues, such as teachers' support and feedback or the young people's feelings towards writing in a new language. In my research, I put the young people themselves at the centre of attention. This allowed me to understand their development as writers in a broader perspective, taking into consideration mobility, migration and their engagement with people across the world. In this way, I did an 'ethnography', telling the story of 13 students attending an introductory class for newcomers in a large upper-secondary school, situated in eastern Norway (Dewilde, 2017; 2018).

Ethnography

The word, ethnography, comes from the Greek term for 'folk description'. Researchers using this approach set out to describe and interpret the behaviour of people by observing their everyday lives and engaging in conversation to try to understand how the world looks from their perspective. The starting point is the fact that people behave in certain ways without reflecting much about what they do and why they do it. Ethnographers believe that behaviour is best studied by observation and engagement, rather than by asking people in formal interviews or by setting up experiments. Therefore, they involve themselves in – even immerse themselves in – people's daily lives over a period of time: watching, listening, discussing and collecting documents, as they try to shed light on the topic of enquiry (Hammersley and Atkinson, 2007). Typically, they study a few cases in depth, rather than a large number superficially.

It is important to realize that ethnography entails more than just describing people's cultural and social behaviour. The approach has roots in the scientific tradition of anthropology, which holds that we interpret and understand people's behaviour according to some basic assumptions. These are interpretivist rather than positivist in nature. Therefore, the researcher does not perceive behaviour as something that is fixed, revealed to and reported by an objective observer, but instead, as something portrayed and interpreted as a social practice in a particular context in an account for which the researcher is responsible (Heller, 2008). Ethnography should thus not be reduced to fieldwork, simply and solely understood as description. Instead, it is 'an intellectual enterprise, a procedure that requires serious reflection *as much as* practical preparation and skill' (Blommaert and Jie, 2010:4, italics in original).

Another characteristic of ethnography is that it is concerned with complexity and multi-layeredness. Whereas other approaches, such as surveys and observation with tick manuals, use pre-defined categories to make sense of the world, ethnography tries to 'describe the apparently messy and complex activities that make up social action, not to reduce their complexity but to describe and explain it' (Blommaert and Jie, 2010:11–12). This does not mean, however, that ethnographers believe that they are able to get the whole picture – Heller (2008) notes that boundaries are always socially constructed and they need to be depicted and interpreted as such. In ethnographies of multilingualism, for instance, researchers are concerned with what counts as a language and who counts as a speaker of a language, as well as what people gain or lose from this categorization. According to this approach, established views of language in society can be challenged (Blommaert and Jie, 2010).

A type of ethnography that may be of particular interest for early researchers is 'short-term ethnography' (Pink and Morgan, 2013), also called 'focused ethnography' (Knoblauch, 2005) or 'rapid ethnography' (Millen, 2000). Like the more traditional long-term ethnographies, which may last for months or even years, this type sets out to gain insight into the everyday lives of people but does so in a different and more concentrated way. It:

> involves *intensive* excursions into [people's] lives, which use both more *interventional* as well as observational methods to create contexts through which to delve into *questions* that will reveal what matters to those people in the context of what the researcher is seeking to find out.
>
> (Pink and Morgan, 2013:352 – my italics emphasize differences to the normal ethnography described so far).

Pink and Morgan strongly argue that short-term ethnography, contrary to what critics may claim, is not some kind of superficial ethnography, but data-intensive, with a clear focus from the start. Also, the ethnographer takes a more central role in the field than is common in long-term ethnographies and engages the participants in the topic of investigation by raising specific issues and setting up activities.

Choosing a setting

Think of some social settings which you might wish to understand better through ethnography, for example, a classroom, lesson or meeting. If you were researching these settings, what activities of participants could you investigate? Which of these settings could usefully be researched through long-term ethnography? Which could be researched through short-term ethnography?

Stages

Ethnographic fieldwork can be divided into three consecutive stages, identified by Blommaert and Jie (2010): prior to fieldwork, during fieldwork and after fieldwork.

Prior to fieldwork

Before entering the field, the ethnographer needs to prepare carefully. This includes finding a suitable context where the focus of the research is likely to occur. Planning to study multilingualism in a monolingual environment, for example, would not be a good idea. At this point, you also need to decide how many sites you have time to cover and how many participants you want to study.

During fieldwork

Entering the field can be overwhelming, even for experienced ethnographers. The site may appear chaotic and without structure and patterns. This is entirely natural, and it is the ethnographer's job to make sense of the complexity of the setting and its participants, before describing and interpreting it. The longer you are in the field, the more you learn and understand about people's behaviour. What appears as messy in the beginning will seem logical after a while. Your role as participant observer also changes, from being an outsider to gaining a more central position. It is also natural that your presence will affect people's behaviour. This is called the 'observer effect', and it is not something that can or should be avoided. It will be strongest at the beginning of the fieldwork, when the participants are still getting used to your presence, and weaker later when you blend in with them (Blommaert and Jie, 2010).

Understanding an episode in its larger context is central to ethnography. In order to achieve this, the ethnographer starts by observing widely so as to get an overall picture, before narrowing down the scope. This process could include observation in the neighbourhood, the school, during lessons, in the playground and in the staffroom during breaks. However, due to time constraints, many researchers adopt what they refer to as 'an ethnographical approach', rather than ethnography itself, spending less time in the field. In these cases, they rely more heavily on formal interviews than has traditionally been common in ethnography (Copland and Creese, 2015). For example, instead of spending time in the neighbourhood to get a sense of the linguistic environment, a researcher might interview the Principal of the school and ask him or her to describe the environment and languages spoken by students in their homes.

An important part of being in the field is recording what you observe and hear by taking fieldnotes, making audio and video recordings or taking pictures, as well as collecting documents produced by teachers and students. Writing extensive notes, for example, may be possible when a teacher is teaching a class and you, the researcher, are observing at the back of the classroom. At other times, however, it may not be so easy. In my study with young refugee students, I jotted down just a few key words in a small notebook while in the classroom but enriched them when I went home in the afternoon. In this way, I could maintain a more active role, for instance by helping students with their tasks, while not having to write very much at the same time.

Audio or video recordings, if they can be made, are important in two ways. First, they help you to remember things after you have completed your fieldwork and are starting to make connections to build your analytical argument. Second, they document your learning process. This is important because once you become accustomed to the setting, it is difficult to remember what you did not know when you entered. Your recordings at the beginning are likely to be longer and more exhaustive (and perhaps subject to confusion and bewilderment) than later in the fieldwork, when they can be more focused and concise. You will also start making connections between different bits of information, contributing to ethnographic understanding and knowledge construction (Blommaert and Jie, 2010). Note that making these recordings, as well as taking still photographs, will require extra ethical permission from an ethics board, participants and possibly others too.

After fieldwork

Because ethnographic data are so diverse, there is no one method of analysis (Copland and Creese, 2015). Central, though, is the discovery of patterns, a process that starts when the ethnographer is in the field and continues after fieldwork has been completed. The researcher will start by identifying an event as important and then consider what other incidents are similar and therefore noteworthy (Emerson *et al.*, 2011). When looking for additional examples, the researcher may find variations or exceptions. Novice ethnographers may experience this as stressful, as ruining their pattern, but the process is an important part of understanding the setting. Moreover, these discoveries should encourage the researcher to reflect upon, change, elaborate or deepen earlier understandings. In the next section, I will describe my observation of a crucial incident of this kind, which encouraged me to look for similar incidents by reading and re-reading the data I had collected. With small samples, this process can be done by marking the incidents that belong to the same theme with a specific colour, for example, all those relating to one issue in yellow, all those relating to another issue in blue. Analysis of larger samples and more extensive data might benefit from the use of software, such as NVivo or Atlas.ti.

Finally, it is important that ethnographic data are interpreted by relating them to ideas in the literature. A theoretically informed analysis helps to connect data to previous commentary and previous frameworks developed by the academic community. Copland and Creese (2015:44) warn that 'if this fails to happen, the research collapses into mere description and will not reach the standards of rigour required in research'. I return to this idea when reflecting on my own research below.

Thinking about your ethnography

Consider the social settings which you listed in the earlier discussion. Choose one which you would like to investigate. Then consider these questions:

1. What would be the exact focus of your research?
2. What activities would you wish to observe and be involved in?
3. To what extent might you adopt an 'ethnographical approach' (perhaps combining ethnographic fieldwork with more formal interviews), rather than pure ethnography?
4. How much time would you need to spend prior to fieldwork, during fieldwork and after fieldwork?

My ethnography

Let me go back to the very first fieldnote I wrote in my study on young students with refugee backgrounds:

> When I enter the classroom, I see 13 young people, six of the girls wearing colourful hijabs. After the teacher has introduced me to the class, he turns to me and explains that they have watched an episode from the Norwegian TV series, *Lilyhammer*, and that he has given them the task to write a diary extract from the perspective of one of the characters. Hoping to get to know the young people a bit better, I walk around and look at their work. It is interesting to see one of the girls writing that she has just been to the bar for a beer – this would probably be an unusual situation for her, although not for Norwegian women themselves.

In this early fieldnote, I try to make sense of an event which came to illustrate a larger pattern in the data. The teacher had chosen the *Lilyhammer* television series because, as he explained to me later, many people in Norway are familiar with it and because it portrays Norwegian life. He was concerned to teach the students about Norwegian language and society, which of course is part of his job. However, he did so a way that ignored the students' own cultural resources. The pattern, therefore, was a strong 'Norwegian-only' discourse in the classroom. The next fieldnote feeds into this too, by illustrating a status difference in the classroom between Norwegian and other languages for learning:

> There is a lively atmosphere amongst the Somali girls when the Norwegian teacher turns to Khushi [one of the girls] and says that there will be a lot of class money. He explains to me that they have a rule in class that the students must pay 50 Norwegian kroner each time they speak in their mother tongue during lessons. The teacher jokingly adds that the money will be used to go on a class trip and that they have so much money that they will be able to travel around the world. Khushi answers that she is willing to pay the 50 Norwegian kroner because she wants to use Somali to explain something.

A third fieldnote shows how a student refrains from including an example from her home country in a text:

> The teacher starts the lesson by telling the students that they will read an extract from *The Diary of Anne Frank* [written by a young German-born Jew who was hiding from the Nazis in Amsterdam]. He says that Anne Frank gave voice to Jews caught in the second world war and draws a parallel to refugees in the world today. However, he does not appeal directly to the students' own experiences, even though most of them come from countries at war. The students are given an assignment which requires them to write a short summary to a friend who has not read the extract. In the conclusion, they can write their opinion. Mina [one of the students] calls on me. She tells me that the extract reminds her of the conflict in her home country between Mongolians and a Chinese minority. When I ask her if she wants to include this in her conclusion, she quickly refrains, saying that this is not important.

Connecting to theory

In this section, I show how I further interpreted the pattern of 'Norwegian-only discourse' I had identified, that is, how I went from merely describing and collating my observations to connecting them to theory. This process means we have to ask questions about the extent to which we can make claims about the outcomes of our study: 'What exactly do ethnographic data reveal? What sort of relevance do they have for "society"? How confidently can you make generalisations from your data?' (Blommaert and Jie, 2010:12). To answer these and similar questions, the most important thing to bear in mind is that ethnography is an inductive approach. To make an ethnographic argument, you need to work from your data towards theory, and not the other way around. To do so, the ethnographer applies what is often called the 'case method': an event in the data is seen as an instance of a larger situation.

More precisely, the ethnographer detects an episode in the data and uses this as a case to make a theoretical claim (Blommaert and Jie, 2010). For example, in the work described above, I used the episode about the prohibition of using the mother tongue to build the notion of language hierarchies in the classroom (with Norwegian on the top and the young people's home languages at the bottom). In other words, I used a unique episode to show that this particular case is part of a larger category of cases, which then allowed me to link the episode to larger and more overarching issues regarding language and multilingualism in Norwegian schools and society.

To then go beyond the description of this pattern, I can turn to literature on 'discourse'. Blommaert (2005) understands discourse as all forms of meaningful, semiotic (symbolic) human activity. He uses critical discourse analysis to offer 'an analysis of power *effects*, of the outcome of power, of what power *does to* people, groups, and societies, and of *how* this impact comes about' (2005:1–2, italics in original). The deepest effect of power is inequality – language is an ingredient of power and can contribute to this. Analysing discourse will give insight into how language (and other semiotic activity) is connected to wider social, cultural and historical patterns. In my analysis of the pattern described above, I connected the description of the pattern to Blommaert's theory of discourse to make sense of the effect such strict, Norwegian-only requirements had on the students' practices, as their larger repertoires were excluded from the main classroom activity. Other international empirical studies (Clyne, 2011; Daugaard, 2015; Rosiers, 2017) also describe this kind of language policing, which helped to connect my study to the larger academic community.

Ethical issues

Each ethnography comes with its own ethical challenges which the researcher needs to address locally, drawing on contextual knowledge and mutual understanding with the participants in the field (Copland and Creese, 2015). Guillemin and Gillam (2004:262) call these challenges 'ethically important moments' – 'the difficult, often subtle, and usually unpredictable situations that arise from the practice of doing research'. One such moment I needed to respond to in my own ethnography was connected to this disallowing of young people's multilingual resources from the classroom.

When I started my fieldwork, the students quickly got a sense of my positive attitude towards their knowledge of languages other than Norwegian, as I would ask questions related to multilingualism while observing and talking with them. Khushi told me that she learnt Hindi from watching Bollywood movies and that she actively used this language for her own poetry and song-writing during her spare time. One day she brought her diary to school and showed me some of her poems. When I asked her if her teachers knew about her writing, she replied that they did not. Later in the fieldwork, the class visited a photo exhibition about refugee children. Afterwards, they were asked to write about their impressions in a genre of their choice. Khushi quickly decided that she wanted to write poetry. She called on me and asked how to write this in Norwegian. Knowing about the poetry she wrote in Hindi, I replied that writing poetry in Norwegian was similar to writing it in Hindi. At first, she was not convinced, but then I suggested that if she wrote the poem in Hindi first, I could help her with a translation to Norwegian (Dewilde, 2018).

This episode was ethically challenging because, by suggesting that Khushi draw on Hindi, I included a language other than Norwegian in the classroom, even though I knew her teacher would not approve. However, as my study was about how young people make use of their multilingual resources for writing in and outside of school, I felt it was important for me to respond to Khushi's needs in a way that was in line with my theoretical assumptions of multilingualism as a resource, and not a hindrance, for learning. Also, at this point in the study, Khushi was one of the two key young people I had decided to follow more closely, which I felt gave me a bit more flexibility when making suggestions that the teachers would not have made. I should add that the teachers made me feel very welcome in the class at all times. If I had sensed that including Hindi in poetry writing in the classroom really could not be tolerated, I would probably have solved the dilemma differently, for example by co-writing a poem with Khushi during an individual interview somewhere else.

Ethical dilemmas

The example in this section illustrates how ethical dilemmas can occur when the researcher is involved ethnographically in what is being researched. What other dilemmas of this kind can you imagine? How might you address these dilemmas so that your ethnographic research is ethically secure?

Some recommendations

As should be clear by now, ethnography is a time-consuming method. As a researcher, you may not, for instance, have time to get to know the neighbourhood before exploring the school and classroom activity. I have already mentioned the possibility of doing more intensive short-term ethnography or combining participant observation with more targeted methods in an ethnographical approach. Another option is to return to a site you already know, for example from an earlier training placement. You may want to study a specific subject or follow one class over a period of time. Be aware, though, that your role will change from being the student you were during your placement to being a researcher, and therefore your relationship with the people in the field should change too.

A good way to get a feel for doing ethnographies is to read those done by others. In connection with my own work on multilingualism and literacy, for example, I found it useful to read Heath (1983), Heller (2006) and Blackledge and Creese (2010). It was interesting to see how they tell their story. Also, ask more experienced ethnographers about decisions they have had to make in the field and about their development as ethnographers.

Janesick (2003) compares becoming a good qualitative researcher with being a dancer. Before you start dancing, you need to do stretching and practice exercises; similarly, with ethnography you have to cultivate your skills in interviewing, observing, writing, reflecting and so on. It may be a good idea to observe a lesson with another student or your supervisor and compare fieldnotes. How do their notes compare to yours? What did they notice and how did they write about it? Perhaps too you have the possibility to be part of a research team; Creese *et al.* (2008) and Creese and Blackledge (2012) in particular have written extensively on the benefits of team ethnography.

The aspect most commonly criticized in ethnographies is that analytical strategies are often not made explicit enough (Copland and Creese, 2015). Therefore, make sure you write about them in a clear and rigorous manner, probably in the methodology section of your report. Do not leave it up to the reader to search in appendices or assume that your strategies are intuitive and obvious. Copland and Creese (2015) provide a number of specific suggestions about this process. First, a good way of making your strategies transparent is by providing one example of every kind of data you have used, for example, a fieldnote, an interview transcript, a picture or the transcript of an audio recording. They note too that 'once examiners [or any readers] understand what materials will provide evidence, they will have more confidence in the analytical arguments that follow' (2015:212). Second, describe the stages of your analysis in detail. How were the data drafted and redrafted, cut and pasted, and moved around? This will give readers an insight into the rigour of your analytical process and how your arguments were developed.

Conclusion

If you are interested in understanding the complexity of a particular context, doing an ethnography is a suitable approach. It requires that you spend time in the field, build relationships with participants and document social activity. In your report, you will want to tell the story you believe warrants your data and to describe your analytical strategies that give evidence to your argument in a thorough manner. The aim is not to claim representativeness for a larger population but rather to demonstrate complexity and produce theoretical statements. Here are some final points to summarize ethnography as a valuable approach to carrying out research:

- The aim of ethnography is to demonstrate complexity.
- Ethnography is not just about description but also very much about interpreting the data by connecting it to theory.
- The ethnographic researcher's close involvement in the research setting gives rise to particular ethical issues which need to be carefully considered and addressed.

Recommended reading

Conteh, J. (Ed.) (2018) *Researching Education for Social Justice in Multilingual Settings: Ethnographic Principles in Qualitative Research*. London: Bloomsbury.

This anthology illustrates a range of methodological principles for ethnographically informed research and provides practical examples of research projects concerning multilingualism and education in diverse settings.

Emerson, R.M., Fretz, R.I. and Shaw, L.L. (2011) *Writing Ethnographic Fieldnotes*. Second edition. Chicago, IL: University of Chicago Press.

An excellent introduction to the writing of fieldnotes and their analysis.

Selleck, C.L. (2017) Ethnographic chats: A best of both method for ethnography. *Sky Journal of Linguistics*, 30, 151–162.

This article describes ethnographic conversations that can be useful when doing a short-term ethnography.

References

Blackledge, A. and Creese, A. (2010) *Multilingualism: A Critical Perspective*. London: Continuum.

Blommaert, J. (2005) *Discourse: A Critical Introduction*. Cambridge: Cambridge University Press.

Blommaert, J. and Jie, D. (2010) *Ethnographic Fieldwork: A Beginner's Guide*. Bristol: Multilingual Matters.

Clyne, M. (2011) Three is too many in Australia. In: C. Hélot and M. Ó Laoire (Eds.) *Language Policy for the Multilingual Classroom: Pedagogy of the Possible*. Bristol: Multilingual Matters.

Copland, F. and Creese, A. (2015) *Linguistic Ethnography: Collecting, Analysing and Presenting Data*. Thousand Oaks, CA: Sage.

Creese, A. and Blackledge, A. (2012) Voice and meaning-making in team ethnography. *Anthropology & Education Quarterly*, 43(3), 306–324.

Creese, A., Bhatt, A., Bhojani, N. and Martin, P. (2008) Fieldnotes in team ethnography: Researching complementary schools. *Qualitative Research*, 8(2), 197–215.

Daugaard, L.M. (2015) *Sproglig praksis i og omkring modersmålsundervisning: En lingvistisk etnografisk undersøgelse (Linguistic practice in and around mother-tongue teaching: A linguistic ethnographic study)*. PhD thesis for Aarhus University, Denmark.

Dewilde, J. (2017) Translation and translingual remixing: A young person developing as a writer. *International Journal of Bilingualism*. [Online] https://doi.org/10.1177/1367006917740975 (accessed 11 June 2018).

Dewilde, J. (2018) 'It's just in my heart': A portrait of a translingual young person as a writer of poetry. In: T.O. Engen, L.A. Kulbrandstad and S. Lied (Eds.) *Norwegian Perspectives on Education and Diversity*. Newcastle upon Tyne: Cambridge Scholars Publishing.

Emerson, R.M., Fretz, R.I. and Shaw, L.L. (2011) *Writing Ethnographic Fieldnotes*. Second edition. Chicago, IL: University of Chicago Press.

Guillemin, M. and Gillam, L. (2004) Ethics, reflexivity, and 'ethically important moments' in research. *Qualitative Inquiry*, 10(2), 261–280.

Hammersley, M. and Atkinson, P. (2007) *Ethnography: Principles in Practice*. Third edition. Abingdon: Routledge.

Heath, S.B. (1983) *Ways with Words: Language, Life, and Work in Communities and Classrooms*. Cambridge: Cambridge University Press.

Heller, M. (2006) *Linguistic Minorities and Modernity: A Sociolinguistic Ethnography*. Second edition. London: Continuum.

Heller, M. (2008) Doing ethnography. In: L. Wei and M.G. Moyer (Eds.) *The Blackwell Guide to Research Methods in Bilingualism and Multilingualism*. Malden, MA: Blackwell.

Janesick, V.J. (2003) The choreography of qualitative research design: Minuets, improvisations and crystalization. In: N.K. Denzin and Y.S. Lincoln (Eds.) *Strategies of Qualitative Inquiry*. Second edition. Thousand Oaks, CA: Sage.

Knoblauch, H. (2005) Focused ethnography. *Forum Qualitative Sozialforschung / Forum: Qualitative Social Research*, 6(3), Art.44.

Millen, D.R. (2000) Rapid ethnography: Time deepening strategies for HCI field research. *Proceedings of the 3rd Conference on Designing Interactive Systems: Processes, Practices, Methods, and Techniques.* DIS '00, 280–288.

Pink, S. and Morgan, J. (2013) Short-term ethnography: Intense routes to knowing. *Symbolic Interaction*, 36(3), 351–361.

Rosiers, K. (2017) Unravelling translanguaging: The potential of translanguaging as a scaffold among teachers and pupils in superdiverse classrooms in Flemish education. In: B. Paulsrud, J. Rosén, B. Straszer and Å. Wedin (Eds.) *New Perspectives on Translanguaging and Education.* Bristol: Multilingual Matters.

Chapter 12

Case study

Tunde Rozsahegyi

Introduction

There is no single, clear-cut formula to apply when making decisions about what kind of overall research strategy to adopt for an educationally focused, empirical investigation. However, development of objectives, research questions and potential outcomes can steer a researcher towards a particularly suitable, overall design. When understood, developed and then persuasively applied, this design can then provide logic, coherence and credibility to the research investigation.

This chapter explores 'case study', one of the more popular but also surprisingly demanding research designs. Key definitions and characteristics of case study are discussed, then issues relating to sampling, data gathering, validity, ethics and generalization are explored, by drawing on experiences of my own research project which used this design. Overall, a pragmatic but critical overview is provided of issues which a researcher is likely to meet when planning, conducting and evaluating case-study research, and when deciding how its findings might inform professional and academic discourse and practice. The chapter will strengthen your understanding of the benefits and the limitations of case study and allow you critically to consider its adoption for your own research project.

What is case study?

Case study is a design for research which is particularly suitable for developing, extending and deepening understanding and knowledge about aspects of the real-life world. The strategy has been used for many years in applied and natural sciences and its roots can be traced back to life sciences, such as criminology, medicine and psychology. It now also has recognition and prestige in the social sciences, providing a flexible basis for political and cultural studies and sociology, and for educational research itself, especially when addressing issues from an interpretive stance. As explained by Punch (2014:124), 'good case studies, especially in situations where our knowledge is shallow, fragmentary, incomplete or non-existent, have a valuable contribution to make in social research'.

Hammersley and Gomm (2000) warn, however, that the term itself is not always used in a clear and fixed sense, and indeed, a degree of ambiguity and uncertainty about what constitutes this kind of design and how it is applied continues to be evident. Current publications tend to use the more well-established definitions from key authors, such as Stake, Bassey and Yin, and these writers have indeed made influential contributions to conceptualizing the notion of case study over the last two decades.

Bassey (1999:47) defined case-study research as 'a study of a singularity, conducted in depth and in natural settings'. Yin (2009:18) has written similarly, explaining it as investigation of a 'contemporary phenomenon in depth and within its real-life context, especially when the boundaries between phenomenon and context are not clearly evident'. A third explanation comes from Swanborn (2010), who claims that whilst other strategies may be extensive and provide breadth to an investigation, case studies are 'intensive approaches', in other words they involve very detailed, explicit enquiries. Then in Yin's (2018:5) conceptualization, 'the distinctive need for case study research arises out of the desire to understand complex social phenomena … and to retain a holistic and real-word perspective'.

Further to this, Stake (2005:444) has provided the idea that 'a case study is both a process of inquiry about the case and the product of that inquiry'. This indicates a way to further unpack the notion, first by exploring meanings associated with the idea of 'the case', then by examining some perspectives about how to 'study' such cases in order to reach the result of the chosen enquiry.

The 'case'

Case-study research is most frequently associated with an examination of characteristics and qualities of human beings, their relations, activities and interactions. Stake (1995:2) suggests that 'people and programs clearly are prospective cases'. Yin (2018:14) provides a more comprehensive list of examples, when suggesting that individuals, organizations, processes, programmes, neighbourhoods, institutions and even events may be considered as 'cases'. Much earlier, Merriam (1988) implied that as well as studying people and organizations, any aspect of real life may be considered as the focus, and Robson and McCartan (2016:152) agree, declaring that 'the case can be virtually anything'. So, for example, physical entities or elements of these, a nursery's facilities for outdoor play perhaps, can be as usefully addressed through case study as the processes and activities taking place within that physical space, such as children's use of outdoor tricycles. Policies, for example, a university's admission framework, may also be explored as a case, as well as the procedures by which that policy is implemented and how it is manifest in practice.

This broad scope can be clarified by delineating different types of case for case-study research. Stake's (1995; 2005) influential publications make such distinctions based on an underpinning rationale of this kind. In his categorization, there are three types: intrinsic, instrumental and collective. In *intrinsic* case studies, there is an inherent interest embedded into the case that invites the researcher to learn more about its characteristics and peculiarities in order to describe and explain it. In this sense, the case is studied for its own merits, for closer understanding, not only of its specific features, but also of any unusual elements that stray from what might be considered normal or average. *Instrumental* case studies, however, do more to exploit in a questioning way the ordinary manifestations of a phenomenon. The aim is to gain a deeper understanding, which makes the research process more exploratory in nature than with an intrinsic approach. The third type, *collective* case studies, uses more than one instrumental case for analysis, 'chosen because it is believed that understanding them will lead to better understanding, and perhaps better theorizing, about a still larger collection of cases' (Stake, 2005:446).

'Study'

As for the process of actually studying the case, Yin (2018) suggests that the researchers have at least two overall options when reflecting this in the design. Depending on the research intent and the nature of the phenomenon under investigation, as well as on conceptual understanding gained from the literature review, either a single-case or multiple-case design may be adopted. A *single-case design* focuses either on a common manifestation of a phenomenon which is frequently evident in everyday life, or on an instance which seems untypical, unusual or peculiar. An example of the former might, therefore, be an investigation into a frequently or long-used reading scheme; an example of the latter would be an investigation into the introduction or piloting of a new reading scheme. The single unit of case-study analysis would be the chosen reading scheme in one primary-school classroom. In this case, the researcher will aim to explore and reveal as many different dimensions and characteristics of the reading scheme's implementation as possible, taking into account a range of views, such as those of teachers, teaching assistants, parents and, perhaps, the children themselves. Expected outcomes of such single-unit investigation will be a detailed descriptive and explanatory account of dimensions and characteristics of the use or introduction of the reading scheme in that classroom.

More complex studies may require a *multiple-case design*, a concept which overlaps with that of collective case studies outlined earlier. An example of this would be if a researcher wished to investigate evidence of values and processes related to inclusive education in the post-compulsory education sector in a local-government authority in the UK. To do this, the researcher might decide to examine two or more types of inclusive practice within that authority, for example, in a further-education college, a traditional 'red-brick' university and a newer, post-1992 university. By examining the characteristics and processes linked to inclusive provision in each of these units, it would also be possible to accumulate understanding and evidence of shared (or differentiated) values and processes which underlie their work.

Regardless of whether the researcher opts to use a single- or multiple-case design, and regardless of whether the study is intrinsic, instrumental or collective, one further feature is usually important in case-study research, that is the 'boundedness' of the case study itself (Stake, 2005). This may be geographical (the setting of the research), temporal (the time period which is investigated, which in education might be a course, a lesson, or even a single episode within a lesson), or conceptual (the idea or entity) being investigated, or indeed a combination of these and others. Case-study researchers appreciate and recognize too that the case or cases, as real-life issues, are always embedded into and influenced by particular contextual circumstances beyond such boundaries. It is the researcher's obligation to decide on, understand and take into account these circumstances, and also to explain them to the reader in their research report.

Whichever type of case-study approach is chosen and whatever its boundaries, Gillham's (2000:32) colourful explanation of the process is very apt: 'Case study research is very much like detective work. Nothing is disregarded: everything is weighted and sifted and checked or corroborated.' Indeed, case-study research can be particularly enhanced by the use of mixed or combined methods of data gathering, involving questionnaires, interviews, observations or other methods. In terms of the type of data collected, quantitative can sometimes be as helpful as qualitative, despite the predominantly interpretivist nature of most research of this kind.

Overall, the primary driver should be the desire to tease out and scrutinize the specifics of the chosen research issue, as it is evident in the diverse realities of research participants (Robson, 2011). The single or multiple units which are chosen provide an investigative platform for this, but should not wholly become the subject of the investigation itself. So, in relation to the examples above, the case study would focus on the reading strategy or evidence for values of inclusive education, rather than on other elements in the classroom or in the chosen post-compulsory education settings.

Design

You wish to investigate ways in which handwriting is taught in schools. Reviewing the literature, you identify some methods which can be used when handwriting is taught. However, this conceptual understanding reveals little about how such approaches are actually applied in practice. You would like to use your research to gain this closer understanding of actual teaching, and you decide to adopt a case-study strategy, in order to achieve this.

1. How might you design the case study? What might be its 'boundaries'?
2. What would be the benefits and limitations of using an intrinsic, instrumental or collective approach?
3. What would be the benefits and limitations of using single- or multiple-case design?

Implementing case study

The chapter now examines specific methodological issues evident in my own case-study research (Rozsahegyi, 2014) and how these were addressed. As explained in greater detail in Chapter 3, the main objective of this investigation was to gather and examine socially and educationally relevant perceptions amongst parents, practitioners and others of the development and learning of children with cerebral palsy. Research questions focused on participants' multiple views about these children's identities, about processes and contexts providing them with support, and about future aspirations and priorities.

Sampling

To operationalize the case study, the geographical area for the research had to be defined. A local-government authority in the West Midlands in England was chosen, where, in line with national trends, a broad range of early-years childcare and education options were available to families with young children with cerebral palsy. This multifaceted profile of services provided stimulus to examine the main research issue under a range of circumstances. Following Yin's (2009) classification, described above, the research was therefore designed in the form of multiple units for data collection, allowing perspectives relating to different types of provisions and different participant roles and responsibilities to be examined.

Six specific units were chosen to represent the range of early-years provision available in this local authority: a private nursery; a local-authority maintained pre-school setting; a special nursery; a children centre; a specialized, charitable 'conductive education' provision nearby, accessed by families on a voluntary basis; and home-based specialist input provided by the local-authority support services. Six children, each receiving provision from one or more of these services, were selected, their parents and practitioners also, as well as representatives of the local authority's specialist services which supported the families and some of the settings which the children attended. Sampling – of units and of the research participants themselves – was, therefore, 'purposive', deliberately chosen to 'illustrate a wide range of the dimensions of interest' (Coe, 2012:49) and to represent maximum variation within the defined geographical boundaries. It was anticipated that this variety would provide relevant and rich data to answer the research questions (Simons, 2009).

Combined methods

As should be the case in every research study, a key concern in this investigation was to select data-collection methods carefully, so that informative data would be gathered, and so that 'gross misfits – that is, when you are planning to use one mode of inquiry but another is really more advantageous' (Yin, 2018:8) – could be avoided. A pragmatic, mixed-methods approach was therefore developed, whereby 'the investigator gathers both quantitative (closed-ended) and qualitative (open-ended) data, integrates the two, and then draws interpretations on the combined strengths of both sets of data to understand research problems' (Creswell, 2015:2). It included an authority-wide questionnaire survey with parents and early-years practitioners, as well as face-to-face interviews with parents of the six children, the early-years practitioners who worked with them and representatives of local-authority support services. Observations were conducted of children's activities and interactions in their early-years settings. Analysis involved, first of all, exploration and interpretation of data from each data source, then comparison and integration of findings from all sources, so that an in-depth and 'holistic' understanding of the phenomenon could be reached (Simons, 2009; Yin, 2009). Credible interpretations and arguments, reflecting similarities and contrasts between groups, could be drawn and the 'story' of the case study as a whole could be conveyed (Bassey, 1999).

Trustworthiness

Strategies to establish trustworthiness and validity of the data were pursued, for instance, through piloting, data recording and data checks. This process sought to ensure, as far as possible, that each of the various data-gathering methods measured what it intended to measure (Coe, 2012), that interpretation of findings could be regarded as truthful (Mukherji and Albon, 2010), and that the study as a whole would be objective, consistent and replicable (Roberts-Holmes, 2005). Furthermore, the investigation was designed to be 'democratic' (Simons, 2009), in that it represented multiple voices of parents (mothers and fathers), practitioners, service leaders and, of course, children themselves as evident in their observed interactions and activities. The whole process captured different outlooks on the same phenomenon and enabled triangulation, the cross-verification of data from a range of sources, to be carried out, an important tool for achieving a sense of trustworthiness in the data and its research outcomes.

Ethics

Respecting and protecting the personal and professional identities of participants was a prominent concern throughout planning, implementation and evaluation of the case study. A range of ethical deliberations were applied for each research method, such as gaining and maintaining informed consent, avoidance of harm and negative experiences, and respect for participants' cultural, social and professional backgrounds. Particular aspects which arose related to ways in which participants perceived and talked about disability and about related professional and personal issues, and also to the ways in which findings were disseminated amongst participants and the academic community once the research was complete.

Taking into account the variety of research participants, their differing roles and connections to the children and their personal or professional relations to each other, anonymity and confidentiality had to be kept in mind all the time. Sensitivity to the views and opinions which participants expressed was a pressing requirement, as they sometimes revealed perspectives which indicated dissatisfaction with other stakeholders' approaches, or personal views on the children's development, or critically evaluative opinions on the support the children received. In handling this complicated process, I realized that the researcher must be, above all, professionally aware of the potential discomfort and difficulty caused by the research if inappropriately carried out or carelessly reported, yet also find ways to reach outcomes of critical value for the educational field being examined.

Planning your case study

Drawing on the example described in this chapter, consider these ideas for your own case-study research:

1. What topic in which you are interested might be suited to a case-study approach? What could be your research questions?
2. What combination of data-collection methods might be appropriate to use to address these research questions? Which participants might the data collection involve?
3. What issues of trustworthiness and ethics would you need to consider? How might you address these issues?

Generalization

Denscombe (2014) encapsulates the relationship between the specific and the general in a frequently-cited phrase about the aims of case-study research: to 'illuminate the general by looking at the particular' (2014:54). Indeed, when case studies are carried out with methodological rigour, they can be an instructive way of informing policy development, professional practice, future research, and even construction of new theoretical perspectives (Simons, 2009). However, case-study researchers can also be open to criticism, often linked to this issue of 'generalization' and arising from both the interpretivist nature of much of the data and the interpretivist research paradigm which underlies most such studies as a whole. As explained by Bassey (1999:44):

> The purpose of research is to advance knowledge by describing and interpreting the phenomena of the world in attempts to get shared meanings with others. Interpretation is a search for deeper perspectives on particular events and for theoretical insights. It may offer possibilities, but no certainties, as to the outcome of future events.

Indeed, my case study did not offer 'certainties', and few, if any, generalizations which might be applied elsewhere. Instead, it created opportunity for readers to gain a 'vicarious experience' (Stake, 2005:454) – in other words, conclusions and recommendations which encouraged them to reflect, make connections to their own experiences and contexts, and thereby assimilate or reject aspects of findings. As a research design, case study raises this kind of awareness and understanding. It is 'naturalistic' (Stake, 2005:454) in its generalization at a theoretical level, more strongly so if its outcomes are in harmony with readers' own contextual, professional and personal experiences (Swanborn, 2010).

In this respect, my research used its investigation of 'the particular' ultimately to argue for a more distinctive pedagogical identity for children with cerebral palsy, one that should be perceived and pursued as an all-encompassing entity and which should reflect strengthened notions of upbringing and pedagogy (Rozsahegyi, 2014). Practical recommendations arising from the study included renewed academic and professional discourse, revitalized training for professionals, and greater practical involvement of parents in early-years provision.

'Naturalistic generalization'

Find and read a journal article which reports on a case-study investigation and which is relevant to your own research interest. Examine the ways in which the researcher conveys and discusses findings and makes recommendations. To what extent does the author exploit the potential of case study, claimed by Denscombe (2014:54), to 'illuminate the general by looking at the particular'? What cautionary steps might you take in the findings of your own case-study investigation, so as to reflect Stake's (2005) idea of 'naturalistic generalization'?

Conclusion

This chapter has provided a pragmatic overview of case study as a valuable framework for research and has illustrated the process of designing, conducting and evaluating such studies. The flexibility and adaptability of case study, within defined parameters, means that it can be used as a research design for both small- and large-scale investigations. To summarize the main points in the chapter:

- The aim of case study as a research design is to make in-depth, holistic investigation within boundaried contexts.
- Case-study design can combine a range of research methods and draw data from one or more sites and sources.
- Findings of case-study research should be interpreted and presented carefully, so readers can assimilate or reject findings and make use of them as appropriate for their own personal, professional or academic situations.

Recommended reading

I was fortunate, when doing the research described in this chapter, that important writers, such as Robert Stake, Robert Yin and Helen Simons, were extending academic thinking about case-study design at around the same time. These authors and their literature remain very valuable for case-study researchers today. In addition, here are some more contemporary, also very useful publications:

Hancock, D.R. and Algozzine, B. (2017) *Doing Case Study Research: A Practical Guide for Beginning Researchers.* Third edition. New York: Teachers College Press.

This book covers in detail the processes of designing, conducting and disseminating case-study research.

Hamilton, L. and Corbett-Whittier, C. (2013) *Using Case Study in Education Research.* London: Sage.

A highly accessible book for those who are comparatively new to case-study research. The semi-formal language and embedded practical examples and tasks will help early researchers apply theoretical ideas to their own research design.

Journal of Case Studies in Education: www.aabri.com/jcse.html

Although publication of this journal has now ceased, its archive gives the researcher access to a broad range of case-study reports.

References

Bassey, M. (1999) *Case Study Research in Educational Settings.* Buckingham: Open University Press.
Coe, R.J. (2012) Conducting your research. In: J. Arthur, M. Waring, R. Coe and L. Hedges (Eds.) *Research Methods and Methodologies in Education.* London: Sage.
Creswell, J.W. (2015) *A Concise Introduction to Mixed Methods Research.* London: Sage.
Denscombe, M. (2014) *The Good Research Guide.* Fifth edition. Maidenhead: Open University Press.
Gillham, B. (2000) *Case Study Research Methods.* London: Continuum.
Hammersley, M. and Gomm, R. (2000) Introduction. In: R. Gomm, M. Hammersley and P. Foster (Eds.) *Case Study Method.* London: Sage.
Merriam, S.B. (1988) *Case Study Research in Education: A Qualitative Approach.* San Francisco, CA: Jossey-Bass.
Mukherji, P. and Albon, D. (2010) *Research Methods in Early Childhood.* London: Sage.
Punch, K.F. (2014) *Introduction to Social Research.* Third edition. London: Sage.
Roberts-Holmes, G. (2005) *Doing your Early Years Project.* London: Sage.
Robson, C. (2011) *Real world research.* Third edition. Oxford: Blackwell.
Robson, C. and McCartan, K. (2016) *Real World Research: A Resource for Users of Social Research Methods in Applied Settings.* Fourth edition. Oxford: Blackwell.
Rozsahegyi, T. (2014) *A Bio-Ecological Case Study Investigation into Outlooks on the Development and Learning of Young Children with Cerebral Palsy.* PhD thesis for Centre for Education Studies, University of Warwick, UK.
Simons, H. (2009) *Case Study Research in Practice.* London: Sage.
Stake, R.E. (1995) *The Art of Case Study Research.* London: Sage.
Stake, R.E. (2005) Qualitative case studies. In: N.K. Denzin and Y.S. Lincoln (Eds.) *The Sage Handbook of Qualitative Research.* Third edition. London: Sage.
Swanborn, P. (2010) *Case Study Research: What, Why and How?* London: Sage.
Yin, R.K. (2009) *Case Study Research: Design and Methods.* Fourth edition. London: Sage.
Yin, R.K. (2018) *Case Study Research and Applications: Design and Methods.* Sixth edition: London: Sage.

Chapter 13

Grounded theory

Mike Lambert

Introduction

Search on the Internet for images of 'results of grounded theory' – you will find quite intricate charts and diagrams. Some of these describe the processes of grounded theory itself, but look instead at those which illustrate the outcomes of actual investigations which have used a grounded-theory approach. Note how these take a large or complicated idea which has emerged from the research and represent it in a flow diagram, using boxes, arrows and other graphics.

Such images help us to understand what the words, 'grounded theory', mean. 'Theory' is what is produced by the research and encapsulated in the diagrams, while 'grounded' indicates that this theory has emerged from data collected during the investigation. The theory is 'grounded in', or wholly drawn from, real data.

The overriding purpose of grounded-theory research is, therefore, to obtain organized, believable ideas from practical investigation. It is a 'theory generating research methodology', the end product of which is 'a set of grounded concepts [which form] a theoretical framework that explains how and why persons, organizations, communities, or nations experience and respond to events, challenges, or problematic situations' (Corbin and Holt, 2011:113). In this chapter we examine how – if you wish to explore and formalize a particular concept or process in this way – grounded theory may be a suitable approach for your research.

Grounded theory

Grounded theory dates back more than 50 years to the work of two American researchers, Barney Glaser and Anselm Strauss, and their seminal work, *The Discovery of Grounded Theory: Strategies for Qualitative Research* (Glaser and Strauss, 1967). Their aim was simple: to show 'how the discovery of theory from data – systematically obtained and analyzed in social research – can be furthered' (1967:1).

Glaser and Strauss set out a range of strategies for this approach. Many were alternatives to quantitative analysis which was dominant at that time. For instance, they advocated 'multi-faceted investigation' (1967:65), that is, the use of what we would now call 'mixed methods', as well as flexibility, saying that data-collection methods need not be pre-planned in advance but can be determined as the project progresses: 'Emerging theory points to the next steps' (1967:47).

Analysis involved what Fontana and Frey (2008:123) later called the 'painstaking emphasis on coding data'. Crucial to this were notions of 'categories' and their 'properties'.

These could be generated by the researcher by noting similarities and differences in the collected data through coding systems, with potential for generalization of the theory which is eventually produced.

Glaser and Strauss urged 'hard study of much data' as part of this approach. Data collection, analysis and theory generation should as far as possible be done together: 'They should blur and intertwine continually and cumulatively, from the beginning of an investigation to its end' (1967:43). In this way the theory solidifies, modifications to it become fewer and fewer, and the researcher becomes committed to it. Verification comes from 'theoretical saturation', when collection of more data results in no further changes:

> When the researcher is convinced that his [*sic*] conceptual framework forms a systematic theory, that it is a reasonably accurate statement of the matters studied, that it is couched in a form possible for others to use in studying a similar area, and that he can publish his results with confidence, then he is near to the end of his research ... By the close of the investigation, the researcher's conviction about his own theory will be hard to shake ... This conviction does not mean that his analysis is the only plausible one that could be based on this data, but only that he has high confidence in its credibility.
>
> (Glaser and Strauss, 1967:225)

After Glaser and Strauss' ideas had set out the basic tenets of grounded theory, further development and adaptation by others swiftly followed. Three decades later, Dey (1999:23) was suggesting that there were 'probably as many versions of grounded theory as there [are] "grounded theorists"'. These variations included ongoing elaboration by the original authors themselves: Strauss (who died in 1996) focused on refining techniques for coding collected data, while Glaser (principally on his Grounded Theory Institute website) still advocates and further develops the classic elements of grounded theory. Among longstanding commentators are Juliet Corbin, Kathy Charmaz and Cathy Urquhart, and new contributors to discussion and development regularly appear.

Not everyone, however, has been enthusiastic about the approach. Particularly strident, critical comment came from Thomas and James (2006), who claimed that there was little in grounded theory to distinguish it from normal qualitative studies. They criticized use of the 'grounded theory' term, when (as they saw it) what is produced in such research is not theory; 'ground' is inaccurate when the process is really about interpretation; and grounded theory itself is less like discovery, more like invention. The approach 'oversimplifies complex meanings and interpretations in data', 'constrains analysis', and makes 'inappropriate claims to explanation and prediction' (2006:768).

Thoughts on grounded theory

Based on what you have read in the first part of this chapter:

1. What are your initial thoughts about 'grounded theory'?
2. What makes it different from other research approaches? What makes it similar?
3. To what extent, in your opinion, can research produce 'theory'? To what extent is it simply about 'interpretation', as claimed by Thomas and James (2006)?

Examples

Despite (or perhaps because of) its flexibility and variety, grounded theory has become a well-used methodology in many areas of research. A simple search in your student-library catalogue will produce a range of journal articles reporting on investigations which claim to have used the approach.

The most common area, worldwide, is the health sciences, for example the investigation by Asemani *et al.* (2015) into medical trainees' approach to clinical responsibilities in Iran. Research in business management also finds the approach appealing, for instance, Packirisamy *et al.*'s (2017) examination of early-career burnout amongst workers in information-technology services in India.

Grounded theory has also been used in studies in education (more, it has to be said, in relation to organizational and interpersonal issues than to curriculum and learning) and writers on research, such as Basit (2010), have often recommended its use in this field. Among international grounded-theory studies published before my own research were Van Sluys *et al.*'s (2006) examination of classroom discourse amongst children in American schools and Thornberg's (2008) development of a category system of school rules in Sweden. More currently, Parker (2018) has investigated development of social identity amongst high-school women's choir participants in the USA, and Karpouza and Emvalotis (2018) have explored teacher–student relationships in higher education in Greece. A similarly themed Master's dissertation by Cullingworth (2014) on Canadian teachers' perspectives on their relationships with secondary-school students illustrates how grounded theory can be used at various levels of study.

Topics

The research studies cited in this section (and others available online) give an indication of the kind of topics which lend themselves to grounded-theory investigation, namely where thinking and practice would benefit from deeper or more systematized, formalized or theoretical understanding. Taking into account current issues and practice in education, as well your own professional and personal interests and experiences, consider some ideas or processes which might be worth investigating with a grounded-theory approach.

Choosing grounded theory

The research for which I used grounded theory was that which I described in Chapter 4 of this book: an investigation into notions of 'difficulty and challenge' in the curriculum of so-called 'gifted and talented' children and young people (Lambert, 2009). Drawing from questionnaires and interviews with children, teachers and others, as well as from lesson observations, I sought to build an understanding of what constituted difficulty and challenge in learning, and how suitable levels were maintained in curricular practice.

My overall wishes in choosing my approach were two-fold: first, to collect experiences and perspectives of those in the field, including children themselves, and then, from these, to formulate some kind of conceptual framework for what constituted curricular 'difficulty and challenge'. Grounded theory seemed to provide a useful methodological framework for achieving these aims, especially as Charmaz (2005:507) had described the approach as both 'a method of inquiry and … the product of inquiry', in other words an all-encompassing concept. It also seemed to take account of my perception that ideas about difficulty and challenge are not totally absent (they exist in the minds of teachers, learners and others already) but are largely unformulated: 'implicit in data, waiting to be discovered' (Cohen *et al.*, 2007:491).

As the investigation got under way, I found there were several further attractions in the grounded-theory approach. The first was that it allowed me to *begin at an early stage* in the process of understanding. There needed to be no preliminary hypothesis, other than that difficulty and challenge seemed complex, of considerable significance to teaching and learning as a whole and deserving of deeper scrutiny and explanation. Nevertheless, the extent to which it was possible to set aside my own prior ideas about the topic, so that I could actually begin at this early stage, had to be confronted, an issue discussed in more detail below.

Second came the approach's *flexibility*, allowing me to use what data were available and what served best the generation of relevant ideas. The overall approach seemed exploratory, largely reflecting a qualitative paradigm, but I found I could also include more positivist elements – numbers, percentages, particularly from the questionnaires – to add to the overall picture which I was seeking. This was accompanied by an element of *elasticity* in outcomes of the research, the notion found in the writings of Charmaz that there is no pre-determined end to the investigation: it simply gets as far as it can. I could match the extent of my data collection and production of theory to the normal dimensions of a doctoral research study.

A third related appeal was that even though outcomes were unlikely to be conclusive, grounded theory offered the prospect of a *single perspective*: '*plausible* relationships proposed among *concepts* and *sets of concepts*' (Strauss and Corbin, 1998:168, italics in the original). Again, this is an issue examined further below.

Fourth, grounded theory allowed me to *combine proximity to practical activity with a critical, academic approach*. Data collection involved going out into Schwandt's (2003:362) 'rough ground' of practice, followed by close critical scrutiny and interpretation of the data collected.

Finally, grounded theory encouraged me to *plan the project as I went along*. It was difficult at the start to work out where the research would go. What ideas might emerge? What data would be useful to extend or test these emerging outcomes? Designing the research was therefore an ongoing process which developed while the investigation was taking place. One step accomplished determined the next to be addressed, and the need to envisage all the stages of my research project at the start was lessened.

This outlining of positives should not be taken to mean that the grounded-theory process was problem-free or even 'problem-light'. Reduced forward planning, as well as flexibility, elasticity and other presumed advantages, meant that there seemed to be even more decisions to take than in a standard investigation. I continually needed to work out what to do, what data to collect, how to handle data gathered, and how to progress to a next stage – and to justify to myself and to others all the judgements that I made along the way.

Issue 1: How to use the literature?

One specific issue which needed a prompt but important decision related to the use of relevant published literature and other research already in the public domain. If my grounded-theory investigation was to start from an 'early stage' in understanding, what place should literature and research done previously by others have in this process?

The usual approach in research projects is for this material to be examined in a literature review before empirical enquiry takes place, thereby providing a background of understanding within which the new investigation can be located. Then later, after data collection and interpretation, the researcher can look back at the reviewed literature and use findings of the new research to confirm, deny or enhance the ideas scrutinized earlier.

Glaser and Strauss' (1967) original outlook, however, was different to this. They advocated that the researcher should begin with the collection of data without taking published literature into account. Theory could then be drawn from these data, and only subsequently, at a late stage, applied to already published ideas. So data collection does not emerge from and then enlighten what is already in the literature but *vice versa*: data come exclusively from the field, early conceptualization is made from these data, then study of the literature comes afterwards to confirm, critically inform and elaborate on the outcomes. As Corbin and Strauss (2015:49) confirm: 'Researchers don't want to be so steeped in the literature as to be constrained or even stifled by it'.

In terms of a research study, this perspective means writing a late, rather than early literature review. Ideas from already published literature are only related back to data gathered and outcomes reached by the researcher's grounded-theory outcomes, rather than informing the focus and process of his or her research itself. The problem with this, however, is that no-one comes to a research topic without having done some previous reading or without pertinent experience. Every researcher has some early notions about the topic which she or he will be investigating. How can these simply be ignored or discounted until the grounded-theory investigation has taken place?

In my case, previous teaching and training experience brought with it plenty of previous practical and academic scrutiny of ideas and published literature about difficulty and challenge in the curriculum. As a university tutor, I was regularly praising trainee teachers for maintaining suitable levels of challenge in their lessons, or advising on how to strengthen this aspect of their practice. In such circumstances, the idea of developing theory 'from nothing except data' was unrealistic. It was better to recognize that my research would actually organize, fashion, change and extend thinking which I already had in diffuse, preliminary outline already.

Even then, the dilemma about how to use published literature remained. To what extent should I review the literature before data collection commenced? A potentially illuminating paper by McGhee, Marland and Atkinson (2007) analysed two sides of the issue. Marland's position was that 'the initial review was essential in showing that this approach had not been taken before and therefore that the results would constitute a unique addition to knowledge' (McGhee *et al.*, 2007:337). McGhee, on the other hand, was concerned 'to avoid any possibility of "forcing the data" through existing conceptual understanding arising out of prior readings and, most importantly, previous professional experiences brought from the field' (2007:338). Unfortunately, and predictably perhaps, their conclusion resolved the issue neither one way nor the other: their conclusion was that the chosen approach may depend on the stage at which a decision to use grounded theory is made.

I decided eventually to take a third, in my view more flexible and pragmatic approach. I would incorporate scrutiny of the literature at any stage of the investigation – preceding, accompanying or following empirical data collection and theory building – wherever it could best enhance the investigation's overall objectives. One set of literature, therefore, provided a political, social and pedagogical context to gifted-and-talented education – this was presented as a short, historical literature review early in the study to set the scene. Then a more diverse range of literature, more pertinent to the issue of difficulty and challenge itself, was used as part of data collection to inform emergent findings and resulting discussion. Sources for such 'literature data' included psychological theories about how difficulty and challenge stimulate learning; taxonomies of learning and thinking tasks; and studies of the structure of difficulty and challenge within learning. There were also more diverse sources, for instance literature on setting and manipulating levels of difficulty in educational testing and, less conventionally perhaps, material about commercial computer games, where providing appropriate figurations of difficulty is integral to commercial success. Integrated with my collected data from questionnaires, interviews and observations, such literature provided extra material for the development of my theory of curricular difficulty and challenge.

Use of literature

Three possible ways of using the published literature in grounded-theory research are outlined in this section: to provide background, to further inform outcomes, or as actual 'data' for the study. How might you use literature in your own grounded-theory research? One of these, a combination, or even a different approach, which to you seems right for your investigation?

Whatever you choose to do, you should first check with your project supervisor that this will meet requirements of your course of study. If it does, then you will need to explain and critically discuss your approach in your written project, so the reader is clear about what you have done and why.

Issue 2: Theory or 'persuasive perspective'?

A second major issue in my research caused me to question constantly the validity and value of the theory which I was putting together from the data. My eventual decision on this would come later in the investigation and would reflect the notion that in research we should be cautious about the claims we make and the terms we use. If we overstate what research achieves, we lose credibility; if we understate it, the investigation's outcomes are less valued.

What was worrying in this respect was the word, 'theory', and the presumption that, in using grounded theory, my humble research would produce one. Darwin had a theory of evolution, Einstein had theories of special and general relativity, but these and others were developed and established on the basis of decades of scientific scrutiny. Would I really – from one single, relatively short-lived doctoral study – have a 'theory' of educational difficulty and challenge?

After much deliberation, I guardedly decided (perhaps under the influence of Thomas and James, 2006) that no, I would not. The idea that my explanation might be exclusively plausible (the truth about difficulty and challenge revealed at last!) seemed extravagant. It was more realistic to accept that the claims emerging from my research might appear real to one person but not to another, 'true ... for one culture but not for another' (Pring, 2004:72). They might also seem valid to one researcher but not to others who might investigate this phenomenon for themselves.

Nevertheless, I did not want to undervalue the investigation by just accepting the idea that my research outcomes were subjective or might just have the same value as other perspectives which could be taken. Surely I could claim something a bit firmer, a formalized outlook which, while not wholly resistant to dispute, would at least make solid sense, one which I could argue fairly convincingly for in the face of alternative explanations. Readers, especially educators themselves, would recognize it as being more familiar or more coherent than another, as seeming real and right. It could at least be a *preferred* understanding of difficulty and challenge, with potential to be valuably shared amongst other researchers, practitioners and wider interests.

With this in mind, I chose in the study to avoid claims of producing a 'theory' and instead decided that the research would produce a 'persuasive perspective' of curricular difficulty and challenge. This seemed neither to overstate nor understate the significance of outcomes produced from the investigation.

Dilemma

Was the decision described in this discussion too cautious? (I am still not quite sure). Does grounded theory produce 'theory', a 'persuasive perspective' or something else? Consider the issue and relate it to a planned investigation of your own.

Outcomes

So what outcomes emerged from the data of my grounded-theory research? In common with the investigations shown in those Internet images referred to at the start of this chapter, I gradually produced a flow chart drawn from my interpretation of the data, illustrating the processes which seemed to be at work when difficulty and challenge was thought about, planned and used by educators, school students and children in curricular activity.

First identified were six basic categories, which I labelled as 'Distance', 'Scope, 'Orientation', 'Pace', 'Cadence' and 'Mediation'. Each then had its own properties, for instance 'Pace' (the speed with which difficulty is presented and addressed) had two: 'Rapidity' (where this pace is quick) and 'Deliberation' (where pace is slowed to facilitate deeper or more meticulous thinking about complex issues). The category of 'Mediation', defined as measures which help and support learners to overcome difficulty and challenge, had many more properties, 25 in total, including 'Explanation, 'Repetition' and 'Resources'.

I also had to show how different elements were connected to each other. So in the diagram there were solid lines to show clear and singular connections and dotted lines to illustrate where these were more flexible and various. I also tried to incorporate the idea that responsibility for difficulty and challenge was not constant – sometimes the teachers set it in their teaching, or assistants in their interactions with children, and sometimes learners sought it out for themselves – and often the process involved a combination of these.

The final chart was quite extensive, with 15 boxes, variously connected and incorporating 60 categories, properties and other elements, each labelled and defined in the written text and in a glossary at its end. For instance, I chose the term 'Distance' to represent the gap between what learners know already and what they set out to learn; and 'Orientation' to show that learning can either take place progressively step-by-step or spread out to achieve a wider understanding. All labels but one were standard words, chosen to encapsulate the concept being presented; the exception was a term which I invented: 'Horizoning', which was the idea that teachers and other educators (and often learners too) may continually look for and anticipate future difficulty and challenge in their classroom interactions.

Elucidation of emerging concepts was gradually built up in the written thesis, with constant reference to the data which I had collected and with stage-by-stage presentation of the chart itself. A final configuration at the end showed the whole, grounded-in-the-data, 'persuasive perspective' of difficulty and challenge. This all took well over half of my thesis text and its gradual development reflected the importance for all researchers of never confusing readers but instead taking them carefully and systematically through data collected, its interpretation and resulting outcomes.

Conclusion

The 'difficulty and challenge' investigation described here was a doctoral thesis, so fairly substantial. It could, however, have been larger or very much smaller – an undergraduate project even. Smaller-scale research would have collected fewer data and produced a more limited chart, perhaps stopping after early identification of the six initial categories. It would still then have been an interesting and useful attempt to gain more analytical understanding of the nature of curricular difficulty and challenge and potentially be a valuable basis for further research. Finally, here are some points to summarize the critical guidance given in this chapter:

- If in your research you are aiming to understand a concept, idea or process more clearly and more systematically, then grounded theory may be useful as a framework for your investigation.
- At an early stage, discuss your intended approach with your project supervisor to make sure that it will meet the requirements of your course of study.
- Taking on the flexibility of a grounded-theory approach means that you will have plenty of decisions to make about what to do and how to do it. Think these through carefully and explain them clearly in your text.
- Cut the cloth of your investigation – its aims, extent of data collection, and outcomes – to whatever time, resources and course requirements are relevant to your project. In research it is better to achieve a little well, than more in an unsatisfactory way.

Recommended reading

Charmaz, K. (2014) *Constructing Grounded Theory*. Second edition. London: Sage.

Not only is Charmaz a foremost writer on grounded-theory research, she also illustrates how the approach has come to mean different things to different people (Denscombe, 2017). Her constructivist stance emphasizes how outcomes emerge from joint understandings of participants and researcher. The text is substantial but accessible, scrutinizing all major stages of grounded-theory research, including data gathering, coding, sampling and saturation, writing up and reflection.

Glaser, B.G. and Strauss, A.L. (1967) *The Discovery of Grounded Theory: Strategies for Qualitative Research*. London: Weidenfeld and Nicolson.

Most academic libraries will have a copy of this seminal work and, despite the host of developments since its first publication, it still provides a clear account of grounded theory's basic principles.

Academic phrasebank, University of Manchester: www.phrasebank.manchester.ac.uk

Choice and use of language are important parts of grounded-theory research, not least when designing labels and definitions for the categories and properties you discover. This online resource may help you in that process, as well as in any more general academic study you are pursuing.

References

Asemani, O., Iman, M.T., Moattari, M., Khayyer, M., Sharif, F. and Tabei, S.Z. (2015) How Iranian medical trainees approach their responsibilities in clinical settings: A grounded theory research. *Iranian Journal of Medical Sciences*, 40(5), 440–447.

Basit, T.N. (2010) *Conducting Research in Educational Settings*. London: Continuum.

Charmaz, K. (2005) Grounded theory in the 21st century: Applications for advancing social justice studies. In: N.K. Denzin and Y.S Lincoln (Eds.) *The Sage Handbook of Qualitative Research*. Third edition. London: Sage.

Cohen, L., Manion, L. and Morrison, K. (2007) *Research Methods in Education*. Sixth edition. Abingdon: Routledge.

Corbin, J. and Holt, N.L. (2011) Grounded theory. In: B. Somekh and C. Lewin (Eds.) *Theory and Methods in Social Research*. Second edition. London: Sage.

Corbin, J. and Strauss, A. (2015) *Basics of Qualitative Research: Techniques and Procedures for Developing Grounded Theory*. London: Sage.

Cullingworth, E. (2014) *Caring for Adolescent Students: A Grounded Theory Study of Teachers' Perspectives on their Relationships with Students in Secondary Schools*. Master's thesis for Simon Fraser University, British Columbia, Canada.

Denscombe, M. (2017) *The Good Research Guide: For Small-Scale Social Research Projects*. Sixth edition. Maidenhead: Open University Press.

Dey, I. (1999) *Grounding Grounded Theory: Guidelines for Qualitative Inquiry*. London: Academic Press.

Fontana, A. and Frey, J. (2008) The interview: From neutral stance to political involvement. In: N.K. Denzin and Y.S. Lincoln (Eds.) *Collecting and Interpreting Qualitative Materials*. Third edition. London: Sage.

Glaser, B.G. and Strauss, A.L. (1967) *The Discovery of Grounded Theory: Strategies for Qualitative Research*. London: Weidenfeld and Nicolson.

Karpouza, E. and Emvalotis, A. (2018) Exploring the teacher-student relationship in graduate education: A constructivist grounded theory. *Teaching in Higher Education*, [Online] DOI: 10.1080/13562517.2018.1468319.

Lambert, M. (2009) *Difficulty and Challenge in Curriculum, Teaching and Learning: A Contribution to Pedagogy, Using Insights from In-School and Out-of-School Education of Gifted and Talented Pupils*. PhD thesis for University of Warwick, UK.

McGhee, G., Marland, G.R. and Atkinson, J. (2007) Grounded theory research: Literature reviewing and reflexivity. *Journal of Advanced Nursing*, 60(3), 334–342.

Packirisamy, P., Meenakshy, M. and Jagannathan, S. (2017) Burnout during early career: Lived experiences of the knowledge workers in India. *Journal of Enterprise Information Management*, 30(1), 96–121.

Parker, E.C. (2018) A grounded theory of adolescent high school women's choir singers' process of social identity development. *Journal of Research in Music Education*, 65(4), 439–460.

Pring, R. (2004) *Philosophy of Educational Research*. Second edition. London: Continuum.

Schwandt, T.A. (2003) 'Back to the rough ground!' Beyond theory to practice in evaluation. *Evaluation*, 9(3), 353–364.

Strauss, A. and Corbin, J. (1998) Grounded theory methodology. In: N.K. Denzin and Y.S. Lincoln (Eds.) *Strategies of Qualitative Inquiry*. London: Sage.

Thomas, G. and James, D. (2006) Reinventing grounded theory: Some questions about theory, ground and discovery. *British Educational Research Journal*, 32(6), 767–795.

Thornberg, R. (2008) A categorisation of school rules. *Educational Studies*, 34(1), 25–33.

Van Sluys, K., Lewison, M. and Flint, A.S. (2006) Researching critical literacy: A critical study of analysis of classroom discourse. *Journal of Literacy Research*, 38(2), 197–233.

Closing words

Decisions, decisions. If there is one thing which shines through this book's examination of practical research methods in education, it is that the researcher's foremost and continuous task is to make intelligent, informed and sometimes innovative choices about the research process they are pursuing. Not just about the big issues: 'What is my topic?', 'What are the best methods to use?' and 'What kind of ethical issues arise and how can these be addressed?', but the smaller, more intricate judgements as well: 'How does my activity as a researcher affect the methodology I am using?', 'How might data from one method relate to data from another?' and 'How much conviction can I have in what I think I have found out?'.

This book has very much shown how researchers can recognize and address these and many other research challenges. The responses which the authors describe in its chapters stem from substantial and continuous critical reflection – making decisions, yes; explaining and justifying them, even more so; but perhaps too, never being wholly comfortable with those that have been reached. Part of doing research is retaining some doubt and reservation about your investigation, as long as purpose and assertion are evidently (and within ethical boundaries) there as well.

All this means, of course, that a single book on research methodology is never going to be enough. Readers will surely be consulting other material as well, perhaps some of the further reading which has been recommended in these chapters. If you would like something more immediate, then search on Facebook for 'Practical Research Methods in Education' – you will find the book's Facebook page. Click the 'Like' button to get regular news, queries, responses and recommendations about research methodology on your own newsfeed.

Finally, some words of thanks. To Sarah Tuckwell, Lisa Font and others at Routledge, also to Kelly Winter and colleagues at Newgen Publishing UK, all of whom have provided excellent support throughout the process of preparation and publication. Also, to the authors of the chapters, who have not only kept admirably to deadlines but also been prepared to share very honestly close scrutiny of their ideas and research practice in this publication. Thank you specifically to Jyothsna Latha Belliappa for her assured, prefacing words which empower all the rest, and to all others who have provided critical guidance during the book's development.

Importantly too, thank you to the educators, students, children, parents and others who took part in the investigations upon which the book's authors have so extensively and bountifully drawn. The contribution of participants is the most vital element of all in educational research and they have contributed in indirect but crucial ways to what I trust is a valuable, energizing analysis of practical research methods in education.

Finally, appreciation must go to you, the early-researcher readers (and the not-so-early ones), for picking up this book, for scrutinizing the ideas in it, and – it is hoped – for using these to inform and guide your own plans, decision-making and educational investigations. Good luck with your research!

Mike Lambert
https://wlv.academia.edu/MikeLambert
March 2019

Index

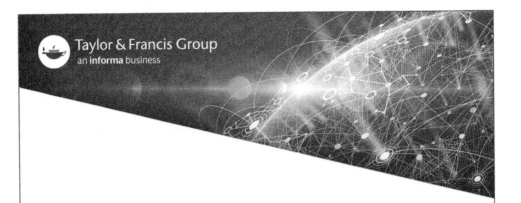

Made in the USA
Monee, IL
11 September 2023

42577685R00096